The Changing World of Gay Men

# The Changing World of Gay Men

Peter Robinson

palgrave
macmillan

First published 2008 by
PALGRAVE MACMILLAN

Palgrave Macmillan in the UK is an imprint of Macmillan Publishers Limited, registered in England, company number 785998, of Houndmills, Basingstoke, Hampshire RG21 6XS.

Palgrave Macmillan in the US is a division of St Martin's Press LLC, 175 Fifth Avenue, New York, NY 10010.

Palgrave Macmillan is the global academic imprint of the above companies and has companies and representatives throughout the world.

Palgrave® and Macmillan® are registered trademarks in the United States, the United Kingdom, Europe and other countries.

ISBN-13: 978-0-230-57395-6 hardback


This book is printed on paper suitable for recycling and made from fully managed and sustained forest sources. Logging, pulping and manufacturing processes are expected to conform to the environmental regulations of the country of origin.

A catalogue record for this book is available from the British Library.

Library of Congress Cataloging-in-Publication Data

Robinson, Peter, 1953 Oct. 8–
    The changing world of gay men / Peter Robinson.
        p. cm.
    Includes index.
    ISBN 978-0-230-57395-6 (alk. paper)
        1. Gay men. 2. Gay men–Identity. 3. Gay men–Psychology I. Title.
    HQ76.R62 2008
    306.76'62–dc22                                                    2008020594

10   9   8   7   6   5   4   3   2   1
17  16  15  14  13  12  11  10  09  08

Transferred to Digital Printing in 2010

*In memory of my father*
*Barclay Charles Robinson*
*1927–2002*

# Contents

# Acknowledgements

First, I would like to thank the students I have had the pleasure to teach in gender, sexuality and sociology classes while working on this book. To my relief, I have often found articulate and politically-aware young people in these classes who believe that the project of achieving gender and sexual equality is not yet complete. I have also been impressed by the conviction and courage of students who are willing to live their lives openly and honestly as young gay people, as exemplars of the gay liberationists' credo to be 'out and proud'.

Then I would like to thank colleagues from various universities who encouraged my research while it grew and took shape as a rather large qualitative inquiry into a sub-culture that has otherwise been the focus of much theoretical scrutiny in the last 20 years. At McMasters University, Toronto I would like to thank Associate Professor Donna Baines for the support she gave me in the lean, early days of my post-doctoral existence—for the fractional research jobs she found me and the jollying along she gave while undertaking her sabbatical in Melbourne. I would also like to thank Associate Professor Clive Moore of the University of Queensland for his kind support and encouragement. At RMIT University, Melbourne, I would like to thank two colleagues who helped me keep up my spirits in the final months of preparing this book for publication, and they are Dr Heather Fraser in Social Work and Dr Helen Marshall in Social Science.

Together with my colleagues, my friends have been a great help as I worked on this book. In particular, I would like to thank Clive Fisher in New York and my friends in Melbourne, including Ian Gartlan, Claire Hedger, Susan Serry, Phillip Siggins, Tricia Tracey, Julie Warnock, Chris Wheat, and Jane Yule—all of whom variously offered thoughtful tips on managing the stress of writing and research, and life generally. Two interstate friends, Humphrey McQueen and Robert Dessaix, helped me recruit interviewees from places other than Melbourne and Victoria, encouraged me in the early stages of the project and then listened as I developed and ordered my thoughts.

Of all the people I worked with on this book, I owe my greatest debt of thanks to the 80 men who agreed to let me interview them, for, without their stories, it would not exist. All gave freely of their time and let me 'blow in' to their lives and then disappear, never to be seen again.

In the space of an hour, sometimes more, we established a unique intimacy, the sort of intimacy that perhaps only gay men can establish with one another. They told me their life stories, which I recorded on cassette tapes, transcribed and then fashioned into the nine chapters that appear herewith. They came from diverse backgrounds, were of all ages and shared two things in common: a strong sense of their own self-worth and their right to be heard. It is for these reasons that I dedicate my book to them.

Finally, I would like to thank a number of staff members from Palgrave Macmillan who helped steer my book proposal then manuscript through the editing and proof-reading stages to production and publication. In particular, I am thinking of Roger Horton from the Melbourne office who initially sent my proposal to Basingstoke, and then Jill Lake who, as commissioning editor, showed me enormous courtesy, gave me the right amount of encouragement, just when it was needed, and wished me all good luck before retiring from publishing. In the Basingstoke office, Philippa Grand directed proceedings while Olivia Middleton promptly and courteously answered my many queries as we communicated via e-mail over a fourteen-month period in 2007 and 2008. Lastly, I would like to thank Shirley Tan of EXPO Holdings, Malaysia for her thorough and thoroughly professional proof reading and editing of the text. Any faults that remain are my responsibility alone.

# Introduction

'I feel *so* privileged to be able to watch *Queer as Folk*.[1] This is the *first* time in my blooming life that I have been able to enjoy a soapie like somebody else. In that sense life has become much more accepting.' Vernon, 75.

Two particularly nasty stereotypes of the gay life course persist in the public mind. The first is that old age is pitiable for gay men because they will invariably be alone and sad, and second, they are seen in youth to represent excessive or deviant sexual practices, as wildly sexual beings. Long-standing public narratives, shared by both heterosexuals and homosexuals, are especially critical of old gay men. In Luchino Visconti's film adaptation of Thomas Mann's *Death in Venice*, for example, Dirk Bogarde represented the central character, an elderly man called Aschenbach, as a desperate and sorrowful figure obsessed with the youthful good looks and playfulness of a young Polish teenager.[2] Other stereotypes draw on the negative aspects of individuals, showing ageing gay men as isolated, irascible and arch (Patrick White), defeated or vilified (Oscar Wilde), or timid, secretive and tentative (C. P. Cavafy, E. M. Forster). Any representations that reflect other stages in the gay life course are ignored or disregarded because they do not fit the narrative's purpose, which is to portray gay men as 'Other'. And in regard to the other pervasive public narrative of the young gay man as a wildly sexual being, whenever television or print media report on gay and lesbian parades, such Feast in Adelaide, Mardi Gras in Sydney or Pride in London, they invariably focus on near-naked, youthful or androgynous bodies that suggest sexual excess or deviance in some form, and overlook the ordinary, everyday gay people who are present.

Powerful and seductive as these images may be, they do not reflect the life stories of men who identify as gay or homosexual, and, as this study shows, few gay men conform to the stereotypes. Gay men come from all classes, belong to all religions, are found in all forms of human settlements, work places and environments, and, importantly, they age and grow old. Their life cycle, which this book also charts, is not—contrary to what the literary works of Thomas Mann, Marcel Proust or Oscar Wilde suggest—one of perpetual youth or of restlessly seeking after young companions for sex or love, or of trying to regain a lost youth—

any more than these are preoccupations of the rest of the population.[3] And, as well, there are gay men from Aboriginal, Indian, indigenous South American and South-east Asian backgrounds—as any quick examination of the community listings in gay and lesbian newspapers shows.

The main source of information for the research on which this book is based was an extended interview with each of the 80 men who volunteered for the project. Questions asked covered aspects of their social, affective and sexual lives and the interviewees revealed a great deal of what Ken Plummer called the 'confusions, ambiguities and contradictions' of their lived experience.[4] To assist in the analysis of the interviewees' life stories, the sample was divided into age 'cohorts'. Men aged 60 and over became part of the 'old' cohort, while men aged between 40 and 59 constituted the 'middle' cohort, and men aged 22–39 made up the 'young' cohort.[5] I then proposed three periods of homosexual and gay social history that coincided with the experience of these three age cohorts.[6] Because the men interviewed for this study grew to maturity in quite different social climates, the purpose of these periods of homosexual and gay social history is to outline the context in which the men grew up, reached social maturity and came out (or did not come out) so as to understand what if any variations existed within and between the cohorts and if these affected the members' lives as gay men.[7] They should be seen as rough guides to the public narratives concerning sexuality and homosexuality that existed at the time the men in each cohort were in their early 20s. In one sense, I was trying to answer the question that Andrew Boxer and Bertram Cohler posed in 1989: 'Regarding the historical changes in the gay and lesbian life course trajectories we may ask, for example: Is coming out in 1987 as a 16-year-old adolescent in Chicago the same process as that for someone who came out in 1970 in San Francisco as a 40-year-old?'[8]

The half-century between 1950 and 2000 was significant for the transformations that occurred in attitudes towards sex and sexuality in the homosexual world and wider society. Along with radical shifts in views on pre-marital sex, contraception and abortion, there was a marked decline in hostility towards sexual difference. A greater tolerance developed in many western countries for gay and other sexual relationships that did not conform to the dominant story of heterosexual marriage and monogamy.

In the previous paragraph, I purposely used 'homosexual' and 'gay' together to raise the matter of terminology used in this book to describe non-heterosexual males. My preference is to use both terms interchangeably, as adjectives and nouns. This usage is not universally accepted.

Some scholars use homosexual and gay separately in order to distinguish between generations of same-sex attracted men. They will, for example, use 'homosexual' to designate only same-sex attracted men in the pre-liberation period and 'gay' to designate only men who belonged to the gay liberation period after c.1970.[9] Jeffrey Weeks has also observed that, in the early days of gay liberation, radicals argued that the terms connoted different identities, that homosexual meant sexual preference and 'gay' meant 'a subversively political way of life'.[10] Then, according to Edmund White, when gay was first used to designate homosexuals and homosexuality, some straights objected that they could no longer use the word to describe something or someone as festive, and gays objected on the grounds that the word was not sufficiently serious: it was 'too silly to designate a lifestyle, a minority or political movement'. For some, too, it may have connoted illicitness since the term was used in the late nineteenth century to describe prostitutes.[11]

White suggests that its popular appeal might lie in its innocuousness: 'One of the problems that has beleaguered gays is that their identity has always been linked to sexual activity rather than to affectional [*sic*] preference. The word gay (whatever its etymology) at least does not sound sexual'.[12] Other scholars use gay to refer to sexual and affective relations between men at any time in the past. John Boswell, for example, used the phrase 'gay persons' to refer to people whose 'erotic interest is predominantly directed toward their own gender' and argued that there were gay persons in most Western societies from antiquity until the present.[13] Among the men interviewed for this study, the vast majority chose gay as the term they use to describe themselves.[14]

Now, to return to the purpose of this book: its focus is the lived experience of 80 gay men. The oldest man in the sample was born in 1922 and the youngest in 1980. Their understanding of what it is to be gay is historically contingent, for their lives span the greater part of the twentieth century: from when homosexuality was invisible and illegal through the less repressive but no less problematic eras of gay liberation and the HIV-AIDS epidemic. Interviewees' private narratives include their experiences of the repression of the Cold War period, the exuberance, and, for some, personal confusion of gay liberation and the disco culture of the 1970s, to the trauma of the HIV-AIDS epidemic. Through the stories of their lives, the men in this sample illustrate the significant shifts in sexual attitudes and culture that Australia and similar western countries experienced in the latter part of the twentieth century.

Many histories of sexuality and homosexuality have been written in the last 30 years. None has used as its primary material the life histories of its interviewees. This book breaks new ground because it shows how three different cohorts of gay men have understood their gayness and have lived their lives as gay men at different points in the last 50 years and under circumstances of varying social tolerance.

# 1
# Collecting and Understanding Gay Life Stories

'I think it is impossible to separate me from my sexuality. It is one and the same thing, and it influences and changes every aspect of my life. As I get older being gay is less of an issue. It is not like a handbag that I carry with me. It is what I am.' Jerome, 49.

## Introduction

The life stories of 80 men lie at the heart of this book. Among two of the more easily remembered stories is one an Aboriginal man told me about how when he came out to his aunties they joked that, as there had been no 'poofters'[1] in the Dreamtime, what did he think he was doing? The second is from a man in his 30s who explained that he did not want to come out to his family in case it upset the inheritance his grandparents had arranged for him. There were other stories from men who had recently experienced anti-homosexual prejudice even though public narratives were now more accepting of homosexuality, and from men who had not come out when they were young because of the hostility then and who had not been able to come out since because they could not identify with today's gay narratives. Unlike Gore Vidal, however, who declared, in the mid-1980s when writing about his old friend Tennessee Williams, that 'there is no such thing as a homosexual or a heterosexual person ... only homo- or hetero-acts', all the men interviewed for this study understood that their sexuality had shaped the lives they were living.[2] How things changed and how they remained the same for gay men in the second half of the twentieth century is the big story this book tells from the life stories of the 80 men who volunteered to tell theirs.

The chapter is divided into three sections. The first section, 'The sample and narrative development', looks at the sample of men that forms the basis of this study, as well as the method I used to interview them. Section two, 'Narrative identity', discusses the theory that suggests our identity is narratively constituted, that is, that we are who we are because of the stories we tell about ourselves. This theory underpins my analysis and understanding of the men's stories and the bigger story this book tells of the changing world of gay men's lives in the second half of the twentieth century. The final section comprises brief summaries of the principal arguments and sources in the book's remaining eight chapters.

## The sample and narrative development

This book is based on a sample of 80 gay men aged 22 to 79. As mentioned in the Introduction, the sample was divided into three age 'cohorts' to assist in the analysis of the men's life stories. The first was called the 'old' cohort and consisted of 22 men between the ages of 60 and 79.[3] The 'middle' cohort comprised 30 men from 40 to 59 years of age.[4] The 'young' cohort consisted of 28 men between the ages of 22 and 39.[5] The interviewees were all drawn from capital cities and country towns in south-eastern Australia. More than half were in relationships of varying duration, 29 for seven years or more and 15 for 20 years or longer. Sixteen per cent of the men in the sample were formerly married and less than one fifth had children from a previous heterosexual relationship. Also, one man was co-parent, with his partner and a lesbian couple, of an infant girl. The sample is fairly homogeneous in terms of ethnicity. The majority of interviewees were of Anglo-Saxon or Anglo-Celtic descent.[6] Almost two thirds of the sample were tertiary educated.[7] Most men in the sample earned their income from middle-class occupations in the public service, or in teaching, accountancy or nursing. Slightly less than one quarter of the sample was retired. A small number of interviewees received old age pensions, and an equally small number were receiving tertiary students' benefits at the younger end of the sample. Some of the interviewees had spent short periods of time on unemployment benefits.

The initial call for interviewees was made through a letter published in a gay newspaper in Melbourne.[8] A large number of men in Melbourne and Victoria responded with requests to be interviewed, in fact, many more than were needed. It was not possible to interview everyone who asked for an interview because in some cases the quota was full for men in their age group or geographic region. The 'snow-ball' technique was then used to recruit interviewees from capital cities and some country towns in other parts of south-eastern Australia. Men from non-urban locations were purposely recruited in order to test a hypothesis, which has since been discarded, that gay men who live in large cities are more likely to have negative views of old gay men because of the gay 'scene' and its emphasis on young bodies and youthfulness. Some groups of men were intentionally sought out. In one capital city, for instance, young men in high-status occupations and retired men were recruited to fill gaps in the age range of the sample. In smaller capital cities, friends or acquaintances were asked to help recruit potential interviewees. The 80 interviews were conducted over a period of approximately 18 months, from December 2001 until September 2003.

Among works on qualitative research and narrative approach that assisted in formulating the interview questions were Richard Sennett and Jonathan Cobb's *The Hidden Injuries of Class* and Lewis Hinchman and Sandra Hinchman's *Memory, Identity, Community*, especially chapters written by Alasdair MacIntyre, Edward Bruner and David Carr. Kenneth Plummer's book on life stories and his later one on sexual stories were also very helpful, as was a chapter by Margaret Somers and Gloria Gibson in Craig Calhoun's *Social Theory and the Politics of Identity*.[9] Further help came in the form of advice from colleagues in Melbourne, Canberra and Hobart who had done similar research or collected life stories and who discussed the advantages and disadvantages of interviews in general and fixed questions in particular.

Once in the field, the same set of questions was used for each inter-viewee and all the interviews were tape-recorded. While this procedure makes the interview a more formal interaction, it also provides for an accurate record, which, from my point of view, is preferable to taking notes and having to rely on memory to reconstruct pieces of the narrative after the interview. Recording interviews also involves transcription, which, even though it makes the job of collecting data extremely labour intensive, does mean the researcher may return at any time to consult an exact record of the interview. In the end, the task was never onerous. It was a great pleasure to set up a cassette recorder and conduct interviews with strangers and to do so in locations that are as diverse as Millswood in South Adelaide, Old Tallangatta, Erskinville and Medlow Bath in New South Wales, Sandy Bay in Hobart, Hackett in the ACT, and East Coburg in Melbourne, to name a few. One final benefit of recording interviews is that they may also be of use to other researchers long after the research they were designed for is finished, provided, of course, that interviewees' identities are protected.[10]

Richard Sennett discusses the dialectic of the interview in *The Hidden Injuries of Class* when recounting his experience of collecting working-men's life stories. While his interviewees were reserved at the beginning of each interview, he found that they became quite warm towards both him and Jonathan Cobb when, in Sennett's words, 'they found our interest was genuine'.[11] Describing himself and Cobb as 'upper-middle-class intellectuals', he sensed their presence was causing the interviewees to lose the 'conviction of their dignity'.[12] Sennett argues that in the presence of people like himself, who wear their self-confidence and articulateness like 'badges' of class superiority, his working-class interviewees felt inadequate, or, as a house painter they interviewed said: 'Whenever I'm with educated people ... or people who aren't my own kind ... I feel like I'm making a fool of myself if I just act natural...'[13] My experience of interviewing was both different from and similar to Sennett's. It was similar in that I also had to overcome my interviewees' initial reserve. Whereas his interviewees kept their distance until they realised that he and Cobb were genuinely interested in their experiences of class, most of my interviewees paid little heed to my 'badge of class superiority'—where it could be said to exist—because of the levelling effect of our shared sexuality. With the exception of 13 working-class men and four non-white men (three were Aboriginal, one was Thai) this sample was almost entirely white, middle class or upper class and tertiary educated.

I would like to think that I adjusted for the effects of class when they were apparent. In retrospect, the 13 working-class men in the sample did seem less relaxed, more 'on edge' during the interview than did the middle-class men. They appeared more concerned to make sure that their answers were correct or what I wanted. They also seemed less inclined to recount stories and instead gave one-word answers or short answers, even when it was clear that a narrative response was called for. This corresponded with the experience of Sennett and Cobb and the conclusion they drew about the effect of class on agency. With hindsight, however, I now realise that I did not interpret their hesitancy as an effect of class but as evidence of a poor aptitude or IQ. I recall that I tried to deal with their silence or short answers by asking more questions in the hope that these would evoke fuller responses from the men. I certainly intervened more than I did with the middle-class men: I would re-phrase questions if the interviewees looked puzzled and encourage them no matter how they answered the questions. In a sense I behaved as I would with a student who had learning difficulties: I treated their hesitancy as a sign of weak comprehension skills.

The interviews lasted for about an hour and were never longer than 90 minutes. The atmosphere was neither too familiar nor too formal—it was almost conversational—which was desirable given the unforeseen responses personal interviews can evoke and the intimate topics discussed, such as sexual experiences, relationships and feelings of acceptance. Interview transcripts varied from 1,500 to 7,000 words in length, the average yielding between 3,000 and 4,000 words. Altogether, the transcripts represent a database of approximately a quarter of a million words, which is substantial and required careful management. The material was sorted by age cohort, according to individual interview question. Each interviewee was allocated a fictitious first name in order to protect his anonymity. Codes used for the interviewees consisted of this fictitious first name and their real age. Other measures to protect the interviewees' true identities included disguising their place of residence and occupation. Place of residence is referred to only very broadly by phrases such as 'major capital city', 'working-class suburb', or 'country town'. Occupations are designated by general terms such as 'community sector', 'public service', or 'transport industry'.

The anthropologist Edward Bruner describes the relationship that exists between researcher and interviewee in terms of narrative development. He understands the relationship as one in which the two participants—the researcher and the interviewee—develop a narrative between them. Bruner claims that the researcher goes into the field 'with a story already in mind' and that this is strongly influenced by what he calls the 'dominant story in the literature'.[14] He also claims that the story the researcher collects is 'co-authored', and that, during the course of their interaction, researcher and interviewee come to share the same narrative or narratives.[15]

My experience of developing a shared narrative with the interviewees was as Bruner describes. I went into the field with twin stories in mind. First, that gay men's relations with the world were affected by their coming-out experience and by the degree of acceptance they reckon on receiving in the daily course of their lives, and second, that they experience age and ageing differently than heterosexuals because gay social spaces are youth oriented. The strong response from many men, of all ages, who wanted to tell their story of being gay and growing old, was evidence the story I had in mind was known and already circulating in the gay milieu. It was certainly being told long before I set out to collect versions of it. At the time I went into the field, there was a widespread awareness among gay men that being homosexual meant more than being young, beautiful and desirable. Our shared sexuality made the task easier, for, as Bruner wrote,

> if the story is in our heads before we arrive at the field site, and if it is already known by the peoples we study, then we enter the ethnographic dialogue with a shared schema. We can fit in the pieces and negotiate the text more readily; we begin the interaction with the structural framework already in place.[16]

As discussed later in this chapter, there are many stories in the academic literature that relate to the topic of this book. They include, for example, stories told about gay identity,[17] the growth of the gay community,[18] as well as those on the coming-out experience.[19] Together, these stories comprise the dominant story in the literature, which is first about the emergence and acceptance of the homosexual or gay man in the second half of the twentieth century, and then about how he understands himself and his place in the gay world and the wider world.

One final point needs to be made about the dominant story in the literature. It is not static because it responds to the changing reality of gay men: 'New stories arise when there is a new reality to be explained, when the social arrangements are so different that the old narrative no longer seems adequate'.[20] In this book, the evolution of new stories that explain homosexuality in the second half of the twentieth century is understood generationally, and the new stories are interpreted by means of the three age cohorts.

## Narrative identity

The concept of 'narrative identity', which David Carr, Alasdair MacIntrye, Margaret Somers and Gloria Gibson, among others, have explored, is central to this study because of what it contributes to an understanding of the self and how it is constituted. It is particularly applicable to the understanding of gay life stories because of the central place coming out has in a gay man's life and the transformation that invariably follows this event. According to MacIntyre, 'man [sic] is in his actions and practice, as well as in his fictions, essentially a story-telling animal'.[21] Kenneth Plummer agrees. He says that all humans are 'social world-makers' and that everywhere we go 'we are charged with telling stories and making meaning'.[22] And Somers and Gibson argue that, when we act, we do so on the basis of 'the projections, expectations, and memories' that we derive from a 'repertoire of available social, public, and cultural narratives'.[23] In other words, we understand our actions, and our actions can be understood, as part of a store of public and private narratives that reach back into the past of which we are conscious and stretch forward into the future we expect to unfold.

Public narratives are the large stories that circulate in any human society concerning, for example, family, class and nation. MacIntyre calls them 'traditions':

> I inherit from the past of my family, my city, my tribe, my nation, a variety of debts, inheritances, rightful expectations and obligations. These constitute the given of my life, my moral starting point. This is in part what gives my life its own moral particularity.[24]

Public narratives on sexuality, and in particular on homosexuality are, of course, central to the formation of the homosexual or gay identity. They are those influential, widely circulating stories in any period or society under study of heterosexual monogamous sex, marriage, prostitution, abortion, homosexuality and paedophilia, to name a few. When gay men come out, they do so in a time that is historically specific. As discussed, below, in the section on Chapters 2–4, the traditions of the time and place of their birth and upbringing will affect how they understand themselves and the story they tell of their gayness. The public narratives that are available to them will include those narratives that are normally available to other people, viz. narratives of family, local regions of birth and schooling, and the public sphere of newspapers, television and social action. They will also include narratives of the local gay scene and gay community (where they existed) on sexual and affective relationships, social interaction, social support or political rights.

As well as public narratives, Somers and Gibson identify what they call ontological, or private, narratives. These are the stories that individuals use 'to make sense of—indeed, in order to act in—their lives'. Ontological or private narratives 'make identity and the self something that one becomes'.[25] David Carr also argues that narrative is 'constitutive', that is, that it brings into being not only actions and experience, but also, and crucially, the self: '[N]arrative ... is constitutive not only of action but also of the self which acts and experiences'. He says in addition that each of us strives to occupy the position of storyteller in our own lives and, crucially for the men in this sample, that our identities may depend on which stories we choose from the available repertoire.

> My identity as a self may depend on which story I choose and whether I can make it hang together in the manner of its narrator, if not its author. The idea of life as a meaningless sequence ... may have significance if regarded as the constant possibility of fragmentation, disintegration, and dissolution which haunts and threatens the self.[26]

This possibility of 'fragmentation, disintegration, and dissolution' haunted many interviewees when they lived in the 'closet' and before they 'came out'.[27] Most said that life became meaningful and purposeful after coming out. The years spent in the closet represented a period in their lives when they did not occupy the position of storyteller. Eight of the men interviewed for this study who are now in their 60s and 70s married, for instance, because it was safer to do so than risk being suspected a homosexual in the 1950s and 1960s when gay people in Australia and similar countries were subject to state persecution and social hostility.[28] In some cases, they waited until their children had grown up before they came out or in other cases until the social climate was less hostile.

In *Telling Sexual Stories*, Ken Plummer describes the interconnected nature of our social world constituted in and by narrative: 'Change is ubiquitous: we are always becoming, never arriving; and the social order heaves as a vast negotiated web of dialogue and conversation'.[29] Plummer's metaphor of a heaving web suggests constant movement, almost like the breath of life. That narrative process is dynamic is an understanding shared by all who write about it. This is the strength and appeal of narrative identity. It allows researchers to map the unpredictability of human lives, individually and communally, to uncover and reveal the interconnected and fluid nature of interviewees' lives, to examine the relationships and stories that give them meaning, and to do so while also being aware that each of these features of life is in constant motion.

## Chapters 2–4

As mentioned in the Introduction, for the purpose of this study I divided the second half of the twentieth century into three periods of homosexual or gay social history: the 'camp' period, the 'gay' period, and the post-liberation period. The principal social and sexual features of these three periods are covered in Chapters 2, 3 and 4, together with the corresponding coming-out stories of the old cohort, the middle cohort, and the young cohort. By so comparing the interviewees' stories with the social context of their youth, it is possible to consider the influence public and private narratives had in the formation of gay men's homosexual identity at the time of their coming out. An important change took place in the second half of the twentieth century and it concerned the extent to which coming-out narratives adapted to changes in major public narratives of sexuality. As sexual taboos and constraints in the wider society were loosened, gay people became more visible and coming out changed focus and meaning. The nature of this change and interviewees' experience of it are central focuses of Chapters 2, 3 and 4.

Today, the term 'to come out' means to declare one's homosexuality publicly to family, friends, and possibly also to workmates or colleagues, depending on the degree of acceptance a person has experienced or witnessed in the workplace. Some theorists reject this definition on the grounds that the very concept is 'heteronormative', that is, it defers to dominant 'heterosexist' narratives and so, in their view, is unnecessary.[30] This was not the experience, however, of the majority of men interviewed for this study. With the exception of a small group of interviewees from the old cohort—who said they had no need to come out, because their homosexuality was obvious to other people—all interviewees had coming-out stories to relate. Other coming-out stories men from the old cohort told included accounts from those who married first and then came out when the social climate was more accepting of homosexuality.

In contrast to the meaning that coming out has today, in the camp period, it carried a variety of meanings—from being presented to homosexual society, in the sense that debutantes were once presented when they 'came out' into 'society', to declaring that one was homosexual, although the latter was relatively uncommon in the 1940s and 1950s. Underlying the notion that a camp or gay person might come out are the associated ideas of 'closet' and 'double' life, which, because of their significance to discussions in much of this book, require some explanation now.

The word 'closet' is gay jargon for the state of being where a person keeps his sexuality secret because he fears he will be the subject of social opprobrium, physical abuse or violence if people learn that he is not heterosexual. As mentioned, a person is said to come out—of the closet—when he declares his homosexuality, his gayness; that is, when he ceases trying to 'pass' as a heterosexual person. In other words, the closet is a place where a person hides or shelters when he is not prepared to make public his homosexuality.

Two scholars who have written on the subject of coming out, Eve Kosofsky Sedgwick and George Chauncey, understand and use the terms closet and double life differently. Sedgwick's influential text, *Epistemology of the Closet*, was published in the early 1990s. In it, she argues that gay people are never fully out of the 'closet', and that, because of a powerful heterosexism narrative in most societies,[31] there will always be people in a gay man's life who will not know his sexuality and might assume he is heterosexual; he must then decide whether he wishes to remain in the closet, or not. As well, there will be those to whom a gay man consciously chooses not to reveal his sexuality because he believes such information may weaken his standing with them. For such persons, 'passing' as heterosexual is preferable to coming out.[32] Chauncey is known for his remarkable social history of gay subcultures in New York from the end of the nineteenth century 'til WWII. He is less persuaded by the usefulness of the term closet or Sedgwick's use of it to describe homosexual life before the 1960s. He dislikes its pejorative connotation and suggests that double life is a better metaphor for how homosexuals managed their identity in the camp period.[33]

Closet connotes invisibility and isolation, which, Chauncey argues, was not borne out in the lived experience of homosexuals before gay liberation.[34] They were not invisible or isolated from other people like them, even if they were to the heterosexual majority. He suggests a number of possible explanations for the origin of the word closet, all of which tend to support another argument he makes, which is that overt homosexuals—that is, men who were relatively open about their homosexuality—used closet to describe covert homosexuals who wanted to keep their sexuality hidden.[35] Nevertheless, as Chauncey points out, '[l]eading a double life in which they often passed as straight (and sometimes married)', had advantages: it allowed such men 'to have jobs and status a queer would have been denied while still participating in what they called "homosexual society" or "the life"'.[36]

### Chapter 2 and the 'camp' period

I called the first period the 'camp' period because camp was one of the terms homosexual men used to describe themselves at the time.[37] The camp period and the coming-out stories of the old cohort are the subject of Chapter 2. This is the period before gay liberation and is when the men in the old cohort reached maturity, that is, from the 1940s until the end of the 1960s. Drawing on the work of George Chauncey, Angus McLaren, Garry Wotherspoon and others, my argument here is that because of the state's interest in 'deviant' citizens, especially during the Cold War, and an associated, more general fear of so-called sexual deviants (prostitutes, homosexuals), homosexual men led closeted or double lives and the homosexual sub-cultures that existed functioned clandestinely.[38]

At the same time, however, as Allan Bérubé and Angus McLaren argue, the dominant public narrative of the period was not entirely or uniformly repressive. During WWII in the USA, for example, the national call-up provided increased opportunity for homosexual encounters as thousands of young men and women were brought together, trained and accommodated in vast single-sex military units.[39] And then in the 1950s, argues McLaren, there was a 'swirl of conflicting social currents' in North America and Europe. On the one hand, the research findings of Alfred Kinsey and his colleagues suggested a greater variety of sexual experimentation in young American women and men, while, on the other hand, the surveillance of citizens during the McCarthy period in the USA focussed special attention on homosexuality, and gay people were persecuted and targeted.[40] As many studies have shown, this focus on and persecution of gay people was not limited to the USA.[41]

## Chapter 3 and the 'gay' period

The second period—the 'gay' period—takes in the decades when the gay liberation movement was established and its influence spread, among gay and straight people alike. It is when the men in the middle cohort reached their social maturity, that is, from the end of the 1960s until the mid-1980s. The principal features of this period are the gay liberation movement and the 'unprecedented' and 'mass coming out' of gay people to which it gave rise.[42] Discussion focuses on why gay activists called on gay men and lesbians to come out, how ordinary gay people understood this injunction and why they acted on it, if they did. As George Chauncey observes, coming out transformed in this period from a private to a public declaration.[43] The growth of the gay 'scene' is also examined, as well as its contribution to the variety of gay public narratives available to those considering coming out.

In this period, gay activists and many gay men of all ages regarded it as axiomatic that a gay person would want to come out. As a result of the efforts of gay liberationists, and the public attention they received, coming out transformed into a public declaration and a political statement—in much the same way that a woman's belief in feminism was regarded politically. Deeply involved in gay liberation at the time, gay theorist Dennis Altman wrote in the 1970s of the liberating power that coming out held for the neophyte, a sentiment which fellow 'gay libber', sociologist Ken Plummer, echoed when writing almost a quarter of a century later about the power of emerging sexual narratives.[44]

One of the notable findings of this study concerns the coming-out stories of the men from the middle cohort. These men belong to the so-called 'baby-boomer' generation and came to maturity in the midst of momentous social movements, such as the women's liberation, gay liberation, and anti-war movements, which had a marked and long-term influence on public narratives in the West. Despite all of this, as is shown in Chapter 3, only two men from the middle cohort (comprising 30 interviewees) belonged to gay liberation groups as young men. In addition, as a whole, this cohort of men struggled with coming out: their coming-out experiences were more difficult than those of interviewees from the other age cohorts. There was evidence in some of the accounts, for instance, of men who experienced trauma or rejection on coming out, while other accounts revealed interviewees afraid to come out, who preferred to wait until they were more prepared to do so or the climate was propitious. The reason for these difficulties relates to the fact that these men belonged to a generation in transition: while they might have been convinced of the rightness of their cause, of their 'duty' to come out, the audiences who would receive their news were not necessarily prepared or willing to hear it.

### Chapter 4 and the 'post-liberation' period

The third period is the 'post-liberation' period, which looks at developments in the gay world and changing narratives of homosexuality between the mid-1980s and the early 2000s. One event overwhelmed gay men in the West during this period—the outbreak and spread of the HIV-AIDS epidemic.[45] During the post-liberation period the men from the young cohort reached their social maturity. Together with the story of the epidemic and its effect on private and public narratives of homosexuality, including the remarkable story of gay men's communal response to the threat it posed, Chapter 4 focuses on different public narratives of coming out as well as the private narratives of the men from the young cohort, which in many cases mirrored these.

In this period, coming out was said to be less important than it once was, an outdated and heteronormative concept; gay men were also said to be *both* delaying their coming out, in the face of the increased stigma HIV-AIDS caused, *and* to be coming out earlier than before.[46] The interviewees' stories reveal that the vast majority of men from the young cohort came out as teenagers or in their 20s. Two prominent themes in the stories they recounted of coming out were first, the importance of their parents' response, in particular the response of their father and second, a related theme, that a significant minority of young men left home or their home town in order to come out.

## Chapters 5 and 6

Chapters 5 and 6 examine the interviewees' involvement with two signal institutions of the gay world, the gay 'scene' and the gay community. As Nancy Achilles, Dennis Altman and others demonstrated, until the 1960s, the organised gay world in many cities such as Sydney and Chicago was limited to public toilets and parks (also known as beats), coffee shops, restaurants and the bars of some hotels where homosexuals could meet to socialise or have sex.[47] Venues catering for gay men expanded in number and kind and became more commercialised in the late 1960s and early 1970s, such that the scene in most large cities in many western countries now comprises bars, pubs, discotheques, clubs and sex venues, among others.[48] Naturally, the shift from a clandestine homosexual scene to a more open, commercialised gay scene did not occur uniformly or at the same time. In Amsterdam, for example, the shift occurred in the 1950s, a decade earlier than in other cities in the West.[49] The influence of the scene on the lives and social practices of gay men of all ages cannot be underestimated, for its venues are the principal locations for gay men to congregate safely in large numbers. Its primary purpose is as a sexual market for young and youthful men.[50] As the discussion in Chapter 5 shows, there was general agreement among men from all the age cohorts that the scene has its shortcomings because it is age segregated, highly sexualised, and its physical environment is impoverished.

The gay community, which is the subject of Chapter 6, is understood in this book to comprise a loose set of organisations with a sense of public service and social awareness. Among these are bodies that focus on helping people to come out or find housing, manage their relationships and understand the gay world, lobby for improved social and legal rights, and, importantly, assist in HIV-AIDS education and provide housing and home care for people living with HIV-AIDS (PLWHA). As the discussion in Chapter 6 shows, almost all the men interviewed for this book reported positive involvement with community organisations of the gay world. The overwhelming majority understood community as the practical work they did to improve the lives of others like them—for example, because they were PLWHA or struggling to come out—or as a participatory experience with other gay men. In particular, they nominated four principal sites of community involvement, which were HIV-AIDS support groups or counselling services, local gay groups, festivals, parades and the scene, and social activism and political lobbying. As their interview narratives show, the stories they tell when working on community tasks with other gay men or mixing with them socially help to shape their understanding of community. In this sense, therefore, their narrative accounts of themselves support David Carr's argument about community formation, which is that it exists 'when it gets articulated or formulated ... by reference to the *we* and is accepted or subscribed to by others'.[51] The final quarter of the chapter is devoted to a small dissident minority that expressed scepticism about the existence or relevance of a gay community. These men either do not agree with or cannot conform to dominant gay narratives. Some of them rejected versions of gayness available to them, having no wish to understand or embrace them.

## Chapters 7, 8 and 9

Chapters 7, 8 and 9 look more closely at the interviewees' intimate lives. Their stories show that the majority of the sample are in couple relationships, friendship is their most valued affective relationship, and that in old age their lived experience is far more social and less lonely or isolated than popularly-held myths suggest. In Chapter 7, the focus is on the couple relationship. The majority of men in the sample were in couple relationships, which were notable for their length and similarity to the companionate marriage. This finding is in line with arguments of Gilbert Herdt, Stephen Murray and Ken Plummer, among others, that, contrary to popular beliefs and humour, gay relationships are not conducted on the basis of a division of female and male roles.[52] In this chapter, the qualities the interviewees value in a couple relationship, such as intimacy and sexual relations are examined. And so too are the features of a lesser-known version of the couple relationship, the so-called 'open' relationship, which allows a greater degree of sexual adventurism within the security of the primary relationship. Chapter 8 investigates the importance to the men in this sample of friendship and family. The interviewees' stories reveal friendship to be the relationship they most value, which is contrary to what generally is the case for heterosexual people, for whom, according to Lynne Jamieson, the couple relationships is the most valued.[53] Together with the reasons for friendship's pre-eminence in the affective lives of gay men, the chapter considers four examples of the 'gay family'. First, in its most common form, it consists of a group of people comprising the children and partner of gay men who were previously married or in a heterosexual relationship; second, a less common form consists of two sets of parents—a gay couple and a lesbian couple—who between them conceive and give birth to a child; third, a relatively recent version of the gay family occurs when a gay couple establish a gay nuclear family consisting of themselves and children; finally, there is the extension of what Jeffrey Weeks calls the 'family of choice', which is a group of people comprising the friends, relatives, lover and perhaps former lovers of a gay man.[54] These four family types are both similar to and different from those that Barry Dank identified among gay people he interviewed in California in the late 1960s, as well as configurations of gay families that Michael Pollak observed in the early 1980s.[55]

Chapter 9, the final chapter in this book is entitled 'Life as an old gay man', and considers what if any connections exist between a man's homosexuality and the ease or difficulty with which he may lead his life as an old man. The majority of men in the sample reported being aware that many homosexual men treated old gay men as Other. This finding is interesting for two reasons. On the one hand, it supports similar observations that historians such as Simone de Beauvoir and Norbert Elias made about the prevalence of ageism in the general population.[56] On the other hand, it reinforces the claim that Raymond Berger and Jeffrey Weeks made, and that I also make in this book, which is that age segregation is more pronounced in the gay world because gay men valorise youthfulness, and that, as a consequence of this, ageism too is also more pronounced.[57] In support of this last point are some of the negative stereotypes that the interviewees' stories reveal, viz. that old homosexuals are worthless (invisible and ignored), contemptible or predatory. And yet, interestingly, the men from the old cohort were less aware of these than were their younger counterparts.

Two themes run through this book and they are the influence of age and sexuality on the lives of the men interviewed for the study. The interviewees' chronological ages allowed me to understand their life stories in the context of the public narratives that were circulating when they were young men and—in the cases of the men from the middle and old cohorts—at later stages in their life course. Those public narratives that were of interest include ones relating to the family, the self, sexuality, and, of course, homosexuality. Public narratives on homosexuality included stories homosexual men told about themselves, their relations and practices, as well as the stories that heterosexuals tell and have told about gay men, their relations and practices. The main concern of this book is to explain how the interviewees understood the repertoire of public narratives available to them, how these defined what it was to be homosexual or gay and then how they lived out or will live out lives shaped by their sexuality.

# 2
# The Coming-out Stories of the Old Cohort

'I have no difficulty crossing between the homosexual world and the heterosexual world.' Maurice, 65.

## Introduction

Between the early 1940s and the end of the 1960s, public narratives of the self, citizenship and sexuality were subject to increased state surveillance as governments worldwide enacted emergency measures to deal with the exigencies of World War II and then the Cold War. In World War II, one of the purposes of this surveillance was to exclude homosexuals from the armed services because of their supposed threat to morale and morals; in the Cold War, its purpose was to contain a supposed threat to state security. The North American historian, Allan Bérubé, has argued that because of the state's concern about the homosexual as a type of person and the homo-sociability of the military, World War II saw the assertion of a stronger gay identity and increased gay social activity, even though the dominant narrative depicted homosexuals as social deviants, criminals or mentally ill. It was during this period and in the midst of these contradictory public narratives that the interviewees in the old cohort reached maturity. These and other features of the period when the men from the old cohort 'came of age' are discussed in the first section of the chapter, 'The "camp" period: from the 1940s until the end of the 1960s'.

For men of the old cohort, coming out meant something quite different from what it came to mean for gay men of later generations. It rarely meant that a person made public his sexuality or revealed his identity as a homosexual to all who knew him. It could mean, however, that he had been 'presented' to gay 'society', for example, or that he had become aware of his sexual interest in men. Notably, it is only in this cohort that there are men who say they never needed to come out because their homosexuality was self evident, or, as one interviewee in his 70s says, because 'it was simply taken for granted'. What coming out meant to the old cohort is discussed in section two of the chapter, 'Coming out in the "camp" period'.

With the exception of two men, all the interviewees in this cohort have come out—in the sense that they now freely and openly admit to being homosexual. This was not the case, however, for the majority of the cohort when they were young men, and few could say that they have been out for most of their lives. Their stories reveal a variety of coming-out experiences and this is discussed in section three, 'Coming-out stories'. There are accounts from the two men who never came out and from men who came out when their marriage ended. One group of men also reveals how news of their coming out was received.

Because the majority of men in the old cohort did not come out as teenagers or young adults, the audience for their coming out was more diverse than it was for the men in the other cohorts, and may have included their parents and their children. As with the other cohorts, their coming-out stories include accounts of rejection by parents or friends and also of acceptance. None reported being rejected by their children.

## The 'camp' period: from the 1940s until the end of the 1960s

The most notable feature of the 'camp' period is that it occurred when public narratives regarding self, citizenship and sexuality were subject to intense scrutiny and strict control by organs of the state. During World War II, there is evidence, as Allan Bérubé shows, of the state's interest in the homosexual as a category of person: the United States military engaged psychologists to assist in screening out 'undesirables' from the armed services.[1] Later, according to George Chauncey, there is evidence of a direct link between the state's anxiety about security during the 1950s and 1960s and its surveillance of citizens, the strict regulation of masculinity and the persecution of deviant sexual minorities.[2] Throughout the period and notwithstanding Bérubé's evidence of increased homosexual sociability during World War II, gay men lived 'closeted' or 'double lives' because the dominant public narrative positioned them as socially deviant, criminal or mentally ill. The 'fairy' or the 'sissy', that is, the effeminate man, was one of the more pervasive stereotypes of the homosexual in the camp period.

When publicly acknowledged at all, they were caricatured as 'fairies' ... [as] freaks whose lives were trivialized as silly and unimportant, so that many ... gay men learned not to take themselves or each other seriously. Such insidious forms of social control worked quietly below the surface of everyday life through unspoken fears and paralyzing shame, coming into view only in sporadic acts of violence, arrests, school expulsions, firings, or religious condemnations.[3]

In the decade before World War II, gay sub-cultures in most cities of the West were clandestine,[4] homosexuals discovered gay life only by accident and many suffered from negative effects of social opprobrium: 'Self-hate, individual pathology, and the social hatred of medicine, law, and religion were commonplace and prevented most gays from gathering and seeking one another'.[5] The camp period takes in the post-war era until the end of the 1960s. In the brief historical sketch that follows, discussion concerns how homosexuals and the gay sub-culture were affected by developments in World War II and the post-war years, with a focus on Australia.

## World War II

Following the work of Bérubé, many scholars now accept that World War II acted as a catalyst in the United States for the growth and development of a gay sub-culture and identity. Charles Kaiser, for instance, likens the role of the army to that of a 'giant centrifuge' that created what he calls 'the largest concentration of gay men inside a single institution in American history'.[6] This is not to say that the US military was a homosexual bacchanalia after lights out or that gay servicemen could openly parade their homosexuality. The point the historians make is that gay men who had previously thought themselves isolated and alone in the small towns and provincial cities of America found in the armed forces that there were others like them. Bérubé argues that the US policy of screening out 'undesirables' from the armed services benefited gay people: 'Ironically the screening and discharge policies, together with the drafting of millions of men, weakened the barriers that had kept gay people trapped and hidden at the margins of society'.[7] He also argues that the changes brought about by the war, such as the 'proliferation of gay bars' and increased awareness of homosexuality, albeit defined by the psychiatric model, would determine the nature of relations that mainstream American society would have with gay men in the 1950s and 1960s.[8]

The war did not affect gay sub-culture and identity in Australia exactly as it did in the United States, nor was the state in Australia as intently concerned about the existence of the homosexual as a type of person or about homosexuals in the armed forces. The Australian armed services did not implement the same stringent screening pol- icies to prevent homosexuals enlisting, and 'most homosexually inclined men who wished to fight did ... get into the forces. They simply kept that aspect of their lives hidden; in the terminology of the time, they acted "square"'.[9] Unlike in the US military, men were rarely discharged from the Australian armed services if they were discovered having sexual or affective relations with other men.[10] However, if they were, its effects were severe, for they 'bore the full brunt of official censure or the tearing apart of their lives that exposure brought.'[11] The unusual homo-sociability created when large numbers of men are forced to live and work together in military units provided some homosexuals with greater opportunities to develop friendships and sexual relations[12] and also created circumstances for 'situational homo- sexuality':[13] 'Many other men who might not usually have been involved in homosexual behaviour, lived day-by-day, expecting to die in battle ... [and took] their pleasures wherever they found them'.[14]

Of all the capital cities on the east coast of Australia, Brisbane was possibly the most affected by the presence of very large numbers of armed servicemen.[15] At the peak of the war, it is estimated that 80,000 Americans were stationed in Brisbane, which then had a civil- ian population of only 500,000.[16] By the middle of 1943 approximately 200,000 US servicemen were in Australia.[17]

Even though most of the capital cities in Australia had homosexual sub-cultures that pre-dated World War II,[18] the effect of the arrival in Australia of large numbers of American servicemen, some of whom were covertly homosexual, while others were willing to have sex with men, was significant and long lasting. Some Americans brought with them and passed on to Australian men their personal knowledge of institutions and practices of gay sub-cultures in cities like Chicago and New York, and this 'played a key role in helping break down the perception among many homosexually inclined men that they were in some way bad or evil or were in an individual predicament'.[19] In Sydney the effect of the Americans was not to change existing insti- tutions such as drag balls and beats, but to increase the number and patronage of others, such as coffee shops and 'sly grog' shops and bars.[20]

One of the older men interviewed for this study had a story to tell of a sexual encounter with a serviceman in Melbourne during World War II. It was Vernon's first sexual encounter as a school-boy. He is from the old cohort and no longer lives in Melbourne. In his account, Vernon uses the word, 'beat', which is Australian slang for 'areas where men cruise for (often anonymous) sexual encounters, frequently parks, beaches and public lavatories'. Robert Aldrich notes that beats have 'a long history as sites of male conviviality'.[21]

> One night when I was seventeen years old a friend and I decided to go down to the gardens across from the Princes Bridge and I was picked up by a soldier and taken home and fucked. And that was perhaps the most significant night that I had ever had. I realised then that a whole world had opened up in a way that I did not anticipate. It was during World War II. Those gardens have been a beat from time immemorial. If those dark flowers could talk they would tell you an awful lot.

The gardens to which Vernon refers were (and still are) less than ten minutes' walk from Flinders Street railway station, the prin-cipal station of Melbourne's suburban rail network. The gardens are at the northern end of the King's Domain, bounded by St Kilda Road, Alexandra Avenue and the Yarra River. In the Domain are Government House and the Shrine of Remembrance as well as statues and other memorials to the dead. The locale is public parkland of considerable ceremonial and civic importance. The spot where Vernon met the soldier was not well lit, was relatively secluded and public, which would make it a perfect location for a beat. Vernon describes his sexual encounter as a life-changing experience, for it showed him a world about which he had not even dreamed. The fact that it was a soldier with whom he had sex is casually stated and unremarkable.

### Post-war period

After the brief flowering of homosexual sociability during World War II, repressive social practices returned in peacetime and intens-ified in the late 1940s and early 1950s as the Cold War began. During the McCarthy period in the United States—and in other Western coun-tries as well—it was no longer safe for homosexuals to be open about their sexuality: it was 'a time of intense persecution of homosexual desire'.[22] Chauncey describes gay men's existence as an oppressed minority:

> [H]omosexuals were not just ridiculed and scorned. They were systematically denied their civil rights: their right to free assembly, to patronize public accommodations, to free speech, to a free press, to a form of intimacy of their own choosing. And they confronted a degree of policing and harassment that is almost unimaginable to us today.[23]

He is not alone in this estimation of the level and extent of anti-homosexual prejudice in the West. Dennis Altman says that '[u]ntil the end of the sixties, to be a homosexual in most Western countries ... was to experience a life that was largely furtive, shameful, and guilt-ridden; most homosexuals shared only too strongly the social condemnations against them'.[24] Ken Plummer observes that in the early twentieth century homosexuality was so disparaged that 'coming out often led to misery, madness or at the very least a life of loneliness'.[25] As well, John Gagnon notes the damaging effects of repression on homosexuals.

> Many ... were 'in the closet' to most of the significant others in their lives; they were properly fearful of the police, their own families, and their coworkers [sic]. Such fears often extended to the people with whom they were having sex, since blackmail and violence were both endemic and not reportable to police.[26]

In the United States, more than half the states passed laws between the end of World War II and the mid-1950s that gave police powers 'to force persons who were convicted of certain sexual offenses, including sodomy—or, in some states, suspected of being "sexual deviants"—to undergo psychiatric examinations'. Punishment consisted of 'indefinite confinement of homosexuals in mental institutions'. Homosexuals thus imprisoned could be freed only if 'they were cured of homosexuality', which, Chauncey writes, 'prison doctors soon began to complain was impossible'.[27] John D'Emilio and Estelle Freedman stress that all levels of American government were involved in a campaign to prevent the growth of a gay sub-culture: 'Especially in the 1950s and 1960s, federal, state, and local governments mobilized their resources against this underground sexual world'.[28] This period of intense anti-gay prejudice was all the more extraordinary and 'traumatic', says Angus McLaren, because it took place after World War II, when, 'an American gay world ... had begun to coalesce as a result of the uprooting of civilian life'.[29] It was extraordinary also because it followed so soon after the work of Alfred Kinsey.

Together with his co-authors, Wardell Pomeroy and Clyde Martin, Kinsey published *Sexual Behavior in the Human Male* in 1948. They interviewed 12,000 men of all ages. Their findings included, for examle, that 37 per cent of the male population would reach orgasm with another man at least once between adolescence and old age. They estimated that 25 per cent of the male population had more than 'incidental homosexual experience or reactions for at least three years' between 16 and 55. Ten per cent were exclusively gay. Four per cent were exclusively gay from adolescence, that is, all their life.[30] Kinsey's contribution to a more tolerant understanding of homosexuals lies in his refusal to accept the psychiatric model that said all homosexuals conformed to a universal type and that their lives were defined by the objects of their desire.[31]

A number of historians have noted that during the camp period frequent 'crackdowns' by police were one of the forms of repression to which gay people were subjected.[32] Evidence from McLaren that gay people were persecuted in the 1950s and 1960s includes 9,000 files that the Royal Canadian Mounted Police opened on suspected gay men; 38,000 convictions in West Germany for homosexual offences between 1953–65; a 'five-fold' increase in convictions for homosexual offences in Britain in the 1950s; and, the discharge of more than 4,000 homosexuals from the US military between 1947–50.[33] In France, Didier Eribon writes, the national legislature amended laws to define homosexuality 'as a social illness alongside alcoholism and prostitution'.[34] Persecution of gay men thus occurred in other Western nations at the same time and with the same intensity as in the United States. D'Emilio and Freedman describe how gay people were treated in United States cities during the period:

> Arrests were substantial in many cities ... [and] fluctuated enormously as unexpected sweeps of gay bars could lead to scores of victims in a single night ... Newspaper headlines would strike fear into the hearts of gay men and lesbians by announcing that the police were combing the city for nests of deviants. Editors often printed the names, addresses, and places of employment of those arrested in bar raids.[35]

These crackdowns suggest a moral panic until one realises that they were state sanctioned and did not cease when the newspapers lost interest. Indeed, if the newspapers did publish the names and addresses of gay men who were arrested in bar raids, they were acting as agents of the state in its persecution of homosexuals. The frequency of police raids and intensity of state surveillance varied according to place and time.

Conditions were not much better for gay men in Australia where they were subject to similar repression following the war. Graham Willett shows that a six-fold increase occurred between 1938 and 1958 in the number of people convicted of unnatural offences in Australia, and that more than 3,000 people were convicted between the end of World War II and 1960.[36] Gay men were arrested as a result of deliberate policies by police forces to suppress homosexual activity, specifically public sex at beats.[37] Other features of the repression included censorship of films, books and plays, and an increased interest by the Australian Security and Intelligence Organisation (ASIO) in the homosexual public servant as a security threat, especially if employed in intelligence 'sensitive' departments such as Defence or External Affairs. Willett notes that the crackdown was designed not to change public opinion—for there was scant coverage of homosexuality in the press—but to terrorise homosexuals, 'and in this it was very successful. Homosexual life during the 1950s was marked by a degree of secrecy and fear and self-censorship that speaks volumes for the effectiveness of the repressive mobilisation'.[38] This 'wall of silence' did not prevent social relations between gay men. It did mean, however, that relations had to be conducted in secret and that the homosexual milieu was by necessity clandestine.

Throughout the camp period an organised, if hidden, sub-culture existed in Australia's capital cities. Sydney then had, and still has, the most extensive gay sub-culture in Australia. In the 1950s its institutions comprised coffee shops, restaurants and hotels in central Sydney that welcomed a homosexual clientele. Towards the end of the decade, 'gay-friendly' businesses began to re-locate to Darlinghurst and Kings Cross.[39] '[T]he downstairs bar of the Chevron Hotel ... was called "The Quarter Deck" and was popular with young sailors and ... the men whose interest was young sailors'.[40] And then in the 1960s the sub-culture embraced drag with the opening of clubs like the Jewel Box, Les Girls, the Purple Onion and the Annexe, and continued to expand, this time into Oxford Street, as bars opened there. These included Enzo's and Chez Ivy.[41] 'The place of Oxford Street as a focus for gay entertainment was further reinforced early in 1969 when Ivy's Birdcage, a major venue for drag shows, opened at Taylor Square.'[42] When it burned down a nightclub called Capriccio's, which had a 3am license, replaced it. An interviewee recalls its pre-eminence among Sydney bars:

> The opening of Capriccio's was a great thrill because until then the gays didn't have a proper place to go to. It had a restaurant downstairs, with a piano, soft music, and a female impersonator who used her own voice. Upstairs, it had a show that was better than Les Girls. It was gay orientated, not touristy.

Perhaps not coincidentally, state-sanctioned repression of homosexuals corresponded with the 'high-water mark' of the nuclear family in Australia.[43] In its ideal form—which conservative governments of the day supported and promoted—the family comprised male breadwinner, female housewife and mother, and dependent children.[44] As well as being the proper institution for raising children, it was the only socially approved site for the satisfaction and enjoyment of sexual relations between women and men. John Murphy argues that the 1950s was not a period of sexual denial for heterosexuals, and that contemporary commentators, such as marriage guidance counsellors and writers for popular magazines, consistently argued that 'sexual expression and what they call "adjustment" were crucial to a stable and happy marriage'.[45] It was not sex that was taboo in the 1950s but sexual relations outside marriage.

Given the extent of repression of homosexuals that occurred in Australia in the 1950s, it is noteworthy that only three men from the old cohort tell of it: two men had direct experience of police raids and a third man says it kept him in the closet. There are a number of possible explanations for the small number of instances. First, what accounts there were of homophobia or repression arose in the normal course of the interviews; when they occurred, I noted them, but did not always follow up. Second, the cohort is largely middle class and, because middle-class men are generally more aware of the social cost of arrest and prosecution, it might be that they are less likely to risk being arrested at beats. Third, a large number of men in the old cohort were in long-term homosexual relationships or in heterosexual marriages and, from the accounts they gave, were faithful to their partners or wives. If they mixed with other homosexuals, they did so in a way that did not attract the attention of the police; thus they had little or no experience of repression to report.

## Coming out in the 'camp' period

In the twentieth century, different generations of gay men understood the expression 'to come out' differently and at times alternated it with the expression 'to bring out'. Depending on the historical context, to come out has meant to be presented to homosexual society, to become aware that one is sexually attracted to men rather than women, to declare that one wants to have or has had sex with a man, that one has social relations with other homosexuals, or that one is gay.

In the 1920s, gay men were said to have come out after they had been presented to the gay world at a drag ball, in much the same way that young women came out into 'society' as debutantes.[46] If, however, they wanted to say that they were aware of a sexual interest in men or wanted to have sex with men, they would use the expression 'brought out', because, according to Chauncey, 'brought out' implies that one has been initiated into social and/or sexual practices by a more experienced person.[47] In World War II, coming out lost the connotation of being introduced to society, possibly because the war disrupted the settled social patterns of homosexual social relations that had developed in established gay quarters in large cities of the United States. Bérubé shows that by 1941 gay people were 'using coming out to mean they had found gay friends and the gay life'.[48]

When Barry Dank interviewed gay American men in the late 1960s, his interviewees used the expression 'to come out' in a number of different ways.[49] They used it to refer to the occasion when they first identified as homosexual and then how (that is, in what circumstances) they met other homosexuals. Dank maintained that it was possible to be homosexual and not develop social relations with other homosexuals: 'self-identification may or may not occur in a social context in which other gay people are present'.[50] In other words, a homosexual identity was independent of immersion in or even contact with the gay world. As well, Dank found that his interviewees used 'to come out' interchangeably with 'to bring out' where the meaning referred to an individual's first enjoyable sexual encounter with a man: 'The statement, "He brought me out," usually meant, "He taught me to enjoy real homosexual acts"'.[51]

In his early influential work, *Sexual Stigma*, the British sociologist, Kenneth Plummer, explained that while coming out had many different meanings, including the public declaration of the gay liberationists, he understood it to mean a process whereby 'individuals ... are "reborn" into the organized aspects of the homosexual community ...

during which they come to identify ... as "homosexuals"'. Crucially, he notes that coming out is 'neither an inevitable step nor a necessary stage in becoming homosexual', because a person may regard himself as homosexual without having to develop social relations in the gay world, but Plummer insists that a person must come out—that is, be 'reborn' into the gay world—if he wishes to take on 'homosexuality as a "way of life"'.[52] For Dank, coming out may or may not occur in company of others and is related to the individual's self-regard, whereas Plummer sees it as a social process where the individual adopts a new 'way of life'.

Before gay liberation when gay identity and the gay milieu became more public, the expression to come out referred to a man's admission to himself and perhaps later to homosexual friends that he was sexually attracted to men rather than women, and that he wanted to have and/or was having sex with men. If he was an overt homosexual, his homosexuality was known not only to his friends but also to other homosexuals who socialised in the bars and clubs of the sub-culture. By today's standards, these men would be described as leading a 'closeted' life or 'double life'.

Many homosexuals were able to make a relatively easy transition between their lives as heterosexuals and the sub-culture, or the 'homosexual world'. While Chauncey acknowledges that passing came at too great a personal cost for some gay men, for those for whom the personal cost was slight, the advantages were considerable. To illustrate how a person might lead a double life, an interviewee from the old cohort explains in the following extract from his interview how over the years he managed to move between two worlds, that is, to pass as a heterosexual man when required and resume his homosexual persona when circumstances permitted. Maurice is 65 and lives in a country town located within an hour's drive of a major capital city.

> I do not mix with a lot of straight people and those I do mix with are totally unaware of my homosexuality. With the homosexual world I do not have to think as much when I am expressing myself whereas with the heterosexual world I have to be a little bit more on guard. The art of getting along with people is being to them what they want you to be. I can mix on all levels, with straights and gays. Of course gays come in 67 different colours. With the exception of the scene, I blend in fairly well.

Apart from having to take more care with the presentation of his self in the company of heterosexuals, Maurice shows no evidence of being oppressed by the double life. It has become his accustomed way in the world. With the exception of the scene, he has no difficulty 'blending in' with all other homosexual cultures. On the scene, his age might possibly make blending in more difficult.

By the time of the gay liberation era in the 1970s, the meaning of coming out had grown, and, as is shown in the next chapter, while it could still mean a gay man's first sexual encounter or his entry into the gay world, it was more likely to refer to the occasion(s) when he announced to his friends and family that he was gay. Of the historical shift in meaning from the 1920s to the 1970s, Chauncey observes '[t]he critical audience to which one came out had shifted from the gay world to the straight world'.[53]

## Coming-out stories

The coming-out stories of the old cohort stand apart from those of younger generations because, as its members reached their sexual and social maturity before the advent of gay liberation, they were not under the same pressure, created by the dominant narrative of the gay liberation movement, to come out. In other words, they did not face the same compulsion to declare their sexuality publicly. What pressure they did experience, however, concerned the decision they all had to make, which was whether to live their life as an overt or as a covert homosexual, that is, how they would manage what Erving Goffman called a 'spoiled identity'.[54] If they decided to live as a covert homosexual, they had to hide the truth of their sexual desire not only from other gay men but also from their siblings, parents and friends, and their wife in the case of those men who were married. On the other hand, if they decided to live as overt homosexuals, and were 'out' to other gay men, they could expect to find emotional support and camaraderie in the gay sub-culture. Such support and camaraderie were available only to those who were able to move between gay and straight milieus without undue psychic distress—that is, to pass while they were at work, for example, and then to be out when they went to a gay bar or were with gay friends. One example is Ronald, who is now in his late 60s. He turned 18 in the mid-1950s and explains the subtle meanings that then attached to being out.

I met men in the ballet who were homosexual and who were out in the limited sense that we understood the term in the 1950s. In other words, they were out to each other and perhaps to other people in the dance world. But they were not necessarily fully out in the sense that we would mean it today.

In the old cohort, half of those who 'came out', as they understood its meaning, did so when they were in their 20s and 30s; the rest came out when they were in their 40s or older. With only one exception, all the men who came out in their 40s, 50s and 60s had once been married. And, with the exception of two men, all the men in this cohort are now 'fully out'. The variety of coming-out experiences their stories represent are examined in three sections that follow. First, there is a small group of men who never had to formally come out because their homosexuality was never in doubt. Second, another small group comprises those who came out when their marriage ended. Third, five men, whose stories are a fair representation of the old cohort's coming-out experiences, reveal how news of their homosexuality was received, that is, how people close to them—their audience—responded to their coming out.[55]

## Never had to come out

Those who said they never had to come out were in their late 60s and 70s. All said they knew from an early age that they were 'different'. Charles (67) was off-hand when asked to tell the story of his coming out. 'I didn't have to', he replied. 'I have always been gay. I am one of the lucky ones.' Geoffrey, also in his late 60s, echoed these sentiments: 'I think I have known all my life even before I knew what sex was. I don't suppose that I ever came out. I was always that way'. Chester (71) is one of a number of children of migrants in the sample. He was born to upper-middle-class parents who moved to Melbourne when he was 14. He is single and lives on his own. He never had to come out because his parents did not think 'such things mattered'. His parents were 'thought to be unconventional in the small, rigid town that is Melbourne'. He said he does not choose friends who are 'bigoted or conventional people who were reactionary in their views'.

By contrast, Reginald (79) was brought up in a working-class family. He explained that being gay was something he could never hide, and, for that reason, he never had to come out: 'I feel that I was always pretty obvious to most people because of my voice. I realised that I could never hide the fact that I was a homosexual because I have a pale pink voice'. But Reginald did tell his father he was gay. The occasion was one of his weekly lunches with his parents. He was 55 at the time. It was the Sunday after the Sydney gay and lesbian Mardi Gras and they were watching television. When the television station broadcast footage of the Mardi Gras parade from the night before, Reginald's hand was forced: 'My father said, "We don't want to watch this stuff". And I said to him, "But I do!" And he said, "But you're not one of those". And I said, "Yes I am". And that shut him up completely'. Reginald did not stop visiting his parents on Sundays and the topic was never raised again.

### Came out after end of marriage

Men who came out when their marriage ended, and therefore relatively late in life, comprise a small but significant group. Their lived experience is significant because it is an example of coming out as a long, slow process of positioning oneself against heterosexual expectations, of learning a new identity at a time when gay narratives were being created and refashioned. They are represented here by the stories of one man in his 60s and another in his 70s. Both came out in the late 1980s when—the AIDS epidemic notwithstanding—the social context was more open, and gay men were less likely to be regarded as mad, criminal or deviant. The gay identity was also less closeted and more accepted and there was less reason to lead a double life.

John (65) explained that he did not come out in the 1950s when he was a teenager because 'there was no conception of homosexuality in the minds of people then'. Also, he saw no evidence of people like him on which he could model his life, and was confused for many years 'without knowing why'. For three years in his mid-20s, however, he had a covert relationship with an older man. When this relationship ended, he got 'involved with women' and within six months was engaged. His decision to marry 'relieved the situation'—of having to live a covert life—'because it was [his] avenue to being normal'. He believes he was not alone in seeking 'normality', as 'so many people would tell the same story'. Then, after more than 30 years of marriage and when he was in his early 50s, he experienced a crisis while on holidays. He came to the realisation that all his involvements were 'a form of running away', and that his sexuality was the reality he was trying to avoid. He contacted a counsellor and thus began the unravelling of his marriage and the end of a coming-out process, which, he says 'had spun out over 30 years'. John believed that he would not have married if he had known more about what it was to be a homosexual when he was a teenager: 'I would have recognised what I was and lived with it'. To finally come out, however, albeit late in life, has made him very happy: 'I shall never forget the sense of relief when I came to terms with my sexuality and the joy I felt that I had found myself at last'.

Leslie is in his mid-70s and was married for more than 30 years. He worked in education before he retired. As a young man, he found himself attracted to his own sex. 'I liked to mess around with men', he said. He was 20 in 1948 when Alfred Kinsey's report was published, but said that he could not see a place for men like himself because 'gay did not have a name then'. And so, like John (above), he got married and hoped that his interest in men would 'go away'. But, over time, it became apparent that his homosexuality was an intrinsic part of who he was: 'I gradually realised this is me'. But he did not leave his wife until relatively late in life.

> I stayed married for 30 years. I did not want to leave while the kids were growing up. In the end, we separated because the relationship had broken down. Brian and I met in 1983 and we moved in together in 1987. Brian is married too. I suppose that it must have been a gradual coming out over a number of years. I had gay friends who said when I was younger: "You have to leave and start a life of your own". Of course they did not have kids. They did not understand. It did happen eventually. I have no regrets. In fact my kids have been heard to say, "Dad has never been happier".

Leslie's decision not to leave his wife might confound people today, gay men included, just as it puzzled his gay friends and acquaintances when he was young. He stayed married because he wanted to take care of his children and keep his family together. In the West—in France, for example, the United States, New Zealand and Canada— men like John and Leslie married women or remained closeted during the 1950s and 1960s and until quite recently because it was simpler to conform to the 'heterosexual assumption'.[56] When they 'came of age', there was no public narrative of homosexuality with which to identify themselves. In many cases, they stayed married in order to look after their children or because of the affective bond with their wife and family.

### Audience response

In contrast to the young cohort, for whom parents constituted the crucial audiences for their coming out, audiences were more varied for the coming-out stories of the old cohort. Because these men did not come out uniformly, as teenagers or young adults, and their life stories are more complex—some were married, most led a double life for some part of their lives—their coming-out audiences are more diverse. In the stories of the five men who represent the old cohort's coming-out experiences here, the first understands his audience to be himself, then two men describe how different audiences—a work colleague and parents—responded to their coming out. Finally, two men tell how their children received the news of their gayness. As is the case in the younger cohorts, whose stories are discussed in later chapters, there are accounts of rejection and also of acceptance.

Maurice came out in the early 1950s, when, as he says: 'homosexuality was extremely undercover, especially where I grew up'. The clandestine nature of the sub-culture that existed meant it was not easy to identify, in his words, 'people who were of that nature' and he felt 'fairly isolated'. Maurice did not mention parents or siblings in his coming-out story. An exuberant, self-confident man, he believes his coming out was not exceptional: 'I do not think my coming out was any more difficult than what the average person went through'. His coming out did not involve other gay men, his friends or family. Also, it did not involve coming out in the gay sub-culture. According to Maurice, he came out to himself and he alone was the audience for his story.

The idea of a person making a public declaration of his or her homosexuality is central to the ideology and practice of gay liberation, discussed in the next chapter. It is less common, however, in the camp period. In this section, two men recount their experiences of making such declarations. The first is Oscar, who was previously married and, like the other men who were married and came out late in life, did not come out until he was in his late 40s—in the 1980s. He came out in the 'post-liberation' period when the social climate was less repressive than in the camp period, although, because of HIV-AIDS, no less problematic. The other man, Ronald, came out as a young man in the mid-1950s. Apart from making public declarations of their homosexuality, the common experience these men share is varying degrees of rejection by their audiences.

Oscar was not out at work, but said that people had 'worked it out for themselves'. No one comes out where he works, he said, 'because that is the end of your career. It is a very conservative industry. Most of them are typical poofter bashers'.[57] Despite this knowledge of his workplace and its *mores*, and his knowledge of the risks involved in coming out, Oscar did come out to his secretary:

We had a long lunch and I had had a few drinks. She had been my secretary for 11 years and I had known her a long time and knew lots about her personal life. She had had a difficult life. But when I told her officially, it was quite difficult.

Oscar has had no dealings with his secretary since that day. In effect his decision to come out to her, based on what he believed to be the strength of their long-standing work and personal relationship, brought their friendship to an end. Other friends also dropped him, 'like a hot potato': 'I did lose quite a number of friends, some of fifteen years' standing. They stopped sending me Christmas cards. Three of my best friends have not spoken to me for fourteen years'. Painful as it was to him at the time and to recall, Oscar's experiences of rejection illustrate Goffman's observation about the 'moral career' of a person who becomes aware late in life of a stigmatised identity: '[W]hen an individual acquires a new stigmatized self late in life … pre-stigma acquaintances, being attached to a conception of what he once was, may be unable to treat him either with formal tact or with familiar acceptance'.[58]

Ronald is in his late 60s. He is from an upper-middle-class family and told his parents when he was in his 20s. His news was received with minimal understanding or interest. His parents did not reject him but nor did they welcome him as a homosexual son. He knew from an early age that he was gay but there was 'absolutely no possibility' he could speak to anyone or do anything about it. And yet, despite his repressed upbringing, he did manage to come out to his parents. The experience was, however, 'quite dramatic and traumatic'. The occasion was his first love: 'I fell in love with someone and that was sufficient to bring me out'.[59] Ronald was still living at home and was forced to tell his parents because they noticed a change in him: 'It involved a confrontation with them and the upshot was that I left home'. His parents suggested he see a psychiatrist, which he says was 'a fairly conventional response then'. Conventional though his parents' response may have been, Ronald was distressed by it. As a teenager he had been a devout Christian and regarded his love affair as a passionate and serious commitment, not a 'condition that needed treatment'.

Two men explain their children's response to news of their gayness. Their audiences reacted quite differently. Clive, who is in his mid-60s, was surprised by his children's acceptance of him, while Gerald (75), struggled with his children's response. Clive was married for more than ten years. He and his former wife have five children. Both have come out as homosexuals. Clive admitted to a 'cautiousness' in his dealings with his children. He did not talk to them about his sexuality but felt 'accepted and loved by them'. Gerald experienced a variety of responses from his children: from being cross-examined by his daughter to being 'cold-shouldered' by his son. He is in his 70s and lives with his partner, Larry. When his children, all of whom are adults, learned by accident of his homosexuality, he expected not to hear from them again. His daughters were, he said, 'a bit doubtful at first but came to accept it'. Between Gerald and his son there had been 'a lot of tension', he said, 'and we had not spoken for years'. At one point, his son wrote and told Gerald that he should leave Larry and go back to his mother, which in Gerald's words was 'simply ridiculous'. Relations improved when Gerald's younger daughter had a child and his son arranged a celebratory dinner and invited Gerald. Since then, they have kept in touch more regularly. Gerald's children live inter-state, and so, while relations are harmonious, he rarely sees them. He and Larry live self-contained lives that are not so different from the lives of most other couples in their 70s.

For some of the men represented here the idea of coming out was redundant. They were never called on to do so because they were 'always that way', and they lived relatively good lives as overt homosexuals in the camp period and thereafter. The men whose lived experience showed greatest variety were the covert homosexuals who married, raised a family, lived a double life and waited for propitious times before they came out. These men also revealed the greatest variety of coming-out audiences. In some cases, they comprised parents, siblings, wife and children. And at least one man—Ronald—anticipated the gay liberation practice and made a public declaration of his sexuality when he was a young man.

## Conclusion

The camp period was notable for the level of state interest in the homosexual as a category of person alongside the gay sociability that World War II fostered in the armed forces of countries like Australia and the United States. The state's interest in homosexuals arose from their supposed threat to the morale and morals of the armed forces and to the security of the state during the Cold War. Yet, an unintended effect of the military's enlistment of men was the development of gay identity and homosexual sociability. Soon after the end of the war, increased surveillance by civilian authorities resulted in repression of the gay sociability that flowered during the war. Censorship of literature and the arts, increased interest in homosexuals as possible security risks, as well as police raids on gay bars and clubs, were features of the repression.

While historians such as Chauncey argue that these actions show the state oppressed gay people in the USA and elsewhere, there is little evidence from the private narratives of the men in this Australian sample that they suffered at the hands of police or believed that they were being oppressed. There was no evidence from their coming-out stories of extreme suffering. While there were accounts of rejection by family or friends, none reported being bashed, pilloried or gaoled.

The expression 'to come out' carried varying meanings in this period. It might mean that a man had admitted to himself or to gay friends that he was sexually attracted to men or that he wanted to have and/or was having sex with men. If he was open about his homosexuality, his friends would know it and so would other homosexuals who socialised in the gay sub-culture. Today, such men would be described as leading a closeted life or double life. The idea of a person making a public declaration of his or her homosexuality, which became a central tenet of gay liberation, was relatively uncommon in the camp period.

Audiences for the old cohort's coming-out stories were therefore more private than they were for the younger cohorts. In their coming-out stories, the men of this cohort reveal a wide range of life trajectories: some men never came out, some had no need to come out and others came out when their marriage ended. Also, their audiences were more varied and could include children as well as parents, family and friends. Coming out was a far less definitive process for this cohort, first, because it rarely took the form of a public declaration, and, on the odd occasions when it did, was rarely mentioned again, and second, because it most often took place between friends who lived double lives and jointly kept secret each other's homosexuality.

# 3
# The Coming-out Stories of the Middle Cohort

'It was a great relief. I felt like yelling out of the car.' Neil, 46.

## Introduction

The men in the middle cohort reached their early adulthood at the end of the late 1960s and early 1970s, a period that was significant in the post-war era for its level of social and political unrest. The fact that they did was critical for their identity and development as gay men because the period took in the movement for gay liberation, the growth of a gay 'scene' and 'community' and the decriminalisation of homosexuality in some Australian states.[1] It also preceded the outbreak of HIV-AIDS in the West.

A gay social movement began in Australia when the Campaign Against Moral Persecution (CAMP Inc.) formed in Sydney and other cities in 1970–71. Then a gay liberation group was launched in Sydney in 1972, quickly spreading to other capital cities. Both CAMP Inc. and gay liberation set up consciousness-raising groups in schools, universities, youth groups and churches and called on gay people to come out of the closet. This remarkable period is the subject of discussion in first section of this chapter, 'The "gay" period: the early 1970s until the mid-1980s'. The idea of 'the gay man' was formed in discussions homosexuals had in consciousness-raising groups as well as in their social relations and sexual relations with other men. Not only did gay men of this period reject the old public narrative of the homosexual as an effeminate, insane, deviant or criminal male, they also rejected the practice of 'passing' or leading a 'double life'.

Gay theorists have understood coming out to be a personal act people take to resolve their sexual identity by integrating it with the rest of the

self, as well as a radical political act to challenge anti-homosexual prejudice. As is shown in the second section of this chapter, 'Coming out in
the "gay" period', the members of the middle cohort, the so-called
'baby boomer' generation, did not regard their sexual identity as contingent. To them, it represented an important element of the authentic
self, which demanded to be liberated. When they told the stories of
their new selves, however, they often found that their audiences
responded with less than equal enthusiasm. The stories of their coming
out, which are discussed in the third section, 'Coming-out stories',
include those from men who never came out, who came out to selected
family members, who waited until they were in a relationship to come
out, whose coming out was accompanied by trauma and, finally, whose
parents rejected them.

## The 'gay' period: the early 1970s until the mid-1980s

The homosexual of the gay liberation period was unashamedly the 'gay'
man. These men abhorred the term 'queer'. As Jeffrey Weeks explains,
queer was the word that their oppressors used to bait and abuse them
and it symbolised their 'accepted oppression'. Gay, on the other hand
was, 'a word chosen by homosexuals themselves—it represented the
new mood among gay men and women'.[2] The anthropologist, Edward
Bruner, believes that new stories, such as the more tolerant story of
homosexuality that began to be heard in the West in the 1970s, arise
'when there is a new reality to be explained, when the social arrangements are so different that the old narrative no longer seems adequate'.[3]
For example, gay men of this period were at pains to reject the 'gender-
inversion images of the past'.[4] They rejected prevailing public narratives
of the homosexual as effeminate and weak and instead developed their
own image of the gay man as masculine in manner and appearance. As
Angus McLaren writes, '[t]he stereotypes of "fairy" and "queen," which
had once been embraced were beginning to be discarded'.[5] New versions of the gay man formed around the 'lusty male etiquette' that was
acted out in 'bathhouse sexual intercourse'.[6] Michael Pollak refers to the
'super virile' gay man and the 'macho man'—characters that were to
become known as 'the clone'. By the end of the gay period, 'the clone',
who appeared with 'crewcut, moustache or beard, and muscular body',
had become the dominant and most popular representation of the gay
man: '[E]quipped with jeans and T-shirts, moustaches and cropped hair,
[he] became the international [leader] in style in the gay community in
the later 1970s'.[7]

In the works of North American and some Australian and British scholars, this period is known as the 'Stonewall' era.[8] In the northern summer of 1969 at the Stonewall Inn, New York, a group of gay men and drag queens refused to be harassed any longer by police and a riot ensued that lasted three days.[9] It is this event from which people date the beginning of the end of the post-war repression of homosexuals and the rise of gay liberation. The name has mythic importance in the history of gay and lesbian activism as a foundational narrative. Ken Plummer explains its symbolic importance for gay people in the West:

> The fact that ... [Stonewall] was not the first radical action by les-bians and gays ... the fact that shifts in the women's movement played at least as central a part in gay liberation ... all these 'facts' are beside the point. Stonewall became a galvanising symbol: a crucial memory in the reconstruction of lesbian and gay stories from the late 1960s onwards.[10]

The novelist, Edmund White, was at the Stonewall Inn when the police raided. In a 1980 article he reflected on its importance as an act of resistance by a minority who until then had never regarded themselves as having rights to defend. At the time of the riot gay men saw them-selves as 'separate individuals at odds with society because we were "sick" (the medical model), "sinful" (the religious model), "deviant" (the sociological model) or "criminal" (the legal model)'.[11] Gay men had in common an absence of pride in themselves:

> [B]efore 1969 only a small (though courageous and articulate) number of gays had much pride in their homosexuality or a convic-tion that their predilections were legitimate. The rest of us defined our homosexuality in negative terms, and those terms isolated us from one another ... [F]ew felt anything but regret about their homosexuality as such.[12]

White reflected on the relatively swift change in self-regard that the Stonewall riot brought about in gay men in the United States. Even though gay liberation was still a new phenomenon in 1980, it had 'already transformed attitudes among homosexuals and modified the ways in which they speak'.[13] He prophesied that gay liberation would cause gay men to become less remarkable, for, in the end, gay men are just like other men: they are, in his words, 'as reassuringly philistine as the bulk of straights'.[14]

In Australia, the evolution of a gay movement followed a similar but not identical path to those in other Western countries in the early 1970s. It did not develop in the context of acts of civil disobedience by gay people or in response to police harassment as in the USA. News of the Stonewall riots and their aftermath did of course reach Australia and were discussed by gay activists. But gay activists in Sydney advised against following the example of gays in the United States, arguing that street marches were not yet appropriate to the times.[15] Indeed, prior to the events of 1970–71, there had been no demonstration or evidence of gay activism in Australia.[16] Until then, the impetus for homosexual law reform came from agitation by some churches, a homophile group in Canberra and sub-committees of the Humanist Societies of New South Wales and Victoria.[17] For example, in 1966, the Methodist Church agreed to 'look into the problem of homosexuality', while in May 1967 the General Assembly of the Presbyterian Church in New South Wales agreed to the proposition that homosexuality between consenting adults in private ought to be decriminalised.[18]

It was not until the formation of the Campaign Against Moral Persecution Inc., or CAMP Inc., in 1970–71 that there existed in Australia a political organisation of and for homosexual men and women,[19] although, the title of the first 'openly homosexual political organisation' must go to the lesbian group, Daughters of Bilitis, which was set up in Melbourne in January 1970.[20] The aims of CAMP Inc. were to agitate for law reform (to decriminalise homosexuality in the first instance), to act as a support group for male and female homosexuals, and also to 'restructure' their place in contemporary society.[21] To achieve its aims, CAMP Inc. wanted female and male homosexuals to come out. And this was revolutionary, 'given that homosexuality had so long been hidden away, not only due to social attitudes, medical perceptions, and church definitions, but also because male homosexual activity was still illegal'.[22]

A little under a year following the formation of CAMP Inc. in Australia, a gay liberation group was established. Influenced by gay and other social movements in the USA and Europe, gay liberation was markedly different from CAMP Inc. In its early days its philosophy was radical, even subversive. In *Homosexual: oppression and liberation*—published in the USA in 1971 and in Australia in 1972—Altman explained that gay liberation shared aims similar to other counter-cultural groups and that together they comprised what he calls 'the movement'.[23] Gay liberation, he argued, would have a part to play in the removal of cultural and social structures of oppression: it would challenge 'the basic cultural norms of our advanced industrial, capitalistic, bureaucratic society ... bringing about changes in individual consciousness and new identities and life styles'.[24] The changes that gay liberationists hoped this movement would introduce were revolutionary. They believed that full liberation would make it possible to create 'a new human for whom ... distinctions [between hetero- and homo-sexual] no longer are necessary for the establishment of identity'.[25]

In Western democracies, generally, this period was notable also for what Gilbert Herdt calls the 'mass coming out' of gay men, which, he argues, was made possible by the social networks of men that developed around gay institutions such as bars and clubs, sex clubs, saunas (bathhouses) and discotheques.[26] It was also assisted by networks that developed around social action groups such as the many gay societies that formed in and on the margins of universities and secondary schools in the 1970s. Ken Plummer describes the mass coming out of the period in the UK and explains why it was unprecedented.

> [T]he 1970s witnessed the growth of gay publishing, gay industries ... gay churches ... Sexual diversity had become the explicit, overt organising point of hundreds of thousands of lives ... Whatever evidence there was for 'gay sub-cultures' in the Middle Ages or for institutionalised homosexuality among certain tribes, it is certain that world history has never seen the organisation of stigmatised sexual diversity on such a massive scale before.[27]

This large-scale coming out took place in a time marked by social unrest in Western society. In Australia, social movements developed to challenge dominant values (the 'counter-cultural' revolution), sexual power and practices (the women's movement and the 'sexual' revolution) and the country's military involvement in the Vietnam war.[28] In North America, the activists of gay liberation were influenced by similar social movements in which many of them were also involved.[29] Thus the various social movements of the time fed into, bolstered and influenced one another. Altman describes how the act of coming out affected gay people's sense of themselves: '[T]he visibility of the new homosexual woman or man was an affirmation that we no longer considered our sexuality a matter of which to be ashamed'.[30] He continues: 'To come out publicly is, according to the liberationist argument, the one potentially radical act for every homosexual'.[31] Australian journalist and bon vivant, Peter Blazey, who died of HIV-AIDS in 1997, saw coming out as an act of 'personal resistance' as well as a 'public affirmation': 'It is one of the only ways we can beat the many forces which still want to keep us isolated, fearful and silent'.[32] The belief these men and others held in the power of coming out to transform the individual and society showed the brash confidence of the 60s and 70s generation. They were convinced that they could make a new world if people only dared to liberate themselves from a repressive social order. And for gay people this meant revealing the truth of their essential self, which they believed straight society forced them to keep hidden: 'In the gay movement I affirmed my affectionate and erotic feelings for men, the particular emotions for which my society put me down—and for which, for so many years, I put myself down'.[33]

Yet, for all the stress on political activism and consciousness raising, many gay men came to understand the nature of their sexual identity in this period through the sexual and social relations they had with men they met on beats, in sex clubs and in bars and discotheques.[34] Notably, of the men in the old and middle cohorts, only three said that they were involved with gay liberation or homosexual law reform in the late 1960s and early 1970s.[35] Not one of them said that he was part of a consciousness-raising group. Two men were members of CAMP in Adelaide. And yet, if the appeal of consciousness-raising groups at the time was limited and few gay people participated in them, it is still clear that they were important building blocks of gay political organisations. They were the revolutionary cells of the gay movement for it was in the consciousness-raising groups that the activists, leaders and future leaders of gay organisations met and formed important friendships, and from which they also recruited supporters and members. Importantly, their work made possible a more open social gay identity and thus increased the social opportunities that were available to more apolitical gay men, such as the majority in this sample.

What happened to the radical agenda of the early gay liberation movement? Over the course of the 1970s, the radicalism dissipated as more gay people came out and, instead of joining consciousness-raising groups, queued for entry to discotheques, dance clubs and saunas.[36] Peter Shapiro argues that in the United States activism waned because 'the discotheque made ... [it] largely irrelevant':

It was never going to change discrimination enshrined in law, but disco culture was the most effective tool in the struggle for gay liber-ation. Disco didn't have to hit anyone over the head with slogans or bore you into submission with earnest missives; its 'message' was its pleasure principle. Disco was born of a desire that was outlawed and branded an affront to God and humanity, so its evocation of pleasure was by necessity its politics, and by extension its politics was pleasure.[37]

The same was certainly true of gay sub-cultures in Australian cities where the opening of the first discotheques roughly coincided with the screening in cinemas of the US film, *Saturday Night Fever*. More significantly, the counter-cultural movement slowed and lost its purpose as society became less repressed. Then, in mid-decade, Western economies faltered in the face of the Middle East oil crisis and the destructive 'stag-flation' that followed, after which social movements seemed to have less appeal.

In drawing this brief sketch of the birth of gay activism in Australia, the intention is to underline the importance of the activists' injunction to come out, which gay people in Australia and other similar countries took up in the thousands. It is also to provide some idea of the context in which this call was made. The period was notable for the transformations that took place. The social and political changes would not have occurred without the activism of gay political organisations, particularly those in Sydney, but, while gay activists lobbied for change, parallel transformations were occurring in homosexual identity and the homosexual milieu. Just as the homosexual identity transmuted into 'this new social category, the gay man', so too did the clandestine homosexual sub-culture transform into the more open gay community.[38] In the mid-1990s, Robert Dessaix recalled the gay culture that in 1978 had developed in Darlinghurst and Paddington, two inner-city suburbs of Sydney, where

> people were experimenting with a new set of rituals and rites, new value-systems, new readings of history and new political agendas, and they were talking to each other about them in their own newspapers and books and in their own cafés and pubs. Homosexuality was being positively celebrated, as well as practised and theorised about.[39]

In Sydney, an increasingly important part of this culture was the 'scene'. During the 1970s, it grew at a rapid pace from a relatively small group of drag clubs and bars into a sophisticated web of bars, saunas and clubs that provided for varying styles of homosexuality.[40] Oxford Street and adjoining suburbs were the focus of the scene once the CBD and King's Cross lost their appeal.[41] But Sydney is an exceptional case in the history of gay and lesbian culture in Australia. Similar developments did not occur in the same way or at the same pace in other capital cities. In Brisbane, for example, the gay market was small and relatively undeveloped, its members never large enough to support more than a handful of bars.[42] Whether because of the tropical climate or because masculinity is less domesticated in northern Australia, beats were (and remain) an important site of homosexual activity in Brisbane and Queensland in general:

> There is no sign of decline in these public displays of male homosexuality [at beats]. The focus may be shifting away from park toilets to shopping centre amenities, but commercial gay venues will only ever attract one section of the gay population.[43]

By the mid-1980s, at the end of this period, homosexuality was no longer spoken of as a single homogeneous identity, but as a diversity of identities. Garry Wotherspoon describes some of the possibilities that had become available to gay men.

> For some, being 'gay' represented no more than being more open about their sexual preferences, being open in their patronising of gay venues, or being able to conform to the new stereotype of homosexuality, that of the 'macho man'. For others it represented questioning the very grounds on which society defined them, a rejection of the views that they were 'ill', and accepting that homosexual desire is as legitimate ... as heterosexual desire.[44]

In large part, this transformation of identities available to gay men had come about as a result of the political and social activism of gay liberationists as well as the growth and expansion of the gay scene.

## Coming out in the 'gay' period

The concept of coming out has been the starting point for analysis of gay lives and identity for the last 30 years, and since the 1970s there have generally been two ways of explaining coming out. On the one hand, there are scholars who describe it as a deeply personal transition or life-changing event while, on the other hand, there are some who, though acknowledging this personal aspect, draw attention to its importance as both a public and a political statement. During the gay period, coming out became the clarion call for an entire generation of young gay people in Australia, Britain, the United States and similar countries. A number of those who were young gay liberation activists— for example, Dennis Altman, Ken Plummer and Jeffrey Weeks—have since written scholarly works on coming out and its meanings. Thus both the historiography and contemporary documentation are richer than for the earlier period.

Typically, those who see coming out as deeply personal regard it as a process. For some men coming out is a life-long process,[45] and there are many homosexuals who never come out. It has been described as 'showing oneself'[46] or as a 'unique life event',[47] as the 'end of a search for identity',[48] a 'rite of passage'[49] a form of 'rebirth',[50] or as 'reskilling',[51] all of which emphasise the personal in the process. For Gilbert Herdt, it represents a profound change. He describes it as a transformation in 'gendered worlds', which involves 'much more of the whole person— body, soul, and mind—than [was] previously implied'.[52] And he equates its significance to the 'social drama ... [of] the initiation rites of small societies in New Guinea and Africa.[53]

Henning Bech also understands coming out as an event of consider- able psychic significance, the implication of which for the gay man is that he must become an outsider. He means by this that all the familiar associations and sense of belonging that the gay man has developed with friends and family must come to an end if he is to become a homosexual. The power in Bech's argument lies in his understanding, examined by few others,[54] of the destabilisation people experience when they realise their experience of 'togetherness' can come to an end:

> The homosexual ... must leave the safe and self-evident socialness he has otherwise become embodied in. He must go out to 'realize himself'. He is no longer with *them*; what he does is somewhere else, in another world ... of which the former know nothing and is [*sic*] unwilling to know anything.[55]

And this experience, says Bech, causes the homosexual to become a loner: 'To this extent he becomes a stranger; by leaving their world he becomes an outsider; he steps out of their fellowship and becomes alone'.[56] Bech qualifies what he has to say on 'the end of togetherness' and the loneliness that homosexuals know. He acknowledges, for instance, that heterosexuals also leave home and also have to separate from their parents and families at some stage in their adult life. But notwithstanding this fact, Bech insists that what young heterosexuals experience when they 'break away' is not as acute or nearly as painful as what gay people go through when they come out. Bech writes about heterosexuals: '[F]or the most part their break-away is less radical: they go from one social world to a similar one, or the various worlds merge into each other with no great dividing lines'.[57] Heterosexuals move in transit between families:

> [T]hey scarcely get the first one [self-evident community] out of their head before they enter the next one. They have to go home to the family. The homosexual, on the other hand, is typically travelling and out in town: he sits there at the café table, alone, gazing out of the window.[58]

In contrast to writers such as Herdt and Bech, who view coming out as intensely personal, are those writers who consider it important because of its political dimensions. These writers refer to coming out as a 'potentially radical act',[59] a transition from a 'secret' to a 'public' existence,[60] and a 'challenge [to] sexual chauvinism, homophobia, and bias'.[61] When Plummer wrote in the early 1980s, he again stressed its importance on a personal level but also discussed its political potential as a means 'to break down ... the hostility and mythology which surround the whole subject'.[62] It is also a matter of personal ethics, for the effect of keeping secret one's homosexuality is that it causes the individual to 'live a marginally dishonest, slightly dissonant existence'.[63] Here is the nub of the gay liberation argument.

Gay liberationists argued that the decision to come out would lead to greater positive well-being for the individual, would help also to break down barriers between homosexuals and straight people and, finally, would allow the homosexual to avoid having 'to live his life as a lie'. Gay people used this as their rallying cry in Western countries then and later. Jeffrey Weeks was a young academic in the London School of Economics in the early 1970s when he came out. In one of his first books, he defined coming out as a combination of the personal and the public: '"Coming out" is usually seen as a personal process, the acceptance, and public demonstration, of the validity of one's own homosexuality'.[64]

In the early 1970s Dennis Altman wrote in *Homosexual: oppression and liberation* that coming out could be seen as the desire by homosexuals to 'integrate their sexuality into a total life style' and to escape the secrecy, the closeted life, or what he calls 'the traditional divided life of the gayworld'.[65] Its political nature varied according to the degree of social hostility that homosexuals faced: 'We are freeing ourselves through the way we live, and as long as homosexuals are oppressed, walking arm-in-arm with one's lover down Fifth Avenue [in New York] is as much a political act as campaigning for legal reform'.[66] Almost 25 years after the publication of Altman's *Homosexual*, Ken Plummer described the political power that flows through stories of gay people's coming out and said that it is something like the personal power that gay liberationists and feminists made work for them and their generation in the 1970s. '*The power to tell a story, or indeed to not tell a story, under the condition of one's own choosing, is part of the political process*'.[67]

## Coming-out stories

The coming-out stories of the men in the middle cohort reveal a greater diversity of experiences than for the men in the other cohorts. This contrasts with the uniformity in the coming-out experiences in the old and young cohorts: of a double life on the one hand, and of relatively trouble-free coming out on the other. In general, the coming-out stories of the middle cohort concern the reaction of the men's families. What is exceptional about this generation of gay men is that they were the first generation to feel the need *en masse* to confess to their families, to say, particularly to their parents, 'I am not who (or what) you think I am'. The generation of gay men that preceded them went to great lengths to keep their sexuality secret. In regard to the diametrically opposed approaches of the two generations, Henning Bech observes that 'just as it was a matter of course ... [for homosexuals of an earlier generation] that homosexuals should not advertise their homosexuality and be provocative, so too it was obvious for the gays of the 1970s that they should'.[68]

While the 'baby-boomer' generation of gay men felt honour bound to proclaim their homosexuality from roof-tops and soap-boxes, on street marches and at campus sit-ins, their coming-out stories show it was not easy for them. They may have believed in the precepts of gay liberation, that coming out was a necessary political statement, but for many making it was easier said than done, and coming out was not always a liberating experience. On the contrary, for some men, personal crises and family trauma accompanied it.

The coming-out stories of this age cohort, arranged in roughly equal numbers, concern first, men who never came out; second, men who came out to some but not all members of their family; third, men who waited until they had a partner before they came out; fourth, men who experienced some degree of trauma when they came out; and, fifth, men who were rejected by their family because of their homosexuality.

## Never came out

Three men in the middle cohort said they had not come out. All were educated in same-sex boarding schools. The reasons they gave for not coming out vary. Two of the men were content they had not come out because, in the words of one, he 'never saw the need'. The other man, Richard, in his late 50s, provided a variety of views on the topic of coming out. Some he derived from his own experience, while others were an amalgam of public narratives that were in circulation in the gay milieu. He believed coming out to be a fairly slow process: 'I certainly could not come out when I was a younger man', he says, and for two reasons. His dead parents held strong prejudices against homosexuals: 'My parents were certainly anti-gay. They did not want to know or talk about it'. He managed his relationship with them by not coming out, which was only partly effective, for, while on the one hand it avoided a confrontation, on the other hand it meant that his mother never stopped asking him when he was going to get married. The second reason he could not come out concerned work. In his 20s and 30s, he worked in a private school for boys and 'did not feel comfortable in coming out'. He said that the school was 'rife with homophobia' and that a member of staff would have been asked to leave if he had admitted his homosexuality. To come out in such circumstances would have meant the end of a career.

Richard's understanding is that he is 'not fully out', that is, he is overt when it is appropriate and covert when it is not. In his words, he is 'out when it is okay to be out' or that he is open about his homosexuality when he feels it is safe to do so; otherwise he is silent about it. This is not how coming out is generally understood and, in effect, Richard is leading a double life. For Richard, the idea of being out is conditional on the company he finds himself in. Whereas the gay liberationists of his generation understood being out to be a permanent state and identity, Richard experiences being out as temporary and subject to the reception he anticipates from his audience. Recently, he witnessed police raid his local gay pub. They had dogs with them and three or four men were removed and searched for drugs. This caused him to reflect on the precariousness of the legal privileges that gay men now enjoy in Australia and to arouse fears of how easily they might be taken away: 'When that sort of thing happens, I feel that they could so easily change the law. Under the present circumstances, I would not be surprised if one day they repealed the homosexual law'.

## Came out selectively

A handful of men in this middle cohort came out only to selected members of their families. Among them is Lionel, who is in his late 50s and was thus in the vanguard of the gay liberation cohort. While coming out was 'never an issue' for him, he admitted on the other hand that he 'went through … [his] straight bit' at university when he dated a woman for six months, and was, in his own words, 'emotionally screwed up' by the experience. Lionel grew up in a lower middle-class family. He was 18 in 1962. After he broke up with his girlfriend, he moved in to share a house with friends from school. He was forced to come out to his mother when she read one of his letters. He said that his relationship with his mother improved as a result because it 'gave her a way into my life, so she could understand me better'. Lionel's mother pre-deceased his father. He never told his father because 'the relationship was not as good as it was with my mother and it would not have improved anything if I told him that I was gay'. He did come out to his brother after his mother died and his brother said that he had always known. His brother advised against telling his father. Yet an intriguing aspect of Lionel's family life is that he introduced to his family every man he was ever interested in. They were all invited to dinner with his family or to stay over-night when he was living in the family house and even to go on holidays with his family. Memories of these family experiences lie behind Lionel's belief that coming out was 'never an issue' for him:

> The men that I had affairs with met my parents, had dinner with them and my parents never asked a question. And because of that, I have never had to sit down with people and say that I am gay. I have never had this coming out thing and have never felt the need to hide anything.

Lionel's understanding of what it means to be out was, like Richard's, at odds with the generally accepted meaning of coming out and he was living a double life with his parents and family when he was at home. We might infer any number of meanings to the statement that he made in retrospect, that his parents 'never asked a question'. This might mean that they never enquired into the nature of his relationship with the men he brought home because they thought it improper or impolite to enquire into a person's personal life. Alternatively, they may have known but did not want to admit it to themselves. What Lionel's complex and ambiguous story most likely means is that even though he kept his sexuality a secret while he lived with his family and until he had to come out to his mother, he felt sufficiently at ease about his relations with his parents and with his boyfriend(s) to sit down together with them *en famille*. It is probable also that because his parents did not pry into the nature of his relationships, did not make insinuations about them or ascribe any meaning to them other than what they assumed from the surface (that they were friendships), Lionel developed an untroubled sexual identity and 'never had to sit down with people and say that ... [he] was gay ... never had this coming-out thing'. He was able to lead what we would call a double life that did not cause him any psychic distress and that allowed him to introduce his boyfriends into the heart of his family where both he and they were accepted and 'there was never a question asked'.

## Came out once in a relationship

Two men waited until they were established in a long-term relationship before they came out. Both men are in their 40s. One lives in the country and the other in the city. Both have professional jobs. Alan is in his late 40s. When he was debating whether and how to come out 20 years ago, a friend advised him to assume that everyone knew. He followed this advice: 'My sisters and brothers who were straight never had to have the "I've got something to tell you" conversation with the folks, so I decided to treat it the same way'. When Alan had a steady boyfriend, who later became his partner, he told friends and family that he had met a wonderful person whose name was Howard. In retrospect, Alan saw what he did as a political act in that he avoided having to apologise for himself: 'I treated it as a positive experience. I did not want to see myself as a victim or as deserving victim status. It's a bit like Jews who refuse to see themselves as beaten and downtrodden. Neither should gays'. Ivan, the other man, is in his early 40s. He met his partner when he was in his mid-20s and they have been together for 18 years. Ivan did not come out when he was at university in the early 1980s, 'for no particular reason except I now know that I needed something secure'. Ivan began to tell his family and friends when he realised his relationship with Paul was more than a casual relationship. He needed to be comfortable about himself, 'about who I was', and to know that he and Paul meant 'the world to each other' and that Paul 'was going to be around for the long haul'.

### Trauma on coming out

Three men reported that some degree of trauma accompanied their coming out. This ranged in severity from moderate discomfort with a family member to intense psychic distress. All are in their 50s and turned 18 between the late-1960s and the mid-1970s. The first man is in his late 50s. On hearing that he was gay, his mother's response was to make an appointment with her doctor in the hope, he now believes, that the doctor would write him a prescription to cure his homosexuality. To please his mother, he saw the doctor who advised him not to worry about it. Although the interviewee made light of the situation, he described his mother as being 'traumatised' by his news, and conditions at home as 'tense and difficult' for about a month while he and his mother 'skirted around each other and did not talk'. They settled their differences when his mother realised that he was not going to turn into 'a monster with two heads'. He has lived with the same man now for 27 years.

The second man was brought up in a devout Christian family. He and his family regularly attended Sunday service. He knew that 'it was wrong to be gay in the Christian sense' and abandoned his Christianity 'the moment [he] accepted his homosexuality'. This man experienced a distressing and prolonged coming out. He first realised he might be gay when he was upset that the crush he developed for a school friend was not requited. Like the first man, he sought help from his family doctor who referred him to a psychologist: 'At this point, I became quite emotionally unwell. I stopped speaking and was unable to communicate at all. I started to stutter and to carry pieces of broken glass around in my pockets'. He experienced a period of intense psychic distress, brought on by the conflict between his feelings and Christian upbringing. He saw a counsellor for 12 months. He had a girlfriend and tried without success to initiate a sexual relationship with her. Finally, towards the end of the year, he 'began to move to accepting [his] homosexuality'. He went to university and threw himself into gay liberation and student politics. The worst was over: 'I started to make new friends and slowly started to come out to them'. Later, as his confidence grew, he became more open and told the world: 'I announced it, as one did in those days, to everyone very publicly, so that in the end everyone around me knew I was gay'. The interviewee and his partner celebrated their 25th anniversary together in 2002.

The third man fell in love and was committed to the psychiatric unit of a hospital. He too is now in a long-term relationship. Brought up by parents who were 'sexually open' and in a house 'that was very open as far as nudity was concerned', he knew about sex from an early age. As an adolescent, he had sexual relations with boys and girls his age: 'I was bisexual because I did not realise there was anything different about them'. Despite his parents' openness and their philosophy that you 'love everybody equally', he learned that it was best 'not to boast' about sexual relations with boys. When he fell in love with a cousin who visited them from inter-state, his parents had him committed to the psychiatric unit of the local hospital. While there, he was sexually abused by one of the medical staff. These events ruined his final year of school. Two years later he met his partner and they have lived together for more than 30 years. At the time, these events taught him that 'if you wanted to get on, you had to live a double life and that coming out is not always a safe thing to do'. He believes that it would have been safer for him if he had come out when he and his partner were together and when they were sufficiently confident of their love and relationship not to care what anyone thought.

### Rejection on coming out

Two men recorded that they experienced some degree of rejection from their family when they came out. Neither, however, experienced the level of psychic distress about which the interviewees in the preceding section spoke. These men risked all, told all and suffered some degree of rejection as a consequence. Both are in their 50s. Roy (aged 58) did not come out until his father was dead and, when he did, he experienced varying levels of acceptance from his siblings. Patrick (aged 53) came out and his father promptly disowned him. Both Roy and Patrick spent approximately 20 years living a double life before they came out to their parents. Both men recalled events from some time in the past. Their accounts are brief, to the point and relatively unembroidered. There was no sound of distress in their voices when they recounted their experiences.

Roy marked the first stage of his coming out when as a young man he asked a friend to have sex with him. Although his invitation was rebuffed and his friend told the rest of their friends, Roy said that this 'was a kind of coming out'. Being gay was never an issue for him at work because he was always out there. But he did not come out to his family until he was 44, by which time his father was dead. Roy is the youngest in his family. When he told his mother, her reaction was: 'My own flesh and blood! How awful!' Once Roy reassured her that he was not a transvestite and that she would not see him walking down the street in a frock and hat, she revealed that it was not a surprise.

'Your father and I always thought you were anyway', she said. His siblings' responses varied from full acceptance to complete rejection. His sister told him his gayness would not make any difference to their relationship and that she loved him all the same. One brother said that he was gay because 'it was fashionable'. His other brother and his wife refused to have anything to do with Roy, and they did not speak for seven years.

Patrick began coming out in the 1960s. His fellow students at college were both interested in his decision and supportive.

> When I was in my first year at college, I decided to tell my group of close friends that I like boys and the response was very good. They were very supportive. In those days, it was a bit like, 'You poor thing' and 'That is sad for you'. I guess I identified with that because in the movies the only homosexuals were the miserable ones and, as this was at the height of existentialism and being miserable was fashionable, you could be gay and miserable and be very happy about it. I suppose I played up on being the 'victim'.

It was not until the 1980s, however, that he came out to his parents. Throughout his early adulthood Patrick led a relatively untroubled gay life: he had a network of gay friends and moved easily in and out of the gay sub-culture in the city. He told his mother when he was in a long-term relationship: 'I had a four-year relationship with a guy that my parents knew and liked and they never guessed'. Then Patrick's mother told his father. His father declared that he never wanted to speak to his son again, that he disowned him and would cut him out of his will.

## Conclusion

This cohort reveals a greater range of difficulties associated with the act of coming out than do the other two cohorts. This may be for two reasons. They were the first generation to regard coming out as an indispensable condition of their homosexuality, and to attempt to come out publicly and *en masse*. As discussed in the preceding chapter, the men of the old cohort did not understand coming out in the same way as did this gay liberation generation. Mostly they did not consider it required a public declaration and they often limited their coming-out audience to people close to them, often other homosexuals, who would keep it a secret. And as we shall see, for the young cohort, coming out was less fraught, largely because the other cohorts prepared the way for them.

The men in this cohort came of age during a time of marked social change in the West when personal and public narratives were being reconfigured. The so-called sexual revolution involved the re-writing of male and female heterosexual roles as sexual relations were liberated from marriage. The anti-war movement seriously challenged the notion of citizenship and authority. As these men came of age, a gay identity was being created in a confusion of liberation ideology and disco fever. And, as scholars have noted, the act of coming out, which gay liberationists enjoined their generation to undertake, was not only a political act, but also an intensely personal process often involving profound transformation of the self.

Many men who belonged to the generation of gay liberation believed, therefore, that it was their duty to make public what had hitherto been kept secret and was only spoken of in whispers, if at all. For this reason, their audiences were not always as ready and willing to receive the new story, as the story-tellers were to tell it. In their zeal to advertise their new self, they often misjudged the power of entrenched sexual hierarchies, which their public declarations challenged—as was revealed in the stories of the men who experienced trauma or were rejected when they came out. Of the 30 men in this cohort, only two were really gay liberationists. Both men are 52 and joined gay liberation in their respective cities when in their early 20s. So, despite belonging to the gay liberation generation, the overwhelming majority of men in the middle cohort did not identify themselves as liberationists.

I believe that an important reason for the greater variety of coming-out experiences in the middle cohort is that this is a generation in transition. The old cohort, if they did come out, came out into the world of a secretive homosexual sub-culture, while the young cohort came out into a much more public and open 'gay community' after 1985. The picture of the men of the middle cohort is of individuals whose experiences of coming out were less consistent and less uniform than were those of the men in the other cohorts. The 'baby-boomer' generation experienced more uncertainty because they were part of a culture in transition. But while they experienced the vagaries and insecurities of transition, they were also the generation that established many of the cultural institutions that now support the gay world and are taken for granted—newspapers, magazines and academic journals, bars and clubs, bookshops and cafés, sex clubs, saunas and discotheques.

# 4
# The Coming-out Stories of the Young Cohort

'Dad was a bit cool when I came out but it didn't change anything.' Travis, 38.

## Introduction

In November 1982, the first case of AIDS (acquired immune deficiency syndrome) was diagnosed in Australia.[1] The first reported death was in July 1983.[2] It took medical researchers in the West until 1984 to determine that the disease was caused by a retrovirus that attacked the body's immune system, the Human Immuno-deficiency virus (HIV). Rates of HIV infection peaked in Australia in the mid-1980s, rising from fewer than 500 diagnoses in 1984 to approximately 1,800 in 1985 and 1,600 in 1986, and then again in 1987, after which there was a gradual decline, until in 2000 the annual number of new HIV diagnoses was around 763.[3] The overwhelming majority of deaths from AIDS in Australia has been among gay men.[4]

The men in the young cohort reached maturity in the period that stretches from the mid-1980s to the early 2000s. This period corresponds with the outbreak, spread and then containment of the HIV-AIDS epidemic in Australia and also in other similar western countries. How it affected gay men and gay communities and how they responded is the subject of discussion in the first section of this chapter, 'The "post-liberation" period: the mid-1980s until the early 2000s'. Despite the devastation, some positive consequences flowed from the epidemic, such as the growth of a stronger, more diverse homosexual community, a greater willingness by gay men to engage in monogamous relationships, the development in the 1990s of a rights agenda, the birth of 'queer' and an increased openness and acceptance of gay men. And because these occurred at a time when homosexuality had been or was being decriminalised in most civilised countries of the West, I have called it the 'post-liberation' period.

Coming out now seems less important than it was in the 1970s and 1980s, though those who do tend to come out earlier. Angus McLaren even refers to reports that, in the late-1990s, there were young gay men in North America who did not understand what the term, 'the closet', meant or what it meant to be 'in the closet'.[5] Some, however, see coming out as heteronormative. It is possible too that during the 1980s gay men may have delayed coming out because of HIV-AIDS. These themes are discussed in the second section, 'Coming out in the post-liberation period'.

Despite a greater level of acceptance of homosexuality in the West and the fact that, for some gay men, coming out is now less of an ordeal, the majority of men from the young cohort in this study still regarded coming out as a major life-course event to be negotiated. Their accounts of coming out are the subject of the third section of the chapter, 'Coming-out stories'. In general, the biggest obstacle they faced was having to tell their family, in particular their parents. While almost none said relations with friends were affected by their coming out, only a small group of men reported their parents receiving the news well and in a positive spirit. On the whole, then, fear of rejection still caused young men anxiety as they approached the task of coming out. Interestingly, the importance of their father's acceptance was a strong theme in their coming-out narratives, as was the fact that, when their parents were frightened or apprehensive, the cause was often a fear that their sons might contract HIV-AIDS.

## The 'post-liberation' period: the mid-1980s until the early 2000s

The AIDS epidemic was the outstanding feature of the 'post-liberation' period. It was the context in which the men of the young cohort grew up and into which many of them came out. Their experience of what it meant to be gay was shaped by the epidemic and its effect on older gay men. All the men in the middle and old cohorts were adults in the 1980s and it was among their ranks—particularly the middle cohort, or 'baby-boomers'—that AIDS took its greatest toll. While the main focus of this chapter is the coming-out stories of the young cohort, a selection of stories about the epidemic from the old and middle cohorts helps explain the historical context.

Infection rates and mortality figures are useful in outlining the extent of the HIV-AIDS epidemic, but they can too often disguise its personal dimension. How did individual gay men respond to it and how were they affected by it? John D'Emilio and Estelle Freedman wrote that, before the discovery of the retrovirus, 'death and dying became endemic' in the gay communities in North America, 'as young men found friends and lovers taken ill, with no prospect of recovery'.[6] The experience for gay men in Australia was similar. A man from the middle cohort, for example, described how his friendship network was affected:

> I am 56. I was sexually active in getting off with a lot of different guys in the early 1980s. I was fortunate not to contract HIV. It was pure luck. Most of the guys I knew in my 20s and early 30s died of AIDS. Very few of them are left.

The disease struck down communities and friendship networks of gay men, and men bore witness to friends' and lovers' suffering and deaths. In Melbourne, for example, historian John Foster nursed and cared for his Cuban lover, Juan Céspedes, until his death on Good Friday 1987. In *Take Me to Paris, Johnny*, Foster tells the story of their relationship. In this passage from the book, he describes his last night with Juan:

> We were at the end now. He dirtied the bed, and when the nurses lifted him into the chair while they changed the linen, his eye fell again on the palm cross on the bed-head, and he instructed me to put it with him in his coffin ... Finally when he was quieter than he had been all day and appeared to be drifting off to sleep, I switched out the light. 'Come to bed, Johnny', he whispered. So I took off my shoes and slipped into the bed beneath the blanket that was draped on a wire frame to spare his body the weight. I cradled him in the curve of my body and listened to his breathing.[7]

His friend and colleague, John Rickard, wrote in an Afterword to the 2003 edition of the book that John Foster died within a year of its first publication.[8] At about the time *Take Me to Paris, Johnny* was launched, a man from the young cohort was diagnosed HIV positive. As he told his story, he was 22 at the time and it was a routine test: 'I did not suspect that I was positive. That ripped me apart. At that point, I thought it meant death and would be the end of everything. I spent the next five years trying to pull myself together mentally'.

## Conflation of gayness and HIV-AIDS

It did not take long before the medical condition of having AIDS was transformed into a moral commentary on the 'gay life-style'. This suited the political agenda of social conservatives and Christian fundamentalists in Western countries. 'Promiscuity was targeted by the press', writes Angus McLaren, and '[i]n the public mind AIDS was not simply transmitted, it was "caused" by sex'. As a result, '[h]omophobia was let loose'.[9] In such an environment, it was difficult for gay men not to think that they were being punished because their sexual and affective relations deviated from the conventional model of monogamous heterosexuality.

Two men in the sample understood AIDS as a moral punishment. The first man was Jerome, who is from the middle cohort. He referred to his experience of 'survivor guilt', which is a common response among men whose friends and acquaintances died and also among those who simply survived the epidemic relatively unscathed, without experiencing death in large numbers or at all. The metaphor of AIDS as punishment helped Jerome comprehend its arbitrary nature.

> I am a survivor and I do not know why I survived and the others did not. It has been explained to me a hundred times why it occurs, but I do wonder why it had to happen to gay men and why we were punished. Because I think it is a punishment. Because it changed everything.

Maurice is from the old cohort and his understanding of AIDS is strongly judgmental. He saw a direct link between gay men's promiscuity and transmission of the virus, while at the same time admitting to his own earlier promiscuity. His explanation for not being HIV positive was that age 'quietened' his promiscuity, which he attributed to the fact that God 'smiled' on him. By contrast, a man from the middle cohort said that he and his partner gradually became less anxious about AIDS as they acquired more knowledge of HIV and its transmission. Like other interviewees, Neil saw his friends die, but he rejected an Old Testament interpretation for the epidemic.

In the mid-1980s, then, not only did gay men have to suffer the pain of living in an epidemic caused by a mysterious virus that was killing friends and lovers, they also had to endure homophobic taunts that they had brought it on themselves, and bear the burden of a more deeply stigmatised identity. Men under 30 in the young cohort were aged between seven and 11 in 1985. Nonetheless, the effect of the homophobia released by AIDS was, according to some of them, still in evidence in 2002 when they were interviewed for this study. Six interviewees, or slightly more than a fifth of the men from the young cohort, reported anti-homosexual prejudice that associated AIDS with being gay.[10] Their views are represented here by three men in their 20s. They live in different capital cities and share a similar understanding of how AIDS has affected the gay identity. Mark (aged 25) was aware of 'blatant insults', such as 'all gays are AIDS carriers', and Myles (aged 24) feared that heterosexuals believe 'all gay people have AIDS and carry the HIV virus'. Meanwhile, Angus, who is 23, recalled what he learned at secondary school in the early 1990s.

> I remember in Year 10 Science we had sex education and the only time HIV was brought up was in respect to gay sex. Otherwise it was not talked about at all. The one time I got to be talked about as a gay man at school, it was to do with HIV. The only picture I ever got of a gay man was to do with the virus.

Accounts of men in the middle and old cohorts, who were adults during the epidemic, confirm the young men's experience. Vernon, who is in his mid-70s, believed HIV-AIDS erased the acceptance gay men had won from average Australians: 'Most people would have thought it was a poofter's disease and that poofters brought it to this country'. Lindsay (aged 62) recalled that during the 1980s he felt 'being gay associated [him] with this dreadful disease', that 'people looked at [him] differently because of AIDS' and that, because of the intense media coverage, he 'tended to feel tainted by this plague'. A man in his 40s said that 'when AIDS blew up, homosexuals were stigmatised'. He felt the stigma acutely because he was trying to come out to his family and, in the town where he lived, some people adopted a 'red neck view' of gay men: 'They believed that gay equals berserk behaviour, such as rampant sex with hundreds of guys, that all of a sudden gay equals fatal illness'.

### Sexual practices

Because of the manner of its transmission—through the exchange of blood and semen—AIDS forced gay men to think about how and why they had sex and in so doing created 'a moral crisis' in the gay subculture: 'AIDS focused attention on just those practices and beliefs which have been central to a coherent gay identity since the 1960s'.[11] Dennis Altman's response to this moral crisis was to argue that while

AIDS would affect sexual practices, it would not alter what he called the 'fundamental reality of homosexuality'.[12] And in many ways he was proved right: some gay men hesitated longer before coming out; others chose celibacy, monogamy or 'safe sex' as their protection against the virus.[13] Even if gay men chose to be celibate for the duration of the epidemic, as some did, their identity was still homosexual, for, as Altman argues, 'any sense of gay identity [is] quite meaningless if we try to deny it is an identity clearly based upon sexual preference, even if this preference is not always acted upon'.[14] Fear of AIDS affected sexual practices among all sexually active people, gay and straight alike, and contributed among other things to people giving greater emphasis to 'non-penetrative forms of sex' in their repertoire of safe-sex options.[15]

In Australia, gay community leaders debated whether sex venues such as saunas should be closed down, but unlike in the United States —where, for example, in October 1984[16] city officials closed down bathhouses in San Francisco—they were able to convince governments that sound policy required that sex venues be kept open, for two reasons. First, they argued that gay men would continue to have sex whether the sex venues were open or closed and that closing them might force gay sex underground once again. Second, sex venues could play a role in educating gay men about safe sex and so perhaps help to change sexual beliefs and practices.[17] As a result, saunas and other sex venues continued to operate throughout the period and are still in business. Initially, however, people kept away from all types of gay venues, partly because the mood in the early days was sombre as gay men and their friends digested the news of the epidemic and its implications, and because few felt like celebrating. One interviewee who is now in his 70s recalled that AIDS caused a marked decline in the 'beat trade':

> Beats went off for about nine months. There was hardly anybody on the beats. I think HIV has caused a lot of guys to be very frightened. We have all lost friends through AIDS—people we have known who have died. Not so many now, but in the early days when the scourge was at its worse. It was a shame. There were some lovely people.

While numbers attending sex venues fell at first, they returned as safe-sex programs were introduced and understood.[18]

Slightly more than one third of the men from the young cohort came out in the 1980s. Approximately half of these, or one sixth of the cohort, came out during the worst of the epidemic, that is, in the early-to mid-1980s. Two men told how AIDS affected their coming out. Joseph (35) came out in the early-1980s, when he was a teenager, and said that at the time 'there was a lot of hysteria and not much good information'. Moreover, because he was 'not comfortable talking about [his] sexuality then', he was not able to gain access to 'good information'. His solution was to join an AIDS support group as a volunteer worker 'as a way of chasing away the bogey-man': 'I wanted to find out about the virus. I wanted to know what was going on and to find a pro-active way of dealing with it so that it did not overwhelm me'. Harry (28) was 15 when he came out in the late 1980s:

> When I came out, I was bombarded with information about safe sex and took on everything I was told. Even though that was helpful at the time, now I find that I forget about it until someone dies or I have a scare with it and think, 'Oh, shit, it really is there'.

### Community response

By the middle of the 1990s HIV-AIDS was under control in Australia. Even though many men were still dying and would continue to die as Juan Céspedes and John Foster died, rates of new infection had declined from the peaks of 1985 and 1986.[19] The personal legacy of the epidemic in a country like Australia included not only the premature deaths of many thousands of gay men and the loss of entire friendship networks but also, as Jeffrey Weeks pointed out in the British context, continuing doubt for people who live with the disease and for gay men in general:

> The person living with HIV or AIDS must live with ... the uncertainty of diagnosis, of prognosis, of reactions of friends, families, loved ones, of anonymous and fearful or hate-filled others. Everyone must live the uncertainty too: the uncertainty bred of risk, of possible infection, of *not* knowing, of loss.[20]

Scholars generally agree that one of the more notable positive effects of AIDS was to invigorate gay communities in First World countries. In the first instance, communities of gay men drew on their own resources in the form of their labour, time and community leadership and then, in the case of some countries—for example, Australia, Holland and Denmark—they were able to work co-operatively with governments in the formulation of health policy.[21] Networks of gay men, whose engagement with gay culture before the advent of AIDS had focussed on the scene, showed themselves capable of sustained and genuine altruism and, as a result, gay communities that emerged at the beginning of the 1990s in Australia and other Western countries were stronger and showed signs of beginning to transform into more diverse and inclusive social structures.[22]

Not only did AIDS cause gay men to reassess their sexual relations, it also caused them to reassess their affective relations. As a result of this reassessment, which began in the mid-1980s, gay men have shown a willingness to engage in a broader range of relationships. Monogamy became more attractive: 'The havoc caused by AIDS having given rise to a nostalgia for family life, an important segment of the gay community increasingly embraced domesticity'.[23] In the middle cohort and old cohort of this sample are men who admitted that monogamy was their principal survival strategy during the epidemic. Barry (aged 62) said bluntly that fear of AIDS probably kept him and his partner together: 'If that dreadful thing had not been around, I might have looked further afield and might have got involved with other people, but I think it helped keep our relationship on track'. Meanwhile, Richard, who is four years Barry's junior, said that he would most likely have contracted HIV if he had not been in a 'fairly monogamous relationship':

> When I think back to the 1970s, when it all started to happen, I was well and truly in the relationship with my partner, and I think that it is just pure luck that I am not HIV. Before that, I was quite promiscuous. I think that I am very lucky that I do not have it.

On the edges of gay communities afflicted by the epidemic, there developed in the early 1990s a social movement known as 'queer', which began with the establishment in New York of a radical gay group called Queer Nation in late 1990.[24] Its purpose was to challenge existing gay community organisations and leaderships because in the eyes of the young queers these were 'overly liberal, complacent, and politically timid', to do away with the binary distinction between heterosexual and homosexual, to destabilise 'any and every identity claim, asserting the irreducibility of difference itself'.[25] Queer came into existence at the same time as less powerful sexual minorities such as transsexuals and intersex people were asking for recognition. But its claim to represent all sexual minorities directly threatened well-established gay community institutions and what Jeffrey Weeks calls, 'the patterns of lesbian and gay life as they developed during the 1970s and 1980s'.[26]

In the end, it did not subvert existing gay and lesbian institutions or the binary distinction between heterosexual and homosexual, possibly because they were too entrenched and the queer movement was too amorphous.[27]

Gay men became more visible as a result of HIV-AIDS because the disease infected and killed more of them than any other category of person in the West. As well, they refused to give in to it or the homophobia that it gave rise to, they lobbied governments and they simply became more noticeable. How successfully gay activists have been able to fight or contain homophobia is debatable. Dennis Altman, for example, believes homophobia transmutes as soon as homosexuals become more visible.[28] On the other hand, Plummer argues we can measure the growing acceptance of gay men by the expanding volume of stories being told by gay men about their lives: '[W]hereas once a silence pervaded film, press and TV, now lesbian and gay issues get regular airings. Most soaps have at least introduced one gay or lesbian character'. More recently, the stories have 'snowballed' to include 'black men, black lesbians, Hispanic lesbians, Hispanic men, Asian men, Jewish women, elderly gays, ageing lesbians, deaf gays and lesbians. And ... the coming out of children to their parents, of parents to their children'.[29] And Gilbert Herdt, writing in the 1990s, observed the relative ease with which young gay men were able to incorporate gayness into their lives:

> Where early cohorts lived closeted and in fear ... and where the ... [gay liberation] cohort is now besieged frontally with the death and grief of AIDS, today's youth—witness to these preceding lifestyles—are in response developing an alternative cultural reality and future life course. Many ... now assume the possibility of achieving unprecedented gay life goals and open social relationships at home, school, and work.[30]

But, as many of the stories of the young men in this sample show, while coming out now might be less fraught than in was in 1959, 1974 or 1982, it is still an important life event for young gay men to negotiate when they are sure that the time and audience are right.

## Coming out in the 'post-liberation' period

Several public narratives of coming out co-existed in this period. There was a strong argument that coming out had become less important than it was in the 1970s and 1980s. Ken Plummer, for example, believes that, while it has been of signal importance to millions of individuals, its importance might have diminished.[31] And then there are some theorists who argue against the idea of coming out because it is heteronormative, insisting that to do so is to acknowledge the existence of a sexual hierarchy where heterosexual desire is assumed to be 'natural' and right and other sexualities are in some way deficient.[32] Then there are scholars who argue that gay men might have delayed coming out because of the effect that AIDS had on the homosexual identity.[33] And, finally, there is research, which is discussed below, to show that people are coming out earlier.

Most of the men in the young cohort came out either as teenagers (12 interviewees) or in their 20s (ten interviewees).[34] The five exceptions were three men who said they came out as children, one man who came out in his 30s, and one who had not and would not come out because he could not 'relate to the gay community'. As well as these, two men did not say when they came out, a man in his early 20s and one in his late 30s, and it was impossible to infer from their transcripts when they came out. Interestingly, no one said that he had not come out because it was heteronormative to do so but one man did discount the notion of coming out because it was a 'baby-boomer' concept but then proceeded to relate an extensive account of his own coming out. The experiences of the men in the young cohort strongly support the pattern observed in the United States, that is, that people are coming out earlier than preceding generations of gay men.

One of the earliest writers on the subject of coming out, Barry Dank, estimated that more than 80 per cent of the men he interviewed in the late 1960s had come out by the time they were 24.[35] A decade after Dank, and recognising the effect that social context has had on the lives of homosexuals, Ken Plummer wrote that the time of coming out was unpredictable. 'Many will find it occurring during their first heterosexual marriage'. Plummer continued: 'some may find it taking place in mid adolescence, and others can move through it in their retirement'. He noted that among North American men in the 1970s it tended to occur between the late teenage years and the early 30s.[36] Gilbert Herdt also agrees that coming out represents 'a lifelong social and developmental change' for gay people, their friends and family, and even their neighbours,[37] and that overall the age at which they come out is dropping.

North American research suggests that between the 1970s and the late 1990s the age at which young gays and lesbians came out fell by ten years. The reason according to Herdt, is '[t]he growing visibility of the lesbian and gay movement … has made it increasingly possible for people to … "come out" at younger ages'.[38] John Gagnon reiterates that the growth and development of the gay world is the reason for gay youth coming out earlier, writing that the gay and lesbian community offered 'new attractions to wider audiences', with the important conse- quence that young people 'now know about gay and lesbian possibil- ities at an earlier age and … are better informed about the content of these life-styles'.[39] Making connections with changes to sexual and social practices in the heterosexual world, Angus McLaren suggests that the lowering of the age at which young gay people come out can be related to the 'speeding up and standardization of life-course events' in Western countries, by which he means that people are participating in social practices at an earlier age with each new generation: 'There emerged in the twentieth century a "right time" (usually earlier with each generation) to reach sexual maturity, to lose one's virginity, to marry, to have children',[40] and, for gay people, to come out. In a study he conducted with Andrew Boxer of young people in Chicago between 1987 and 1988, Herdt found that 16 was the average age at which young males and females came out.[41] They found evidence of 'same gender attraction' in people as young as ten. This makes coming out, 'for the first time in history a matter of adolescent development'.[42]

## Coming out in childhood

Those who dated their coming out from when they were children are of special interest, partly because western society is coy about recognis- ing or talking about sexuality in children. One man interviewed for this study explained that he and a classmate were 'outed' by the rest of the children in Grade Six and that they were then, 'gay bashed at the traffic lights after school'. Adam is now in his 20s. He is an intelligent, sensitive and articulate man, who is enrolled in a university course as a mature age student. This homophobic attack forced him to come out when he was 11 years old. He explained: 'They labelled our relation- ship for me and after the bashing I felt that I had no choice but to say that this is what I am. I did not want to hide or let other people tell us what we could or could not be'. His account might be influenced by the narratives of discrimination and homophobia he encountered when he was at secondary school and as a young adult at university. It is possible also that he reconstructed a signal life event while his self- identity as a gay person formed and as he told the story of his coming out to other gay people and friends and family. This is not to say that he has invented the story; rather, it acknowledges the important part that ontological narrative plays in the formation of our identity. Adam strongly believed that what he experienced as an 11-year-old was a 'gay bashing' and that this event precipitated his coming out at a relatively early age. He did not say how he experienced being gay at 11.

Harry, like Adam is a man in his 20s. He said that he 'always knew' he was gay and also that he was having sex with boys his own age when he was four or five years old. Harry said that, after these experiences, 'the feelings and the sex' went away until he was 13 or 14. Then he experienced something similar to Adam's 'gay bashing'. His classmates suspected that he was homosexual and started calling him 'poofter'; and thus began what he describes as 'a hard few years and one or two traumas as well'. The term, 'poofter' is a fairly general term of abuse among males of all ages in Australia. Teenagers will often use it without understanding its meaning. For young gay men, however, its meaning is painfully clear and is not as easily shaken off. When a dominant group labels an outsider, especially a male whose perceived deviancy is sexual, the person may carry the hurt for many years after.

For Harry, the occasion when he was labelled 'poofter' marked the beginning of not one month or one school term of abuse, but the beginning of, in his words, 'a hard few years'. The homophobia that he experienced caused him eventually to rebel against his tormentors. He came out, he said, because, 'I got tired of all the crap'. At this point in his gay career Harry told some friends that he was gay, began to meet other gay people and, in his words, 'to feel a bit more comfortable about who I was and who I was with'. This stage in Harry's coming out is significant for the sociability and sense of belonging that seems to have accompanied it. Several scholars have written about the importance in the coming-out process of the neophyte's social interaction with, and acceptance by, other homosexuals who are out.[43] If his coming out began when he was four or five—which is probably unlikely given what we know about childhood sexuality and how we understand coming out—and then went into abeyance until he was a teenager, realisation was forced on him by the homophobic labelling he received in secondary school.

The third man who said that he came out when he was a child is Jason. Jason is in his 30s and says that, like Harry, he 'always knew' he was gay. His sexual awakening occurred when he was in Grade Five or Six in primary school. He said that he and his best friend used to 'play around'. Their sexual relationship came to an end when Jason's friend moved to another town. Jason's sexual career then followed a similar pattern to Harry's, that is, there was a period of inactivity until he reached puberty. Jason is emphatic, however, that he did not know what gay was or what it meant until he was 14. As he tells the story, there was an occasion when the teenager who was then his best friend 'found himself a male lover who was much older', and this friend and his older lover introduced Jason to gay clubs and bars. This was his first 'identifying experience'. He was 16.

Harry and Jason believe that the sexual experiences they remember having when they were children were the beginning of the coming-out process. They may be better understood, however, as early sexual awakenings that they have interpreted in their personal narratives as their first gay sexual experience. It might therefore be more accurate to describe these experiences as markers that they have retrospectively selected as starting points in the story that they tell of their coming out rather than as evidence that they actually did come out when they were children.

## Coming-out stories

The greatest difficulty the majority of men from the young cohort faced when coming out was having to tell their parents. In the main, their friends expressed surprise that they had waited so long to tell them. A handful of men said coming out was an event of no great significance, but they were distinctly in the minority.

Not surprisingly, fear of rejection caused young gay men the greatest anxiety as they approached the task of coming out to their parents. In the stories they told of how they arranged to reveal their homosexuality to their parents—on Mother's Day in the case of one 24-year-old—the emotions they recalled were at best tentativeness, at worst, cold fear. Most commentators are agreed that the chief obstacle to overcome in the process of coming out is what Ken Plummer calls the 'heterosexual assumption',[44] which has also been called the 'presumption of heterosexuality' and 'heterosexual ethnocentricity'.[45] The assumption that people are born heterosexual and grow up heterosexual is, I would argue, *the* dominant public narrative in the West and many other human societies. It is expected, says Plummer, 'that every adolescent will find a partner of the opposite sex, settle down, get married, ultimately procreate and raise children'.[46]

In the past, generations of gay men found they were under pressure to conform to the heterosexual assumption. As discussed in the previous chapter, they lived closeted or double lives and passed as heterosexual. Many got married. In middle age or later, they were likely to face a set of problems, which Plummer enumerates as ones of: 'marital disharmony, of spouses who reproach themselves for the relationship, of divorce, of the custody of wanted and unwanted children and of gay parents'.[47] In the following extract from his life story, the historian Garry Wotherspoon spells out the damaging effects for gay men of the heterosexual assumption.

> I was in my late 20s when, once again, I fell in love, and this time it was requited. The relationship lasted for about three years and ended ... in what I saw then as failure. Both he and I were utterly 'untrained' for the situation we found ourselves in. We ... had no collective past experience—relating to homosexual relationships—to fall back on ... We tried to apply the only guidelines we had learned, those taught by the heterosexual culture, where the roles and categories at least had a relevance to reality. But nothing in all my past reading, or my previous emotional involvements, or my sexual encounters, was adequate preparation for that situation, for that relationship, for what it went through.[48]

Wotherspoon was born in the early 1940s and so was in his late 20s at the beginning of the 1970s.[49] He would consequently belong in the middle cohort and the gay period. Today the gay identity is less stigmatised, and there is more visible evidence of gay men's capacity to form affective relationships that provide role models for others and to develop stable life paths.

### Parents' response

The importance to the young men of their father's acceptance was a strong theme in their coming-out stories. Moreover, because of the father's position in the nuclear family and the associated struggle between fathers and sons, other members of the family often mediated the news of the son's homosexuality. In the stories, it was common to hear that a mother or sibling had offered to be a go-between and to tell the father on the son's behalf, or advised the son not to tell his father about his gayness, or to delay telling him. Fathers' responses varied from acceptance through denial and rejection. What the stories often revealed, therefore, were long-standing and pre-existing structures of power within families that were not sufficiently flexible to incorporate a gay son.

A small number of coming-out stories told of parents who were frightened by news of their son's gayness, often because they feared he would contract HIV-AIDS. When one man who is in his 30s told his mother about his boyfriend, her first question was, 'Has he got AIDS?' For the men in their 20s, the reaction was similar if more dramatic. The mother of a 24-year-old man told her son, 'You will get HIV and die', while a man in his early 20s was told that he could do whatever he wanted to do, but he had to wear a condom and he must never catch AIDS. The latter is Jack and his reflective response to his mother's concerns deserves longer consideration. He lives in a capital city and grew up in a large provincial town. He almost completed a university degree and now works in politics. He is 22 and single.

> Fears about HIV dominated my mother's thinking about my sexuality. Her attitude was, 'I do not care what you are; I love you; just do not get AIDS. You have to wear a condom'. The thought never enters people's minds that sex between men does not necessarily involve anal sex or condoms and therefore I might not be at the risk that they think I am. I have a rule about safe sex and I have kept to it fairly strictly but it is a scary proposition as well. I have never been tested [for HIV] and that concerns my friends who say I am an idiot. I have been making commitments for over a year to do it but it is a big psychological thing. I don't think that I have put myself or anyone else at risk of anything being transmitted.

It is clear that his mother's concern for his well-being is important to him and that he interprets it as a sign of love. He is well informed about transmission of HIV and safe sex, and he is unlikely to be putting himself or his sexual partners at risk. But Jack is frightened. Like people who fear the prospect of having a colonoscopy, mammogram or pap smear, Jack is afraid of the possibility the medical procedure may reveal a fatal disease. His mother's fear is mirrored in his own response.

Among the remaining examples of parental responses are two that concern credulity. Robert is in his late 30s. He came out when he was 27. When he told his family, his mother refused to believe him and would not listen to what he had to say until the girlfriend he had at the time spoke to her and convinced her that he was indeed gay. The other interviewee, Ian, is ten years younger than Robert. His parents accepted his word when he told them that he was homosexual but asked him why he thought they needed to know and then wanted his assurance that he was not a trans-sexual.

In the small group of men whose parents accepted the news of their son's gayness unconditionally and in a positive spirit were a man in his mid-30s and one in his early 20s. The parents of the man in his 30s were divorced. When he told his mother about his homosexuality, he also told her that his sister was not 'handling the news well'. His mother replied that his sister would learn to accept his homosexuality or she would have to leave home. The other man, Troy (aged 24), arranged to meet his father in a city restaurant for a father-and-son conversation. As Troy tells the story, his father, whom he described as a 'powerful, domineering man', stood up when Troy told him that he was gay. Troy continued: 'I thought that he was going to hit me or walk out but he held out his hand and said that he thought I was more of a man to tell him than to keep it a secret'. Troy was overwhelmed by his father's response and even more so when he learned that his father broke down in private and cried. Now, his parents want to know whom he is going out with and are more interested in 'what is happening in my life'.

### Having to leave home to come out

The group of men who had to leave their family home or home town in order to come out comprised five men in their 30s and three in their 20s. Those who left country towns seemed more worried about peers than parents. They are represented here by Robert, Vincent and Daniel who are in their 30s, and Ian who is 28. In almost all cases, the men left town also to go to university or technical college or in search of work. Often they grew up in non-urban regions where anti-homosexual prejudice was not a thing of the past. In the United States, for example, the existence of homophobia continues to make coming out a struggle for some people, and there is no reason to believe that the situation is different in other western countries:

> American society and western cultures in general have changed in the direction of a more positive regard for gays. This does not mean, however, that the hatred and homophobia of the past are gone or that secrecy and fear of passing have faded away. People still fear, and rightly so, the effects of coming out on their lives and safety, their well-being and jobs, their social standing and community prestige.[50]

Moving away from their family and home town provided them with an occasion to develop, as Ian says, 'a circle of friends who were more likely to be accepting', which is code for 'friends who are less homophobic'. When Vincent left his home town, he began drinking because of what he described as the 'heart-ache of having to live a double life'. Once he came out he stopped drinking. Most of his family have accepted his homosexuality. The 'red-neck cousins' who do not accept it and who, he now suspects, were the reason he wanted to leave home when he was a teenager no longer bother him.

Daniel also left his home town because he knew it would be safer to be a gay man elsewhere. He returned to the country town where he grew up when he had a partner and chose, as he said, 'in the full flight of love', to come out to his family. Their response was mixed. Some of his relatives had suspected and were not surprised; others were happy for him. One group of relatives, however, told him that his 'life-style' disgusted them and, said Daniel, 'I still have difficulty with a couple of family members who have not come to terms with that part of my life'. He described the region where his family lives as 'a safe place to grow up' and as 'politically and socially conservative because of the influence of fundamentalist Christian beliefs'. Daniel remembered anti-homosexual marches in the neighbouring town when he was in school.

Unsettling as is Daniel's account, it is an isolated experience of the men in the young cohort. The general pattern is that coming out is a life-course event that they may expect to negotiate without fearing ostracism or social opprobrium. Nevertheless, it is worth underlining that a significant minority of the young men did wait until they had moved away from family and their home town to come out. There are a number of possible explanations for this.

On the one hand, it could be argued that there is nothing special about their decision because the time they left home—for further education or work—is a standard stage in the life course of young adults in Western society, a time when they begin to assert their independence. It is understandable that young gay men would take this opportunity to come out. On the other hand, it could be argued that these men purposely waited until they moved away because they knew any public declaration of homosexuality would attract less negative attention or censure if they came out somewhere other than where they grew up and their family lived. Coming out would be safer if they waited until they had settled in a new town or city and, as one interviewee said, had had time to make friends with people more likely to accept them.

## Conclusion

The general pattern to emerge from the young men's experience of coming out is that, while it is a life-course event that causes some anxiety, they were generally able to accomplish it without the risk of being ostracised or having to sever relations with family and friends. This was not always the case in the past. In this regard, their experience corresponds with that of young gay men elsewhere.[51] 'The hardest thing', said an interviewee in his late 30s, 'was telling my parents'. These men have benefited from the gradual reduction in anti-homosexual prejudice over the last 20 years. Instead of the social opprobrium of the past, the greatest anxiety these men faced was that their parents might reject them because of their sexuality. And, yet, the fact that a notable minority of men chose to leave home before they came out shows that homophobia persists in parts of Australia.

It is difficult to be definitive about the effect of HIV-AIDS on the coming out of this generation. While slightly more than one third of the cohort (12 men) came of age during the 1980s—when the epidemic was at its worst in Australia—half of these waited between three and 12 years to come out. And while this may suggest that the stigma of AIDS caused them to delay the decision, none said so in his interview. HIV-AIDS nonetheless dominated the context of their coming out. Some interviewees reported knowledge of heterosexuals conflating AIDS and homosexuality, others spoke of their parents' fears they would contract the virus.

The men related a variety of responses from parents, ranging from full and unconditional acceptance to incredulity. One notable finding is the importance of the father's acceptance and the strategy a number of men adopted to tell one member of the family—often the person they felt closest to—and then tell the others by stages or let the information seep out via their confidant. Finally, there was a handful of men for whom coming out was an event of no great significance, a relatively matter-of-fact experience. One man, for instance, let his family know via a telephone call. Meanwhile, another man made a casual announcement at his 21st birthday when, at the end of the night, he said, 'Thank you all for coming and, by the way, I am gay'.

# 5
# The 'Scene'

'I would not be rejected at any gay venue because the gay male psyche is conditioned to accept anything young and pretty'. Troy, 24.

## Introduction

An upper-middle-class interviewee from the young cohort joked that the gay life course was a progression through four stages: 'Lycra, leather, rice and rent'. As the material from which bicycle shorts, swimming trunks, gym clothes and vests are made, 'lycra' represents the athleticism of youth. The remaining three terms signify stages of decline, from middle age to old age and destitution. 'Leather' is for a style of dress that mimics service uniforms or signifies an interest in sado-masochistic sex (S&M);[1] 'rice' signifies a penchant for young Asian men as sex or relationship partners; and 'rent' refers to the final stage of a gay man's life when, according to the cynicism of the joke, he is reduced to buying sex, and perhaps affection, from male prostitutes. Such attitudes are understandable in the context of the dominant narrative of the gay scene, which is that a gay man's most valued qualities are his youthfulness and beauty.

The gay 'scene' is a site of physical and youthful display, where young men are to be found in greatest number and are valorised for their youth and beauty. The principal argument of this chapter is that age mostly determines how gay men engage with the scene. As they age, gay men have less in common with its values and activities. They feel less at ease on the scene. It satisfies fewer of their needs.

The scene and the gay community are two parts of what in previous chapters has been called the gay (or homosexual) milieu, the gay world, or the homosexual (or gay) sub-culture. The scene consists of businesses that provide spaces where gay men socialise and may consume alcohol, drugs or sex. These are social and recreational spaces such as bars, pubs, discotheques, clubs and sex venues. The gay community, on the other hand, largely consists of not-for-profit organisations whose focus includes providing assistance for gay people coming out or having difficulties with relationships, lobbying for improved political and social rights, and the provision of housing and care for people living with HIV-AIDS, all of which are discussed in the next chapter.

In major cities, the centre of social life for many gay men is the scene. It is a world oriented towards young men, with a premium placed on beautiful bodies and the latest fashions. All sites of gay sociability are sites of consumption, where 'sexual fantasies and pleasures [are sold] as commodities'.[2] While the commodification of sex is not limited to the gay scene, and is a feature of Western capitalist societies generally, anyone wishing to participate on the scene must have a high disposable income, for night clubs, sex clubs, gymnasiums and dance parties all charge substantial entry fees, and, in the case of dance parties, are very costly to attend.[3] Writing in the early 1980s, Kenneth Plummer commented that, in regard to the scene,

> the homosexual 'poor' are ignored—it is all very well to counsel homosexuals to become involved in the gay scene, when the cost of membership, entrance, travel, drinks and cosmetics are so high as to preclude those who live at or below the breadline.[4]

Scholars who have examined gay social practices in Western countries describe the scene as a competitive place, familiarity with which will not necessarily guarantee gay men social success or emotional support.[5] In support of this observation, a man interviewed for this study, who is in his mid-30s, said he could not go out when he broke up with his boyfriend because 'the gay scene as a whole felt threatening. I was not being hugely harassed but I was aware there might be one or two people in a club who made the whole thing feel really toxic'.

To outsiders and to many gay men who have recently come out, the scene is the most visible form of gay culture. As Vincent, a man in his 30s, explained, young gay men commonly confuse the scene and the gay community:

> The gay community is obsessed with youth and beauty and the perfect body. In some ways I feel let down by coming out into the

gay scene. We need to let young gay people know that the gay scene is one part of the gay community and the gay culture of night clubs, sex, gyms and dance parties is not all there is in life. I have had this weird experience of being sucked into it but also on some level knowing that it is crap. I put too much energy into body image sometimes.

Vincent reveals a strong ambivalence towards the scene. He is drawn to it because it is a site of youthful display but he also knows that its values are insubstantial. His ambivalence helps explain the continuing importance of the scene: the physicality and beauty of men on the scene attracts others to it. In the end, however, most gay men tire of its superficiality and the contrived illusion of perpetual youth.

A word is needed about terms used in this chapter. 'Bar' and 'pub' are social spaces where alcohol is consumed and people socialise. Originally, bar was a North American word for a social institution peculiar to that culture; now it is used to designate any social venue where alcohol is served.[6] While the pub (public house or hotel) has a long history as a working-class venue, its representation has been ambiguous. It has had a variety of purposes, political ones included: in gay pubs, entertainment may include drag shows. The fact that most gay socialising has taken place and continues to take place in bars and pubs affects the way gay men relate to and regard each other, chiefly because social interaction in such venues most often involves consumption of alcohol. A 'club' is a more private venue where an entry fee may be charged and space provided for dancing. Pubs may also be called clubs if they have extended licensing hours and a dance floor.[7] In the gay world, clubs have often been necessary for members' safety, especially if they are meeting for sex. Sex venues include saunas and what are called sex (or fuck) clubs. Their primary purpose is to enable patrons to have sex in public, as well as in booths and private rooms, without fear of assault or arrest. Sexual relations that occur in sex venues are known as 'public sex' and have a longer history at beats.[8]

As suggested in the previous chapters, the scene that exists today in Australia's largest city (Sydney) evolved by stages from the 1920s and 1930s. Between the wars it comprised a small group of hotels, cafés and coffee shops where homosexuals were tolerated or welcomed. These venues expanded during World War II with the influx of servicemen from Australian, American and allied armies. Repression followed with the Cold War and the scene became more clandestine. It remained relatively hidden and clandestine until the mid-1960s when by degrees social exclusion of non-heterosexuals began to abate and the variety of venues available for homosexuals expanded. The emergence of Camp Inc. and gay liberation coincided with a rapid growth in the 1970s of bars, saunas and clubs, which in Sydney has continued since then, slowed, though only in its early days, by the advent of the HIV-AIDS epidemic.

The men interviewed for this study were equally divided in their view of the scene. Equal numbers expressed negative views and positive views, and almost one quarter of the sample held both negative and positive views—in other words, were ambivalent about it.[9] Notably, more than a third of the men said they did not go on the scene, the majority from the middle and old cohorts.[10] This fact underlines the main argument of the chapter, which is that age determines most gay men's engagement with the scene: as men grow older, the scene appeals less to them and has less to offer them. Its social practices are for young or youthful men. This is consistent with other published research.[11]

With the exception of men from the middle cohort, relationship status had little bearing on interviewees' views of the scene. Single men were almost equally divided in their view of the scene, as were men in relationships. At first sight, this appears counter-intuitive but, unlike in the heterosexual world, where social life is more domestically oriented after the formation of couple relationships, in the gay world, social involvement in the scene does not necessarily cease when gay men pursue permanent couple relationships. Interestingly, in the middle cohort, twice as many men in relationships held positive views as held negative views of the scene. One reason for this may be that these men were of the gay liberation generation, who came out as the scene was being formed and helped create it. As a result they seem to have a higher regard for it than the men from the old cohort who preceded them and the men from the young cohort who followed them.

Almost two thirds of men interviewed for this study participated in the scene. The largest group consisted of men from the young cohort where more than 80 per cent reported participation, followed by almost three quarters of the men from the middle cohort, and slightly more than a quarter of the men from the old cohort.[12] Scene participation drops gradually between the ages of 20 and the late 50s and then declines rapidly when men are in their 60s and 70s. Edmund White noted a similar trend in the 1980s: 'In the United States, and especially among gay men, this period of adolescence is being extended for the first time in history into the 40s, 50s, even 60s. It has become a way of life'.[13] What White observed in gay men was a more visible example of a universal condition, which, according to Phillipe Ariès, began to develop in Western society after World War I, when marriage no longer brought to an end what he called the 'privileged age' of adolescence: 'the married adolescent ... [became] one of the most prominent types of our time, dictating its values, its appetites and its customs ... We now want to come to it early and linger in it as long as possible'.[14]

Gay men may appear to experience a more prolonged adolescence than is available to the rest of society because the social sites available to them—where they are free to conduct social relations without fear—are mostly limited to those of the scene, that is, venues where they typically drink, dance, or have sex.[15] To observers, therefore, it may seem that drinking, dancing and having sex are the sum of gay social practices. Their life trajectory may appear to be an extended adolescence. And yet, as this research shows, while a small group of gay men continued to participate on the scene in their 60s and 70s, and many did who were in their 40s and 50s, a significant minority of the men interviewed for this study did not participate on the scene at all. Moreover, a significant proportion of those who did participate on the scene held ambivalent views about it and disapproved of many of its social practices.

## Positive views of the scene

Not surprisingly, interviewees' positive views were contingent on their having had, and being able to recall, rewarding experiences at gay venues. More than 80 per cent of interviewees with positive views of the scene were from the middle cohort and the young cohort.[16] Both of these groups included men who were satisfied with the venues, as well as men whose satisfaction and participation were conditional on finding spaces where they could 'be themselves'. While also expressing some positive views, the men from the old cohort generally offered only faint praise for the venues.

This section begins with a short discussion of the views of the men from the old cohort and the middle cohort. Then there follows a section on men who use sex venues, the majority of whom are from the middle cohort and the old cohort. It is notable that, with the exception of two men, none of the interviewees from the young cohort referred to sex venues in their accounts of their participation on the scene. The final section concerns the positive views of men from the young cohort.

## Old and middle cohorts

In the old cohort, a small group of six men expressed mildly positive views of bars and pubs, and they are represented here by two men in their 60s. Drawing on his memory of an earlier time and gay scene, Charles (aged 67) could only offer that 'the pub scene was better than the disco scene'. Lindsay (aged 62) is still a fairly active participant on the scene. Not long ago, he joined a 'leather' club[17] operating from a pub because he hoped by doing so to make new friends, but went infrequently because, as he said, he 'did not find the people particularly interesting'.

In the middle group, interviewees with positive views of the scene were either satisfied with the venues and what they provided or were more selective about their participation. 'An easy place to meet friends' was a common sentiment about the scene. One of the men described it as 'time out' from the straight world, while another said he liked 'being amongst other gay men', whether in a sauna or a club. A man in his mid-50s recommended gay bars when travelling because he can 'be himself' and he knows that he will be welcomed:

> I always feel safe in gay venues, not that I necessarily feel unsafe elsewhere, but at some kind of level you can relax because everyone knows exactly the situation. I have never been hassled in gay bars or any other kind of gay establishment. So while travelling it was nice to check out gay venues for that feeling.

Five men from the middle cohort specifically stated that their enjoyment of bars and clubs was conditional on being with their own age group. They disliked young men's venues: in the words of one, the scene was 'great fun', as long as he 'kept clear of kiddies' bars'. The sixth man in the group is upper-middle class and in his late 50s. While his account was generally positive, it suggested that the presence of other gay men was incidental to his enjoyment of a 'night out at the pub': 'I enjoy going to gay pubs because you can go in and out. I love going in to watch a drag show. It is good light-hearted fun and you are not going to come across the same people again'.

## Public sex and sex venues

In this section, two groups of men, principally from the middle cohort and old cohort, relate their experience of sex venues. The first group consists of those who limited their participation on the scene to sex venues, while the second group consists of men who included them in their range of acceptable venues.

Public sex is not a recent phenomenon. It has existed for as long as male and female prostitutes have practised their trade. James Boswell, for example, wrote about the sex he had in public with female prostitutes he picked up in St James's Park in London in the 1760s.[18] In the early twentieth century, public sex—both homosexual and heterosexual—was common in working-class neighbourhoods of large Western cities like New York because, as George Chauncey explains, it was impossible for young unmarried people to have sex in the 'tenements, boardinghouses, and lodging houses' in which they lived. Their recourse was to 'construct some measure of privacy for themselves in spaces middle-class ideology regarded as "public"'. When gay men 'cruised'[19] public spaces for casual pick-ups, therefore, they often found that they were sharing them with 'young heterosexual men and women, who sought privacy in them for the same reasons ... Both groups [of gay and straight young people], for instance, found ... [New York] city's parks particularly helpful'.[20]

Following the 'sexual revolution' of the 1960s, and as the gay liberation movement developed, the Sydney scene transformed, like others internationally, into a sophisticated sexual market that included bars, clubs and sex venues, which provided for varying expressions of sexual desire. Michel Foucault described the sex venues he discovered in San Francisco and New York as 'laboratories of sexual experimentation'.[21] At this time of 'increased sexual freedom and stress on individual gratification', argues Dennis Altman, sexuality was 'incorporated into the marketplace':

> [G]oing to the baths to have sex represents an integration of sexuality into consumerism in a way that encounters in parks or streets do not ... As gay bathhouses have both proliferated and become more luxurious, they are being recognised as central institutions of male gay life ...[22]

In contrast to these views, there are other commentators, such as Sheila Jeffreys, who are highly critical of sexual practices that developed in gay sex venues: 'Sex clubs, bathhouses, bookstores and bars with backrooms promoted the sex of "cruising" as the liberated sex of the new era, and the burgeoning gay porn industry, whose stock-in-trade was "public sex", served as propaganda to this end'. Her attack on public sex arises from her belief that too few AIDS activists or queer theorists admitted a link between gay men's sexual practices—in particular, 'multi-partner sex in commercial clubs'—and the spread of HIV-AIDS. She was incredulous that in the mid-1990s gay activists in the United States continued to promote and defend public sex, in particular the practice known as 'bare-backing', or unprotected anal sex, and argues that its implications for others outweigh the rights of gay men to have sex in public:

> The model of sexuality which underlies the queer promotion of 'public sex' is one which is profoundly problematic for women, children, and vulnerable and marginalized men and boys internationally. If the interests of constituencies other than privileged white American gay men are to be taken seriously, then this kind of sexuality needs to be transformed, rather than protected. [23]

A small group of five men from the old cohort and middle cohort had stories to tell of their experiences at sex venues. The social practices they revealed suggest high levels of conviviality, even intimacy, in public spaces. These men did not frequent bars or pubs; their involvement in the scene was limited to sex venues. They are Leslie and Clive from the old cohort, Noel and Bob from the middle cohort and Alex from the young cohort, and their ages span five decades. The youngest, Alex (aged 37), was critical of the scene and his account is discussed in Part Two, below. The remaining four men are middle class with diverse relationship experiences. Three are single, one is in a relationship of more than 20 years, and two were formerly married; three are university educated, two are retired, all are or have been in full-time employment.

There is, in addition, a group of six men who *included* sex venues with bars and clubs in the variety of venues they attended on the scene.[24] Mark (aged 25) is the youngest, and his experience of saunas is discussed in a later chapter on the intimate life of gay men. The remaining five men are from the old cohort and the middle cohort, and, in common with the first group of men, are middle class and university educated. All but one are in relationships and all work in education or the public service. The views of both groups of men are represented here by the accounts of Leslie and Bob from the 'sex venues-only' group, and Alan and Lindsay from the 'wider variety' group.

Once a month Leslie (aged 74) and his partner go to a special night at their sauna for men over 55. It is a form of 'mass sexual encounter' similar to the 'jack-off' parties that began in the United States as a preventive measure against HIV-AIDS.[25] Leslie described one of the encounters he attended:

> You pay a fee. You get your gear off and go into a room where there can be up to 60 guys. Everybody is talking, wanking, hugging and so

on. There are rules: 'No fucking' and 'No lips below the hips'. It is
sensible and it is friendly. We have met some very nice people there.

A frequent accusation made against sex venues is that they are sites
of impersonal sex but Leslie described a mass sexual encounter that
was sociable, and an intimacy of sorts in a public setting. The three
remaining interviewees also referred to the sociability they experienced
in saunas, as did Dennis Altman, in the early 1980s, when he remarked
on their effect on social relations between gay men. He described the
atmosphere as egalitarian, where there existed 'a desire to know and
trust other men in a type of brotherhood far removed from the male
bonding of rank, hierarchy and competition that characterizes much of
the outside world'.[26]

Slightly confused private narratives were revealed in the second interviewee's account of his experience in sex venues. Bob is in his late 40s.
He goes on the scene when he is looking for sex, but is impatient with it
because, as he said, he 'cannot be bothered with the pick-up line that
begins with "Let's have a drink". Also, I am not a great drinker and I
hate getting pissed'. Then, when he does go to a sauna, it does not
always involve sex:

> When I was going there it was mainly to get in touch with my
> Russian friends. There were about five of them who used to go there
> every Friday night. I used to go to practice the language on them
> and to help them with English. It was quite funny. We would go
> into a cubicle and smoke dope and come out ripped off our tits and
> then be struggling through Russian and then struggling through
> English, which was often more enjoyable than hunting around and
> cruising for sex.

Bob is dissatisfied with the artificiality of the scene. He cannot talk to
strangers and prefers to be with friends. Avoiding conventional meeting places, Bob uses a sex venue to socialise with friends, and have
drugs. His difficulty in talking to strangers is not uncommon and is
raised, below, in section two, when the discussion turns to men who
are frustrated because they cannot find a community on the scene.

Alan, also in his 40s, shared Bob's views about the predictability of
social interaction at bars. But, as mentioned, unlike Bob, he does not
limit his gay socialising to sex venues only. He likes saunas for their
conviviality and the direct interaction they allow: 'There is music and
you can talk if you want to. It is warm and you can act on impulse

instead of playing games. I do not feel as vulnerable grabbing someone as I would at a dance party'. Other published research shows a similar relation between gay men's dislike of the artificial social interaction in bars and clubs and their attendance at saunas.[27]

In the early 1970s, Lindsay discovered saunas on a trip to the United States; since then, they have been, in his words, 'part of my life in a way'. Almost 20 years older than Bob and Alan, Lindsay said that he visited saunas on his own, or, like Leslie, with his partner: 'On a trip interstate we will both go to one as a kind of holiday outing'. When in his hometown, he restricts his use of saunas because 'it can get totally out of hand. I try not to become part of the furniture. I suppose I go to one every month or so'.

The picture these men reveal is of moderate involvement and participation in public sex at saunas. Their accounts are notable more for the conviviality they enjoyed there than for any evidence of 'wild' sexual excess. These men are, as well, fairly representative of mature, middle-class gay men. What mention they make of sex in saunas suggests that, while it may be anonymous, it is not their sole motivation for being there. Younger gay men may tell different stories, but, as mentioned in the introduction to this section, only two men from the young cohort referred to sex venues when they discussed their participation in the scene. This relatively small number may be a measure of either the success of the scene as a source of sexual partners for young men or a decline in interest in public sex.

## Young cohort

Slightly more than 60 per cent of men from the young cohort reported positive views of the scene.[28] Their accounts are notable for the diversity of the young men's experiences, and also the range of bars and clubs available to them, which is discussed separately below. At one end of the spectrum were two men in their early 20s whose views on the gay scene were unqualifiedly positive. At the other end was a group of seven men whose participation was conditional, whose views, while positive, were more qualified. Their participation on the scene depends on being in the company of friends. For these men, gay venues are enjoyable only from within a circle or 'bubble' of friends or in a social space on the scene where they could 'be themselves'.

Troy and Lachlan have entirely positive views of the scene. Both are in their early 20s. Troy believed he would be welcome wherever he went, because 'the gay male psyche is programmed to accept anything that is young and pretty'. Lachlan works in the finance sector and has a high disposable income. He recounted very positive experiences of the scene:

> I think of the gay community as the scene. I get involved in it weekly and sometimes more than once a week and it is lots of fun meeting people and having good times with my friends. If it is a work night, I rarely venture out of the house. I have a routine, which is work, gym, home, dinner and bed. Friday night is different. I would have dinner with friends; we would have lots of wine, then we would go to a club where we can stay out until 9 am and have some drugs. But that would be the exception. Normally we would have lots of drinks, get drunk and head home at 3 am.

From Lachlan's account, the scene was the stage for social interaction, chiefly with his friends. It was also the stage for drinking a lot of alcohol and occasional drug taking. In no sense does Lachlan feel isolated or lonely on the scene. Rather it performs a community function for him because it is the place where he and his friends can express their fraternity and socialise.

At the other end of the spectrum of positive experiences and views of the scene was a group of men whose enjoyment was contingent on their being with friends or finding a venue where they can 'be themselves'. The group comprises men from different class and ethnic backgrounds, and is represented here by the accounts of one working-class man, two non-Caucasian men and one middle-class man.[29]

The working-class man is in his early 30s and lives in the country. When he visits a nearby capital city, he goes to the public bar of a small pub in an inner-city suburb where the drag is good and whose owners refer to the bar as 'their "lounge room downstairs"':

> They welcome their friends and regard the rest of us as their friends as well. I used to go out a lot more but I have found that if you do not have 'the look', you are not welcome. And yet at this pub you can be old or young, fat or skinny and they accept you because you are who you are.

The non-Caucasian men were in their mid-30s and late 20s. The older one lives in an inner suburb of a major capital city and the younger in the country. The older man and his friends avoid venues for young gay men because of their experience of racism, and, instead, they go to an 'alternative' club where 'there is no discrimination on the basis of your nationality or the clothes you wear or how you look, and the bar staff are friendly'. When the younger non-Caucasian man 'goes to town', he prefers a small, quiet pub on weeknights because 'it is just people socialising. It is not a meat market and the staff are friendly there as well'.

The middle-class man is in his early 30s and likes to go on the scene to dance and have fun with his friends. He was aware, however, that it is a lonely place for single people: 'I go with friends whenever I go out and that makes it easier. If I were going out by myself, I would feel uncomfortable in a lot of places'. This comment is revealing because, despite the appearance of conviviality, the scene would appear to be a lonely place for single men. All of the men interviewed for this study said that they went on the scene with friends or as a couple. While it may give the impression of comprising large numbers of active, energised men, and give the illusion of individualism, it is more likely to consist of a lot of small friendship groups and couples.

## Negative views of the scene

The interviewees' principal complaints about the scene concerned its impoverished social and physical environments. The majority of men interviewed for this study said that it was difficult to develop genuine social relations on the scene, often because of the poor physical environment of gay venues. More than 70 per cent of men from the young cohort reported negative views of the scene.[30] Because of their age, one might reasonably assume that these men, as the principal 'target market' of owners and managers of gay venues, would be more positive. But many of them were disenchanted, and almost half of those with negative views cited poor physical environment and social relations at venues. The remaining criticisms concerned the regulation body image of the scene and its sexual nature.

That the men from the young cohort were so critical of the scene can be attributed to the fact that, as mentioned in the introduction to this chapter, more than 80 per cent of them participated on the scene. It is their playground, and the number and strength of their criticisms reflect the level of their involvement in it. For this reason, this section begins with the young cohort's views on the physical and social environments of the scene, followed by their accounts of regulation body image and sexualised relations. It concludes with a summary discussion of the views of the men in the middle and old cohorts.

### Impoverished physical environment and social relations

Criticisms of the noise, crowds and smoke at bars and clubs are to be expected from men in middle or old age, but are unusual from the young. And yet, a vocal minority of men from the young cohort complained about the physical environment of the scene.[31] Their views are represented here by the account of a man in his late 30s, which encapsulates the range of the others' criticisms. Robert is caught between a desire to socialise on the scene and his dislike of its environment.

> I hate gay bars because of the loud music, cigarette smoke, people getting pissed, looking unhappy or getting out of it on drugs. It is not my scene. I do not fit into it. That is what made it really hard when I was coming out. It is the most visible place for gay men to meet. It is not just a characteristic of the gay community. A lot of straight people get off on the club scene; others feel alienated by it. What do you do? Join a knitting club? Female friends who are my age and are not married have found it a huge problem to find a man.

The fact that his female contemporaries also criticise straight 'singles' bars' says much about the anonymous nature of social intercourse in big cities and the corresponding anonymity of institutions set up to deal with it. For gay men the situation is more acute because, as mentioned, the social sites available to them are almost entirely limited to the scene. In earlier times, gay men and women who were not married by the time they were in their 30s would have been 'on the shelf' and referred to as 'dedicated bachelors' or 'old maids'. Writing about family life in the post-war United States, Elaine Tyler May argues that unmarried people were seen as deviant: 'Single women and men faced constant suspicion that there was something abnormal or dangerous about them'.[32]

A relatively small group of four men from the young cohort complained about the poverty of social relations on the scene.[33] Of special interest are the stories of two men, Jason (aged 35) and Mark (aged 25), who were frustrated because they expected to find a community on the scene. Jason is a working-class man in his mid-30s. After a number of different jobs, he is now studying at university. He dislikes gay venues because he finds the people insincere:

> Gay venues are full of pretension. They are full of people who are trying to be someone they are not, and when they do that they

isolate themselves from everyone else. I do not think that there is an openness among gay men. Occasionally you find it. It is not a tightly knit community like what you find in the heterosexual community. The bars and the clubs can be cold places. Even though the bar is full of people, you can feel isolated.

For men like Jason, the scene is all they know of the gay world. It is the focal point of their engagement with gay culture and represents for them a community of sorts.[34] Middle-class men probably have greater agency in this regard. They are more likely to be in a position to 'dip' in and out of the scene and treat their engagement with it as a 'special occasion' or 'time out' from their working life or social life or from their involvement in the more serious activities of the gay community. This point is underlined by Michael Pollak: 'Although the collective nature of homosexual life tends to blunt social distinctions, class origins and membership affect the ease with which an individual succeeds in integrating with the milieu'.[35]

Mark is a young middle-class man. He was educated at a private school and is a university graduate. Ten years younger than Jason, he also expected to find a community on the scene. And, in a sense, this is understandable because, for young men who like dancing, drinking and looking for sex, the scene *is* their community. Large numbers of gay men socialise there on weekends, just as do young heterosexuals in straight or 'mixed' clubs and bars.[36] Mark was disappointed, however, that his generation was not more involved in making the scene their own.

The gay scene was more progressive when I came out but now it is more backward looking. It focuses more on 'baby boomer' music when the 'baby boomers' were in their 20s, like Abba, for example, which is irrelevant to me and not played for people like me. People who come out now are expected to listen to old music and do it the way people used to do it. And because the [political and social] rights have been won, they are not as keen to take control and create a community they can be involved in and will participate in.

Behind his disappointment is a desire for generation change, for not only was the music on the scene out of date and irrelevant to Mark, but so also was the style of homosexuality it represented.

Another reason men like Jason and Mark may expect to find a community on the scene is that gay pubs and bars have a long history as meeting places. In the decades before gay liberation, they were the only community institution for gay men and, as Dennis Altman noted, they were often the first place where they met like-minded people, and were 'able to express themselves in ways denied in other areas of their lives'. As well, gay bars and clubs provided 'a sense of identity and even community that only a relatively small number of homosexuals find in alternative institutions'.[37] However, as gay community organisations proliferated, and the scene expanded, the gay bar gradually lost the central community function it once held for gay men. And yet, even though a stronger and more visible gay community exists today, with opportunities for involvement at many levels, and homosexuality is more integrated into mainstream society, some men still look on the gay scene as their community or look to the scene to provide them with a community—and these are generally young men and working-class men.

The remaining criticisms of men from the young cohort concern the regulation body image of the scene and its sexualised nature. Relatively small numbers of men raised these matters. Five referred to body image and two complained about the scene's sexualised nature. These are not large numbers but the views are significant because of the conviction with which they were expressed and because the men expected a better social environment.

### Body image

In the young cohort were men who, although physically, socially, or financially powerful, still felt inadequate on the scene because they did not measure up to its regulation image. They are represented here by two interviewees in their 20s and two in their late 30s.[38] Their experiences and expectations of the scene, though varied, reflect a shared understanding of the scene's requirements and where as individuals they fall short of them. The two men in their 20s are university educated and live in different capital cities. Although the scenes they frequent are sophisticated and specialised, their stories reveal dissatisfaction with the social environment. At 24, Myles is at an age when he can dance all night and still enjoy the next day. His youth does not protect him, however, from being inhibited in a club that attracts the body beautiful: 'It is a fabulous club but it is so intimidating socially. When I walk in, a wave of insecurity sweeps over me. I think, "What am I doing here when there are men like that running around?"' Angus (aged 23) is also aware of the dominant narrative of youth and beauty but doubts people his age are responsible for perpetuating it: 'It is sad that men in their 30s call themselves "gay boys". There is constant representation in gay media of young men. And the images are not only of young normal men but also young perfect men'.

The two men in their late 30s come from opposite ends of the socio-economic spectrum. One earns a medium to high income and has a high-status occupation, while the other has spent most of the last decade in casual jobs in various towns and cities. The latter is Andy. He works in the hospitality sector and has a strong, solid build. But he has to choose where he goes because, although relatively young, he does not have 'the look' and has been refused entry at gay clubs: 'I have a beard. They take one look at me and, going on past experience, I guess they are edgy about people with shaved heads and beards'. Neville is also in his late 30s. Both he and his partner have experience of the scene in Sydney, which Neville described in the following manner:

> If you talk about a fairly narrow group of people attached to the gay community, it is a *Peter Pan* culture. It is also non-reflexive. It is not just age; it is also race. The way Anglo gay men constrain and diminish Asian men and black men is racist. It is also partly to do with consumption. Sexuality is what you consume so anything that deviates from a narrow model of gym-bunny is less desirable.

His observation that gay men as a group are racist—'Anglo gay men constrain and diminish Asian and black men'—is borne out by Australian autobiography and research. Tony Ayres is a Chinese Australian film-maker and writer. His family migrated to Australia from Hong Kong in 1964. At gay clubs in Australia, he has experienced 'a wearing, subtle, almost imperceptible feeling of exclusion … It is the demoralising feeling that I am, in the eyes of the majority of the gay male population, as undesirable as a woman'.[39] He elaborates the layers and subtlety of the racism at work in the character of the so-called 'rice-queen':

> Caucasian men primarily attracted to Asians are called 'rice queens.' Because of the lowly status of the Asian within the gay community, the term 'rice queen' is a term of disparagement. The implication is that 'rice queens' are not desirable enough to cut the mustard in the mainstream scene so they have to resort to having sex with Asians. Within the race-power dynamics of the gay scene, these Caucasian men become second class by default.[40]

Almost 30 years ago, Raymond Berger observed that the gay scene in the United States was 'overwhelmingly dominated by white males'.

He was uncertain if the reason was 'the inhospitality [*sic*] ... [or] racism ... of the established gay community, or ... a lack of interest on the part of women and minorities'.[41] More recently, Australian research found that men from South-east Asian backgrounds reported being treated as Other at gay venues in Melbourne.[42] There is no reason to expect that the treatment of non-Caucasian men is any different in other Australian capital cities.

All these men were conscious of the worship of young men's bodies on the scene and the regulation image. Their discomfort with the valorisation of young men was not a form of self-hatred. Rather, it is recognition of the arbitrariness of the scene's hierarchy, which rewards white men with beautiful young bodies—of the 'gym bunny' variety to which Neville referred—and disregards and diminishes others.[43]

## Sexualised social relations

A persistent stereotype of gay men, often used to discredit their way of life, is that they are only interested in sex.[44] While it is mischievous to see all gay men as obsessed with sex, it is equally a mistake to discount their interest in it because, as Kenneth Plummer explains, 'the cornerstone of homosexual experience ... has to be—by definition—an emotio-erotic relationship with one's own sex'.[45] This 'emotio-erotic' relationship is nowhere more in evidence than on the scene, where sexual exchange dominates gay men's social relations. Michael Pollak used the metaphor of the market to describe its primacy: 'Of all the different types of masculine sexual behaviour, homosexuality is undoubtedly the one whose functioning is most strongly suggestive of a market, in which in the last analysis one orgasm is bartered for another'.[46]

The scene, then, comprises not only bars and pubs but also sex venues, where patrons may have sex in public without fear of assault or arrest. Many of the men interviewed for this study were aware of the sexualised nature of the scene—some referred to it as a 'meat market', others referred to practices such as 'cruising' and 'picking up'—and yet only two men, both from the young cohort, identified it as a reason for the impoverished social relations on the scene. The men are Vincent (aged 30) and Angus (aged 23). Both men live in a major capital city, are university educated and are employed in professional occupations.

Vincent has had relationships in the past but is single now. He believes that social interaction is severely limited at gay venues because they operate as sexual markets. He would like to go out to gay venues with women he knows but does not do so because of previous experiences:

> Female friends and lesbians say that at dance parties people treat them like shit and they believe it is because the men see them as not 'fuck-able'. It is the same invisibility old gay men complain about. That is why our obsession with sex rather than relationship or intimacy is sad. We miss out on a lot of things because of it.

Later in his interview, Vincent said gay men treated one another as sex objects because they confuse sexual freedom—the freedom to express their sexuality—with promiscuity. For Vincent, promiscuity prevents gay men from learning how to be intimate with each other.

In his early 20s, Angus believes that men his age and younger are belittled by what is expected of them on the scene. Young gay men are seduced or forced into a role allotted to them, which is to be 'young and pretty'—code for sexually desirable.

> I get annoyed when I see young guys fitting the role of what is expected of them and not questioning it. They are at the same club every week, off their faces [on drugs] on the podium and they go home with a different guy every week. That annoys me. It seems to me they are filling a role without even thinking about it or what it is doing to them.

Angus uses the argument of an earlier generation of feminists. If he could, it seems he would exhort his contemporaries not to see themselves or allow themselves to be seen as sex objects by older, more powerful men. Angus is angry his peers seem blind to the fact that the role they are given is demeaning. Just as feminists of his mother's generation demanded that women be proud and aware of who they were, Angus wants gay men his age to show more pride in themselves and resist the role of pretty, young sex object. Both he and Vincent were critical of the scene because it is sexualised and hence inimical to the genuine social intercourse they seek.

As mentioned, the views of these two men do not necessarily reflect widespread criticism in the young cohort, or the sample of interviewees in general, about the sexualisation of the scene. That being said, they are remarkable because they are the personal judgement of young men, who are the target market of the businessmen who run and control the scene. They disliked the social environment they

found there because it was impoverished and prevented social intercourse or the development of genuine social relations.

## Old and middle cohorts

By comparison with the young cohort, the men from the old cohort
and the middle cohort had fewer criticisms of the scene, most likely
because it is less important to them. Their criticisms were limited to
the two principal ones to which all interviewees referred, viz. the
impoverished physical environment and the poor social environment
of the scene.

### *Impoverished physical environment*

Eight interviewees criticised the scene for its crowded, noisy and smoky
environment, and are represented here by one man from the old
cohort and two men from the middle cohort.[47] The man from the old
cohort, who was born just after World War I, said that he never felt at
ease in the public bars of hotels because of his parents' views about
drinking in public. Reginald is 79 and lives with his partner. His
upbringing in a working-class suburb shaped his views of what is
appropriate behaviour for a man of his class.

> I have never, ever cared much for the commercial gay venues. I do
> not feel happy in them at all. I do not feel happy in an ordinary
> pub. I think it goes back to my childhood. My parents were not pub
> goers. Both of them used to say, 'If you want to drink, you can bring
> your friends home'. I suppose that is why I feel out of place in a
> hotel or a pub.

Reginald's prejudice against pubs is understandable. His parents saw
the pub as an unacceptable social venue for respectable working people
like themselves, which, until quite recently, was also the case for many
middle-class men.[48]

The two men from the middle cohort are both in relationships and
both work in the education sector. Apart from these similarities, their
life histories are quite different. The first man, Michael, is in his early
50s and is one of two men from this sample of interviewees who was
involved in the gay liberation movement in the 1970s. He is also a
PLWHA carer and has been in a relationship with the same man for
28 years. The second man, Scott, is in his mid-40s, has a teenage
daughter and was once married. He is in a relationship of eight years'
duration and prefers not to define himself by his sexuality.

Michael rarely goes on the scene but, as the following extract shows, while he is drawn to it because of its busyness, its physical conditions make it impossible for him to relate meaningfully to others there:

> I go to the pubs occasionally but I do not feel at ease in them any more. I find the music really boring and it is now too loud for me. But I like to be there because I feel it is where it is happening, and it is fun, sexy. When I have been to venues, I have only stayed an hour and then I have thought, 'It is too noisy. I have had enough. I have seen it all'. And because I am not picking up anyone, because I am going to watch and maybe dance and have a drink, after a while it palls. I like to talk to people but I do not like shouting clichés into some one's ear for two hours.

For much the same reason, Scott simply does not go on the scene: 'I do not think that I would feel uneasy in any venue, other than being uneasy because of the dreadful music and the smoke and too many drunk people. I am not into it, not interested'.

*Poor social environment*

One man from the old cohort and two men from the middle cohort represent the views of the interviewees who objected to the social environment of the scene. [49] Oscar is 65 and was married for more than 20 years. He works part-time for his former employer. He lives with his partner and they have been together for 18 years. People would call Oscar a man's man. He is fit and athletic and commands respect when he enters a room. But he dislikes some gay bars:

> I feel more comfortable in bars that have a wider cross-section of age, where there are more men over 35 than under 35. As people get older they seem to be more at ease talking to people like me who are older. There are a number of bars where I feel ill at ease. I find bars full of young gay men synthetic, and I never feel that comfortable in them. And they are probably the only places where I have sometimes felt old.

Oscar is not being overly sensitive when he says that he feels excluded in a gay bar. He is used to commanding the respect of other men, including the young: 'I am used to mixing with a lot of young people, at work. It's just that I don't feel comfortable in "Twinky"[50] bars or bars where young and beautiful men between 20 and 30 parade their bodies'. If nothing else, a gay bar is an entirely masculine environment. It is supremely male. Apart from the ethos and spirit that pervade all-male sporting clubs or military barracks, no other space is more exclusively masculine than a gay bar, and yet in this quintessentially masculine space a man like Oscar felt shunned.[51]

The two men from the middle cohort are in their 40s and both object to the unvarying nature of the scene's social practices. Trevor is 49 and has no patience with the artificiality of the scene. In particular, he dislikes its predictability:

> It is the same faces all the time. It is the same inane conversation. The crap they go on about: 'How big is your dick?' 'Do you want to go to bed?' I like having sex but I am past the silly games they play. Gay guys are so stupid that they have made it part of their life. It is just not real. They live in this fantasy world where there is a 20-inch dick just around the corner, but it is not going to happen.

James dislikes the scene because he has found many of the people there superficial. James grew up in the country, is 45 and lives in a capital city. He lived overseas in his 20s where the gay scene was less pressured than in Australia. He is critical of the conformity of the gay men on the scene:

> When I am in the mood, I go out with a friend to these places but I find them boring. All the people have got their shirts off dancing. In the 1980s if you were gay, you were outside and that was the exciting thing about it, but now it is extremely conforming in terms of looks, behaviour and expectations. It is the Americanisation of the gay thing.

For James gay was once a symbol of rebelliousness, a sign of a person's outsider status and non-conformist values. His subsequent disenchantment now seems to spring from what he regards as the ordinariness and unquestioning conventionalism of much of gay men's behaviour, and of what it now means to be gay.

## Conclusion

Gay men participate in the scene when they want to socialise with friends or when they are looking for a sexual partner or a man with whom to have a relationship. Some men 'dip in' to the scene immediately on coming out or as part of their initiation and then never return. Others spend their late teenage years or early 20s on the scene and leave once they find a partner or when they realise that it is not the place to find one. There are others again who come out of the closet, go on to the scene, and spend most of their 20s and 30s drinking, having sex and taking drugs. For them it approaches something like a community, but it will not and cannot provide them with the lasting *communitas* they may be looking for, because, in the end, it is a market place.

The scene is not designed as a space or set of spaces for gay men to entertain their siblings or parents, their heterosexual or lesbian friends. Its primary participants are men with fit youthful bodies, and its primary purpose is as a sexual market place. To participate on the scene a man needs dedication, discipline, energy and a high disposable income. He also needs to be young or youthful, for its social practices are geared to the young and age determines the level of a gay man's engagement with it. It was not surprising, therefore, that more than one third of the men interviewed for this study reported that they never went on the scene, and that at least half of these were from the old cohort.

In fact, interviewees of all ages were divided over the worth and value of the scene, and those who most frequently engaged with the scene, the men from the young cohort, expressed the strongest views. On the whole, the men with positive views of the scene were either entirely satisfied with its environment, and they were relatively few in number, or restricted their participation to occasions when they were with friends or were able to socialise in a space where they could 'be themselves'. This applied to all venues, including sex venues. Negative views about the scene related to interviewees' experience of discomfort at gay bars, clubs or pubs: many felt marginalised when they were on the scene or, at best, ill at ease. A significant minority of the sample (one fifth of interviewees) complained about the noise and crowds at commercial venues, which restricted genuine social intercourse. As well, a small but articulate group of men from the young cohort criticised the scene for the emphasis on body image and its sexualised nature.

The commonly expressed complaints about the impoverished social and physical conditions seem to be causally connected—that is, social relations on the scene are weak and poorly developed because its physical environment, designed to facilitate sexual exchange, restricts real social interaction between gay men. This is significant because, unlike heterosexuals, gay men cannot assume that they may congregate and socialise where they please. In the main, if they wish to socialise with other gay men, they must do so on the scene, and, for the reasons outlined in this chapter, the fact that most gay socialising takes place in bars, clubs or pubs affects how they relate to and regard each other.

# 6
# Community Life

'Some people I know will only go to a gay plumber or a gay dentist.' Jeremy, 33.

## Introduction

Whether out of a sense of politeness, linguistic shorthand, or 'political correctness', many of the men interviewed for this study used the word 'community' to describe all social institutions of the gay milieu, from those with a very clear commercial purpose, such as bars and sex venues, to those staffed by volunteers or with a strong sense of public service and awareness, such as HIV-AIDS telephone help-lines and other counselling or support services. As mentioned in the previous chapter, the gay community is understood in this book as a loose collection of organisations with a sense of public service and social awareness.[1]

The term, 'community', was also used, however, by scholars writing before gay liberation to describe the gay world then, when it mainly comprised bars and clubs, and these provided a community function for gay men.[2] And, as discussed in the previous chapter, there are still men today, mainly from the young cohort, who regard the scene as their community. In the early 1980s, Dennis Altman wrote in the North American context that a gay community was much more than the businesses that comprise the scene. He listed the social and cultural institutions as 'political and social clubs, publications and bookstores, church groups, community centers, radio collectives, theater groups ... that represent ... shared values and a willingness to assert one's homosexuality as an important part of one's whole life'.[3] This description takes in most of the institutions and organisations that are features of the contemporary gay community in Australia and other similar countries.

Often staffed by volunteers, gay community organisations focus on providing assistance to people coming out and in developing relationships, fighting homophobia, lobbying for improved political and social rights, and the provision of housing and home care for people living with HIV-AIDS (PLWHA). There are telephone counselling services in most capital cities in Australia and many with facilities for reaching people who live in the country. The National Gay and Lesbian Archives in Melbourne is also an institution with a strong and clear community purpose and representation.

One other example of an important community organisation, mentioned by a handful of interviewees, was the gay and lesbian community press and radio stations. These media have a vital function in the creation and maintenance of community identity, even if they are mostly run for profit. David Carr argues that a community forms where there is a narrative account 'of a *we* which persists through its experiences and actions'.[4] Such an account may be spread via the gay and lesbian media as well as through the personal and public narratives that gay men tell about themselves in HIV-AIDS support and counselling groups, their local social group, or at festivals, parades and on the scene, with other lobbyists or activists, and in written works such as their plays, poems, novels and university papers and theses. As Carr puts it, the idea of community 'exists when it gets articulated or formulated—perhaps by only one or a few of the group's members—by reference to the *we* and is accepted or subscribed to by others'.[5] Kenneth Plummer too believes that in order for a community to flourish, there must be stories of the community, told by its members, that 'weave together their history, their identity'.[6] Again, the gay and lesbian media have been instrumental in achieving this, as has the increased social acceptance of gay men and lesbians, which has assisted in the wider dissemination of these stories.

The interviewees' accounts of their experience of or involvement in the gay community revealed two prominent attitudes. First, as the discussion in section one shows, a large majority of men gave positive accounts of their experience of the gay community. A significant minority, comprising more than a fifth of interviewees, was, however, critical of the community. These interviewees either did not agree with or could not conform to dominant gay narratives; some questioned the existence of a gay community. Their views are examined in the second section of the chapter.

## Positive experiences of community

The overwhelming majority of men interviewed for this study told encouraging stories of their experience and involvement in the gay community and community activities. In their accounts, four principal sites of community emerged. First, a group numbering 22 men said that involvement in the gay community consisted of the work they did with HIV-AIDS support groups and with telephone and other counselling services.[7] Second, an equally large group of 22 men said that they expressed their gay community involvement through the local social group.[8] Third, a slightly smaller group of 18 interviewees said they were involved in the gay community when they participated in gay festivals, street parades and the scene.[9] Finally, a relatively small group of eight men said their experience of gay community was through social activism and political lobbying.[10]

### HIV-AIDS support groups and counselling services

More than a quarter of interviewees said that their community involvement was represented in the voluntary work that they did with HIV-AIDS support groups or with telephone and other counselling services. More of this group came from the middle cohort, that is, the 'baby-boomers', than from either the old cohort or the young cohort, but there was not a marked preponderance. Men from all cohorts saw work with HIV-AIDS support groups as an important community involvement or experience. That this was so underlines the point made in the chapter on the coming-out stories of the young cohort: gay men's response to HIV-AIDS has been remarkable because they responded as a community, and this impulse has not significantly slowed.

For men in the old cohort, the level of their involvement with HIV-AIDS support groups, telephone and other counselling services ranged from membership of umbrella organisations, such as the AIDS Council of New South Wales (ACON) or the Victorian AIDS Council (VAC), to volunteer work in running the service. One example was Geoffrey, aged 69, who, with his partner, became involved in supporting PLWHA through their local gay social group: 'We were very involved with the local gay group because that's when we started doing work when AIDS hit. We collected funds and did a lot of work to help those people [i.e., PLWHA]'. Men like Ronald (aged 68) and Douglas (aged 63), on the other hand, contributed financial support for HIV-AIDS organisations. Said Ronald: 'I have been a member and on the board of the AIDS council. I occasionally go to an annual meeting. But I must admit my involvement has not been enormous'. Douglas is less self-deprecating. He said of his contribution: 'I have been subscribing to ALSO and to the Peter Knight centre since their inception'.[11]

Two older men who have been personally involved at 'grass roots' level are Leslie, aged 74, and Lindsay, aged 62. Both have spent ten or more years with counselling services. Together with a group of men in their locality, Leslie and his partner operate a telephone service for gay people. It provides men of all ages with information about coming out, social groups and the scene.

> We operate a gay telephone counselling service from homes rather than an office. People ring and they hear a five-minute message. If they want to talk to anyone in confidence or clarify anything they heard on the message, which is packed with information, there are numbers they can ring. We have been doing that for fifteen years.

Those in the middle cohort tended to be the most actively involved and are represented here by the accounts of two men in their 50s: Samuel, aged 56, and Graham, aged 52. Samuel works part time in paid employment and devotes a great deal of the rest of his time to volunteer work with PLWHA. As a member of his local support group and as a carer, he has experienced all aspects of this volunteer-based organisation, from being the cook to providing palliative care for the dying. Samuel found the work he has done with PLWHA to be life-changing.

> Being an HIV-AIDS carer is an important part of my life. I had no intention of getting involved with it and it was an impulsive decision when I started. I became very involved and was on committees and got involved with the PLWHA centre. I used to cook lunches for them. I guess it has made me come to terms with dying. I never cease to be impressed with the people with HIV-AIDS and the way they handle the prospect of death. I have found people who I have been with when they died very courageous. It has been something that they have given me without knowing.

Graham also worked as a carer for PLWHA when the epidemic first broke out in the early 1980s. His partner, Charlie, is still looking after the man he was assigned to care for in the 1980s, and has been with him for almost 15 years. Graham spoke of the work he did as a volunteer with the VAC:

> The client load was almost unmanageable. Marvellous, almost visionary people supported us. It was dynamic but fraught with tragedy.

The people who led things died. It was a hard time and the stigma was huge. It is a tragedy that AIDS is still an unpopular cause. It has gone back into the shadows again, even though the gay community educated people and kept them informed.

Graham's account recalls early days when gay people struggled to deal with an enormous crisis, when leaders died, and the work that he and others did made meaning of community.

The experiences of the men in the young cohort were as varied as those of the older men and are represented here by two men in their 30s. One has a highly paid job in the finance sector and the other does low-paid casual work. Jeremy is 36, single and ambitious. He explained how he supported the gay community:

I have done work for all sorts of community groups but now I am more likely to work for the AIDS Trust than for anything else. It depends on what my friends are doing and we tend to do it together. Last year for the Mardi Gras parade, two of us took the bucket around and collected donations for people with AIDS.

He speaks of this contribution without elaboration. He and his friends see community support in terms of charity and the sort of charity work that is acceptable in the circles in which they and people like them mix. In a sense, for gay men like Jeremy, it is just something that one does. By contrast with Jeremy's somewhat 'hands-off' attitude, the other man from the young cohort, Jason, aged 35, has a more visceral connection because he is a person living with AIDS: 'It has included getting involved with friends who were dying. For example, wiping their arses, cleaning up their spew [vomit], changing their beds, feeding them, because their families did not want to be involved, did not want to touch them'.

The significance of these stories lies in the range of meaning the men derive from their voluntary work and their level of involvement in it. Age and class do not always explain meaning or involvement. For instance, the assistance that middle-class men like Ronald, Douglas and Jeremy made to HIV-AIDS causes was removed from the physical presence of PLWHA and mainly consisted of donating money or collecting it. Far greater was the number of other men who devoted considerable time and energy to caring for PLWHA, and these were drawn from all classes. As mentioned in an earlier chapter on the coming-out stories of the young cohort, one of the remarkable effects of the HIV-AIDS epidemic has been the willingness and ability of gay men in

Western countries to respond to it communally. It was, according to R. W. Connell, '[t]he most impressive men's health initiative in any field in recent decades'.[12]

## Local social groups

In country towns and regions, local social groups play an important role for gay men, who would otherwise be socially and culturally isolated. A group of men, equivalent in number to the previous group, said that they showed their involvement in the gay community through the local social group. Typically these are men from smaller capital cities or rural areas. All age groups were fairly evenly represented among those who defined gay community in this way. In *The Hidden Injuries of Class*, Richard Sennett asks how people protect themselves when they feel vulnerable in relation to those who are 'respectable': 'There is the old way to do this, which is to withdraw into an enclave'.[13] In the main, this is what people who belong to minorities have done and continue to do in order to preserve their identities and protect themselves. Gay community can be seen in this light, particularly in small cities and country towns.

The positive experiences of the men from the old cohort are represented by Barry's story. Barry, aged 62, and his partner, Eric, aged 69, belong to a gay social group in the country that still holds an annual gala ball. But, as he explains, they are less involved now than they used to be:

> When I was younger and until the last few years I was always on our local committee. We used to have balls and lots of entertainment. We do not go to them now. The entertainment still goes on but it is a different style. Like everyone else, we do not like changes. We know what it used to be like and it is not as good as it used to be. They do not seem to get the same number of people we used to get when we did it.

Barry understands the changes he has witnessed in recent years as part of a natural hand-over of responsibility from one generation to another but he also hints at a reluctance to be pushed aside, which is expressed in his wistful remembrance of how much better things used to be when they were younger. Given his age, the balls that he and his friends organised are likely to be the same balls that George Chauncey and Garry Wotherspoon argued were an important part of the subculture before gay liberation—as discussed in the earlier chapter on coming out in the old cohort.

A number of men in the **middle** cohort emphasised the role that the local group plays as an alternative to or substitute for the scene, which, as was explained in the previous chapter on the gay scene, can be the centre of social life for gay men who live in big cities. Thomas, for example, who is 52, saw his local social group as a venue where gay men can meet without feeling the need to perform. He referred also to his own experience of feeling isolated on the scene: 'Our group is important because it helps to establish the normal face of being gay and to provide opportunities for normal contact between ordinary gay men. I have been to Sleaze and Mardi Gras parties and sometimes I have found them isolating, disappointing events'.[14] Thomas lives in the country with his partner of 20 years.

Kevin (aged 52) also has reservations about the scene: 'The social life is the bars and the pubs but it is not satisfying. It lacks substance'. He used to work in the finance sector and is now looking for a new career. He is single and lives in an inner-city suburb. In place of bars and clubs, he has found an alternative in a local group that holds monthly drinks for gay men who work in the central business district.

> When I started going to social events for working gay men five years ago, there were forty people in a hall. The idea is that people go there for a drink after work. Now they get crowds of three hundred once a month. You often see faces that you do not see in the clubs or pubs. It is a great social outlet. It is not as intimidating as the clubs. There is a greater sense of equality because they are all business people, which makes it easier to mix together.

Kevin's account of the advantages of this social group suggests that gay men with conventional working lives might feel out of place on the scene, perhaps even at a disadvantage, and that, when an opportunity is provided for them to meet others like themselves and dressed presumably in suits and ties, there is, in Kevin's words, 'a greater sense of equality'. This is, of course, a limited notion of equality, one that exists when people are among their own kind, in class terms.

Almost one third of the young cohort said that their involvement with the gay community consisted of activities within their local social group.[15] Their stories are represented here by the accounts of three men, two of whom are in their 30s and one who is in his 20s. The first man is Drew (aged 39), who is a committee member of his local social group. Outgoing by nature, he has invited straight friends and acquaintances to the group's social functions, to 'make more people aware of it and show them that we are like a sporting group or any other type of group'. He is serious about his responsibilities and the purpose of the group:

> We try to raise funds. I do not think people realise the extra work the committee does in counselling and AIDS support. Some think that we are just a social group so we can have rave parties. That is not what it is about.

Also a committee member of his local gay group, Mick (aged 33) is working to develop stronger bonds between lesbians and gay men. He admitted, however, that there were difficulties, similar to those between generations: 'The older guys and younger guys ostracise one another. They like their tea parties alone but, as a community, we have to stick together because united we stand, divided we fall'.

Adam is the third man from the young cohort. He is 24 and has recently moved to the country. The gay and lesbian community that he found in the country was not as he had imagined.

> I had a dream when I was growing up of a gay community that would look after me if all else failed. But as with other communities that has not always been the case. If we want to have a community, we have to accept it warts and all and accept that we are a diverse lot of people. What we have in common is this one thing that no one can put a finger on. But if we stick together our lives will be better. I learned here that it was possible, which I never found in the city. We are all gay and lesbian people and that is what matters. It is almost like a nationhood experience.

In this short but important extract, a young man explains how he reconciled utopian expectations with the reality of the gay community that he discovered in the country. He also demonstrates a more complex understanding of community as embracing difference and sometimes conflict. The group of people he found was less supportive than he had dreamed they would be, and more diverse. He has also learned that there is strength in unity, an experience he was not afforded when he lived in the city. As well, Adam confirms Benedict Anderson's perception of community and nation as largely imagined.[16]

The common experience these stories suggest is that in small cities and country towns the local group is the hub of gay men's social activities, and this has not changed significantly over time. Even though he might criticise the *style* of present-day balls, the man from the old cohort cited here is not marginalised by contemporary gay social practices in his milieu, for the balls he and his friends organised were the precursors of those today. As well, there is a sense that the men from all three cohorts, as represented by these accounts, have greater agency in shaping their social relations, which is in contrast to men in large cities, who, according to the discussion in the previous chapter on the gay scene, have to rely mostly on the scene for social contact with other gay men and who seem powerless to influence its social practices.

### Parades, festivals and the scene

The third group of men with positive stories to tell of the gay community said that they experienced it when they went to street parades or festivals or on the scene.[17] Other festive occasions and locales where interviewees experienced the gay community included dinner parties with friends, sporting groups and warehouse (or dance) parties.[18]

Gay and lesbian parades and festivals are held in most capital cities in Australia as well as in some provincial cities and towns. The leading gay and lesbian festival is the Sydney Mardi Gras.[19] Parades and festivals have a crucial role to play in the construction and maintenance of gay men's 'social memory', which Kenneth Plummer describes as:

> the common stories talked about and heard within particular groups that often come to have a life of their own ... [and] help in the construction of this 'memory' ... The gay and women's movements, for instance, came to develop their own folklore of stories which get transmitted in part from generation to generation, complete with ritualistic days and marches ... which help to provide a sense of shared history.[20]

Two men, one from each of the young and middle cohorts, are representative of those who cited parades and festivals as their community activity. Michael (aged 52) has enjoyed going to Melbourne's Midsumma festival because it allows him to be himself in public: 'As a rule, my partner and I do not hold hands in public but we do at the carnival because it is a totally safe environment'.

Held in a public park during daytime, Midsumma carnival provides an occasion for gay people and their families and friends to take part in carnival activities in a relaxed, safe atmosphere. There are tents for community organisations and political parties, dog competitions, carnival rides, food stalls.[21]

Joseph is 35 and works in the health sector. Like Michael, he enjoys Midsumma's carnival day for what it allows him to do and to be, in his case to have a picnic in public with his children: 'I have been every year and I enjoy it. It is a great event that I can take my kids to as well. It is a positive event for everybody'. Later in his interview, Joseph said that the carnival is unusual because it does not involve cruising and sex, which he said normally occur when a large group of gay men congregates.

While it is undoubtedly true, as Plummer observes, that annual festivals and marches continue to build the gay community's social memory, the accounts of these two interviewees suggest that they are also valuable because they provide a social space where the men can 'be themselves'. For Michael, the festival allows him to 'be himself' with his partner free of the threat of homophobia, whereas Joseph enjoys the freedom of being among large numbers of gay men in an environment that is not sexualised.

## Political activism

Articulate and well-organised lobby groups exist—mainly in the capital cities—with a mixture of political aims, including gay migration (which assists couples to establish their bona fides where one is an Australian citizen and the other is seeking residency status), gay law reform and gay marriage.[22] A relatively small group of men interviewed for this study expressed their community involvement through social activism, and their views are represented here by the accounts of two men from the old cohort and two from the middle cohort.[23]

One of the most politically active men is also one of the oldest men in this sample. Gerald (75) lives with Larry, his partner of nine years. Gerald has been a political activist most of his life. When he was married, as he was for more than 30 years, matters of social justice were his chief concern. Since coming out in the early 1990s, he has been involved in HIV-AIDS support and wider issues of legal rights for gay men and women. In the following extract Gerald explains how central to his life and that of his partner is their political commitment to rights of homosexuals and general issues of social justice:

My partner and I became carers for people living with AIDS. I was also doing meals on wheels. We are involved with the federal anti-terrorism bills and also in the age of consent issue in New South Wales. We produce and send out a newsletter for lesbian and gay solidarity. Also we discovered that, for instance, the AIDS memorial garden is in a terrible state. There was a letter in a gay newspaper and we are working on that too.

Gerald also explained how he and his partner use the Internet to lobby parliamentarians on matters of human rights and gay and lesbian rights. 'We do a lot of work on the Internet and it's actually becoming an important part of our lives. We send letters to ministers of parliament and things like that, and email has become very important to enable us to do that'. Gerald and Larry are incensed by injustice and motivated by a determination not to be silenced because they are old men: 'The general community regards old homosexuals as old queens who should go away and die quietly. We ageing homosexuals are not going to do that. We are still here and making our voices heard and intend to continue doing so'.

Charles, who is 67 and has a partner of 35 years, spoke of an involvement with the gay community that stretched back more than 40 years and began when police raids were common events in clubs and bars.

> I worked in one of the very first gay bars, which was a wine bar where we sold everything else but wine. We used to get raided regularly. I have always worked for the gay movement. We always supported gay people and gave advice and financial advice to people who were in trouble. I have been in jail three times for gay rights.

Part of the cohort of men who came out before the gay liberation movement, Charles was a businessman before he retired. He spent much of his working life as the manager of a number of clubs that were part of the clandestine sub-culture. There is no doubt that he regarded the bars and clubs as an integral part of the gay community. If he was sent to jail for operating illegal premises—a gay bar in the years before decriminalisation of homosexuality—this is less important than that he believes he was sent there in support of 'gay rights' and that the bar was his stand against the state's persecution of homosexuals.

In the middle cohort Donald (52) said that his experience of the gay community began when he was a young man in the late 1960s. Because of the politics of the time, more was at stake: 'gay liberation was my first gay community experience and that was hugely important, as well as the gay lib[eration] ideologies. I am so glad I was part of that'. Des (aged 50) said he often finds he cannot 'help himself' when he hears a 'demo' is being planned:

> Politically I have been active at all levels. I will take to the streets and blow whistles. I have been violent in demonstrations. I am a passionate person and even though it may not be lawful I believe that you have the right to demonstrate. If that means violence, like in the Vietnam War moratorium, and if it means throwing flour bombs at police, I would do it again. Not that I have anything against the police. It is a statement.

Not coincidentally, most of those who expressed their sense of community through political activism are from the camp generation or the 'baby-boomer' generation. They were actively involved in the movement for gay liberation in their 20s and 30s when it was part of wider social and political movements, and the political beliefs they developed then are now the articles of faith by which they lead their lives and that give them meaning.

## Critical views of community

A significant minority of slightly less than a quarter of men interviewed for this study was critical of the gay community.[24] A number of themes emerged from their stories. Principally, they were disappointed by social practices they had observed, such as 'bitchy' or cliquey behaviour and had difficulty identifying with gay men in general. Others had experienced dismissive or irresponsible behaviour from gay men and saw this as peculiar to the gay community because they regarded it as a characteristic or attribute of gay men in general. Their views are represented here by the accounts of seven interviewees, three from the young cohort and two from each of the middle and the old cohorts.[25]

### Young cohort

The life experiences of the three men from the young cohort are varied. The first man, Jack (aged 22), is single and lives in an inner suburb of a capital city. The second man, David, is 28. He is Aboriginal, also single and lives in the country. Both men have full-time employment and both work for the public service. Jack is a university graduate and David left school after he completed Year 12. Neville (aged 37) is the third man. He is a university graduate also, and works in the education sector. He and his partner have been together for 12 years. Like David, he too is Aboriginal.

Jack is suspicious of gay community organisations because they are unrepresentative of gay men and are not accountable for their actions:

> When my friends and I talk about 'the gay community', we are referring to a bunch of narrow-minded and self-selected gay activists or community organisations that operate in a world that feeds into itself and is publicised in the gay press. It is a very small, intensely wasteful and bitchy community. I do not find it fulfilling at all; in fact I get quite annoyed.

For Jack, the self-proclaimed altruism of support communities holds no appeal because it is too claustrophobic and comfortable. In addition to being suspicious of these organisations, Jack is sceptical that any unity or sense of common purpose exists among gay men. Later in his interview, he described two beliefs, which he said were common to gay men. Some believed, first, that they were no different from straight people and that gay people should simply assimilate into what Erving Goffman called the world of 'normals'.[26] Jack was critical of them because they are apolitical. Second, there were other gay men who believed themselves to be victims of discrimination.

> Some people believe that there is no discrimination against gay people and that we should assimilate into a straight world. And then there are the other people who think that the world is against them and that they deserve special favours.

The second group of gay men who, according to Jack, believed they were entitled to 'special favours' are similar to the category of person Erving Goffman described as using their disadvantage 'as a basis for organising life'. With their own kind they may 'develop to its fullest ... [their] sad tale accounting for ... [their] possession of the stigma'.[27] For such people, a stigmatised identity is central to their sense of self and to their relations with others. They have a vested interest in retaining it.

Like the other men whose views are discussed in this section, David has struggled to identify with gay men in his milieu. He lives three hours by car from the nearest big city and is critical of the gay

community for the overt performance of gayness that he has seen per-
petrated in the country:

> Here in the country my experience of gay community has been
> absolutely horrible. I find gay country folk annoying. It is as though
> they feel they have to prove something to mainstream society. They
> are looking for acceptance from the wider community here and they
> push the boundaries right to the limit. Instead of being a normal
> human being, they have to tart it up or fag it up and they do it to
> annoy rather than to gain acceptance. There is not the same beha-
> viour in the city. People do not aim to annoy other people or to say,
> 'We are here'. They do it because it is how they like to dress or like
> to act. But here or in country towns, and I have lived in quite a few
> of them, they feel they have to do it in protest.

In David's eyes, the overt behaviour of these gay men is designed to
draw attention to themselves. Presumably, it is also to show that they
are not afraid of the response or reaction they might get, and, in fact,
they might even be motivated by the desire to shock. However, for
David the performance is forced and unnecessary.

As mentioned, Neville, like David, is an Aboriginal man. Neville's
criticisms of the gay community concern the homogeneity of gay commercial culture and the insular lives that some affluent gay men lead in
large cities.

> We occasionally go out to a gay night club or gay bar or do the
> dance parties or Mardi Gras. I do not like that life-style. There are
> people in [the Sydney suburb of] Darlinghurst who live in apart-
> ment blocks that are full of gay men. They are completely absorbed
> in the night club scene, go to dance parties, work in the area. I find
> that too constraining. Also it is so Anglo, which I do not find a cul-
> turally friendly environment. I participate in it but I feel like a con-
> sumer at the time. You go in there and shop around for whatever
> you want and then go home.

Neville's most damning criticism was of the ghetto that many gay men
have created for themselves in Sydney. This insular life is more pronounced in Sydney but there is evidence of its growth in other capital
cities. In Melbourne and Sydney, there are districts in the inner city
where the tenants of old, renovated factories and warehouses are predominantly gay men, and similar enclaves exist in cities such as

Birmingham, Hamburg and Paris, Chicago and Toronto.[28] Men who earn medium to high salaries, and whose life-style is, as Neville implies, wholly defined by their sexual identity populate the gay ghettos. He finds it 'too constraining'.

## Middle cohort

In the middle cohort are two men with stories of irresponsible behaviour that they see as characteristic of gay men. Richard is 58 and lives in a large capital city with his partner. Matthew is 42 and single. Both men are middle class in education, income and occupation. Richard's lament concerns unspecified business dealings that he has had with gay men.

> I find that a lot of gay men are unreliable. If you cannot depend on them, what is the point of putting your energy into that? A lot of them are unreliable emotionally and in business. They change their minds. I am generalising but they do not have sustained opinions on things, so you never know where you stand with them. I cannot be bothered putting my faith in that.

There was no note of bitterness in Richard's voice during the interview. In fact, his manner was sanguine, even resigned. There was a strong sense, however, that he did not feel part of the gay community. He also said later in his interview that if there were a directory of gay businesses or service providers—for example, if he needed furniture moved, or his house renovated or painted—he would not make use of it.

Matthew's reservations arise from deeply personal experiences and concern the reckless and irresponsible behaviour of some gay men in their 20s and 30s, of men who despite their age are immature, but who in other contexts would be regarded as adult.

> I do not know whether it is because everyone is having a hard time, but there is a fair bit of dysfunctionality in the community. Many people are not coping well with their finances, their lives, or their sense of balance. They are mostly in their late 20s to mid-30s. I see a lot of people who are just dangling on the edge.

> For example, I had a bad experience with a man I went out with for a year. He was a sexy guy and I used to stay with him every weekend. But he lied to me about his HIV status. I was okay, but it was the worst experience I have had. He lied because he thought I would

leave if he told me. I would not have left but, because he did not tell me and we had been having sex for a year, I had to leave.

At other times, I have lent money to guys who have not repaid it. My experience of gay men is that as they get older, they are more balanced and that is one thing that I like about older gay friends.

As Matthew admits, it is difficult to know why some men lead chaotic or disorganised lives. But he suggests that the gay milieu does not provide the support young gay men need to keep their lives together. And sadly, because of the need to be seen as 'cool' if their social space is the scene and their social circle comprises other people who are on the scene, the young men who are 'dangling on the edge' might not know how to call for help or whom to call.

It is also difficult to know, from Matthew's account—indeed, from the accounts of any of the men in this sample—how widespread reckless and irresponsible behaviour is among gay men and whether they are any more likely than other men their age to be involved in high risk social practices. From Matthew's observations, it would seem that it is not uncommon to see gay men whose life projects do not follow steady trajectories. Furthermore, alcohol and drug taking seem to be common ingredients of their lives. R. W. Connell uses the phrase, 'rebellious masculinity', to describe this sort of behaviour when it occurs among young heterosexual men. Rebellious masculinity is not discredited masculinity; in fact, it is close to its obverse, exemplary masculinity, the masculinity of athletes and sportsmen. It is a version of masculinity that is constructed from being out of control: '[D]oing reasonably dangerous things with drugs, trading on ... physique and youthful energy'.[29] For young gay men, high-risk practices might be their way of rebelling against the constraints they feel a heteronormative society imposes on them, and possibly also as a means of gaining acceptance from the 'in-group' on the scene. If this rebelliousness becomes endemic, however, they can seriously put at risk the stability of their life trajectory.

The story that Matthew tells of his relationship with a man who was HIV positive points to the importance of trust and shame in human relations and how easily the latter can undermine the former. Matthew believes that the man concealed his HIV status from him because he was ashamed of it and feared that if he revealed it he risked losing Matthew's affection or their relationship. In *A Select Body*, Lynette Lewis and Michael Ross raise the dilemma HIV-positive men face. On the one hand, they are morally (and legally) obliged to disclose their HIV status to potential sex partners, while, on the other hand, many know that if they do, the other man may terminate the encounter or relationship.[30]

Matthew's experience cuts to the heart of how we see ourselves as human beings and how we conduct relations with others whom we wish to treat as people of equal standing and regard. Of course, if this experience is relatively common, it might explain the suspicion with which some gay men regard others in the community.

### Old cohort

In the old cohort there are stories from two men in their 60s who had hoped to find a communal spirit among the gay men with whom they worked or mixed socially. In the first instance there is Brendan (64), who is a public servant. His partner is 18 years his junior and they have been together for 20 years. Some time ago Brendan and his partner were actively involved in a gay lobby group. Brendan's experience of gay political activists soured his view of the gay community. He found factionalism and a mood of exclusiveness in the actions of people who were younger than he:

> It is a very narrow element within the gay community that abuses power. It is a bitchy, vicious thing. And more people are talking about it. They can be so political and so dismissive of other people. They have this horrible dismissive view of older people or people that are not politically correct.

His account of small mindedness and in-group versus out-group behaviour, which Norbert Elias discussed in *The Established and the Outsiders*, can be a feature of 'grass-roots' political or 'community' organisations of all colours and persuasions. The members of an in-group will often maintain their identity as 'superior' people by attributing to themselves 'super human characteristics' and by pinning a 'badge of human inferiority' on the members of the outsider group. [31] This may be the social process that lay behind the dismissive behaviour Brendan witnessed. And, although Brendan saw it as a characteristic of gay culture, and similar experiences of gay community organisations have been referred to in published research, it is not exclusive to it.[32]

Oscar (aged 65) is the second man from the old cohort who has a low opinion of the spirit of community among gay men. Oscar was married for 20 years. He has lived with his partner, Henry, for 18 years.

On the basis of his experience both as a heterosexual man and as a homosexual man, he believes that he has a good yardstick for comparing the social *mores* of gay and straight people. In his experience gay men are less trustworthy than heterosexual people:

> The one thing my experience in the gay community has taught me is that there are more superficial people in the gay world than there are in the 'straight' world. There are more bitchy people, more gossips. I have found that a lot of people in the gay world think it's wonderful when relationships break up and that is probably because they have never had a decent relationship in their life. I have had a lot of wonderful experiences in the gay world, but I think that because of the difficulty of acceptance in the 'normal' world, there is a lot more superficiality in the gay world than there is in the 'straight' world.

Oscar feels that he has been let down by his gay friends and acquaintances. In a previous chapter, Oscar was described as a 'man's man'. He said it was only in gay venues that he felt old and out of place. On the matter of a senior gay man's adjustment to the social and moral demands of the gay milieu, Michael Pollak has argued that few gay men succeed in freeing themselves from 'the socializing influence imprinted on them in childhood, an influence totally oriented towards a life of heterosexuality'.[33] Oscar was married for 20 years. As a result of the long time spent as a heterosexual, perhaps he believes that only a long-term relationship is a 'decent relationship'.

One explanation for the difficulties these men experienced and their critical views of the gay community may lie in its failure to meet their social needs. Another explanation may lie in their inability to find a suitable niche. And yet, as the discussion in section one showed, there are many gay community organisations and their activities are varied. Another, perhaps more convincing explanation may be that, as Erving Goffman has suggested, while people who share a stigmatised identity might socialise together and would be seen by outsiders as all the same, the cohesiveness between them is an illusion because they do not necessarily have a 'capacity for collective action' or a 'pattern of mutual interaction'.[34] It can take time for members of a minority to achieve a degree of tolerance and acceptance of their own kind, and of themselves:

> When the individual first learns who it is that he must now accept as his own, he is likely ... to feel some ambivalence; for these others

will not only be patently stigmatized, and thus not like the normal person he knows himself to be, but may also have other attributes with which he finds it difficult to associate himself. What may end up as freemasonry may begin with a shudder.[35]

## Conclusion

When asked to explain their experience of or involvement with the gay community, almost two thirds of the men interviewed for this study nominated their work with HIV-AIDS support groups, counselling services, their involvement with a local social group, or their work in social activism or political lobbying. Then a group of almost one quarter of interviewees said their community involvement occurred when they participated in gay festivals, street parades or the scene. Involvement thus consisted either of the work they did for community organisations as counsellors, PLWHA carers, activists or lobbyists, or when they socialised or participated with other gay men in social groups or public displays of solidarity or celebration. In other words, they understood community as either the practical work they did to improve the lives of others like them or as a participatory experience with other gay men. In both cases the gay community that they knew was visible to them and had a concrete reality.

On the whole, interviewees who worked as counsellors, PLWHA carers, activists or lobbyists were drawn from all classes and all age groups. Other findings included that gay men in small cities and country towns appeared to have greater agency in shaping their social life because of the role of the local social group and their access to it. And festivals and parades contributed to the perpetuation of gay men's shared history and provided non-sexualised social spaces that were free of homophobia.

The accounts of the remaining interviewees, comprising just over one fifth of the sample, represented a significant, dissident minority. These men either do not agree with or cannot conform to the dominant gay narratives. A number of them have rejected the version of gayness available and have no wish to understand it. There is a case to say that all communities include similar dissident minorities. Richard Sennett cites an argument of Lewis Coser that conflict is essential to the maintenance of community,[36] since it forces people to pay attention to one another: '[T]he scene of conflict becomes a community in the sense that people learn how to listen and respond to one another even as they more keenly feel their differences'.[37] If Coser is correct, it is possible that with time the voices and views of dissidents such as these men may effect a change in the number and range of stories that circulate in and comprise the gay community.

# 7
# Couple Relationships

'He has provided huge stability and gives me huge freedoms.'
Lionel, 59.

## Introduction

Banned from openly expressing their affective relations for most decades of the twentieth century, gay men invented other ways of relating, created couple relationships of varying duration and configurations to suit the circumstances forced on them or to circumvent prohibitions against them. These have been variously characterised as experimental, difficult to sustain, or similar to heterosexual marriage.[1]

Most of the men interviewed for this study regarded a relationship as an important source of meaning in their lives.[2] Not coincidentally, perhaps, the majority of men in the sample were also in couple relationships, which, as the discussion in section two, 'Permanent relationships' shows, are notable for their longevity and for the similarity they bear to the companionate marriage. More than one third of interviewees were in relationships of seven years' duration or longer. Importantly, nine men had been in relationships longer than 25 years.[3]

One piece of Australian research suggests that gay relationships are less common than the experience of my interviewees would suggest, especially among working-class men. Hard to attain but greatly desired, their prevalence is, according to these researchers, '*hegemonic* rather than the *normal* thing' in working-class milieux.[4] This view is corroborated by other Australian research on gay relationships. A recent report suggests that male homosexual relationships, especially among working-class men, seem more fragile and fraught than lesbians' couple relationships, and that tensions arise between the demands of the scene and their affective needs.[5] There is a perception, as well, that gay men's relation-ships are short-lived, that they founder too easily. As Gary Dowsett writes: '[C]ommon parlance reviles the homosexual relationship by depicting it as inherently unstable or by judging its worth against a heterosexual norm'.[6] One explanation for the short duration of gay rela-tionships, discussed later in this chapter, is that they developed this way in times of social hostility as a defence against homophobia.

In this chapter, and throughout the book, two terms are used for the partners in a couple relationship: 'boyfriend' and 'partner'. They are used intentionally to distinguish between relationships in terms of duration. Often the term 'boyfriend' will be used in the initial period of a gay relationship, while 'partner' is reserved for the members of a couple relationship when it is more established. For example, gay men are likely to refer to the man they have been going out with for six days or six weeks as their boyfriend. After six months or a year, however, the title is likely to change to partner. Another term, 'lover', was more common in the 1970s and 1980s but is rarely used nowadays.

The argument of this chapter is that there are two principal stories of gay relationships. The dominant story concerns the practice of the majority of interviewees, which is to conduct permanent arrange-ments that mirror heterosexual marriage, or to engage in serial mono-gamy. A powerful secondary story concerns the practice of a small group of men who maintain more fluid or 'open' relationships. Why and how relationships are meaningful to interviewees is discussed in the first section of this chapter. In the second section, the dis-cussion concerns interviewees' experience of permanent relation-ships. Finally, in section three, the discussion turns to the 'open' relationship.

## The relationship as a source of meaning

The principal reason a relationship is meaningful to the men in this sample of interviewees is because it is both the central focus of their life and a project they jointly develop with their partner. More than two thirds of the men in the old cohort and slightly less in the middle cohort said a relationship brought meaning to their lives, while less than half the men from the young cohort made the same claim.[7] In the discussion that follows, the idea of a couple relationship as the central focus and as a joint project is first examined, after which its significance is analysed as the site where men can experience love, companionship, intimacy and sexual satisfaction.

## Central focus and joint project

Two men in their 70s and one in his early 60s represent the views of the men from the old cohort. Two are in long-term relationships, one of 20 years' duration and the other 30 years.[8] The oldest man is Leslie (aged 74). Married for more than 30 years and in a gay relationship for longer than 20, he believes that a solitary life lacks meaning: 'Without our relationship, I would not be sharing my home with anyone and, as far as home is concerned, it only has meaning when I share it with someone'. Harold, who is 71, also enjoys a shared life, even though he and his boyfriend live apart: 'Not a day goes by but he rings. We have a wonderful relationship. He and his daughter are very important to me'. Lindsay (aged 62) expressed similar intense feelings:

> The most important thing in my life is my relationship with my partner of the last 30 years. We moved in together in 1972. That is fundamental. We live in the same house. It is impossible to imagine what life might have been like without it. It is so important.

As a group, the interviewees from the middle cohort expressed themselves with more certainty than those from the young cohort when asked to explain the meaning of couple relationships. Four men in their 50s represent those views here. None of the men was previously married and all are in couple relationships of 20 years' duration or longer.[9]

Graham and Lionel are each in relationships of more than 25 years' duration. For Graham (aged 52) his relationship is his life's focal point: 'Everything in my life really *hinges* around my primary relationship with my partner and that is the context for everything else'. Lionel is 59 and lives with a partner he describes as 'a real kind and gentle fellow', who has been 'an incredible stabilising influence'. While sex is less important now, their sexual relations were 'terrific for the first fifteen years!' He also enumerates the many other ways in which his partner makes sense of his life:

> If I want to do something around the house or in the garden I just do it. I talk to him and he accepts and lets me go. I never argue about whether we'll have this colour on the walls or this carpet. We share interests in football and opera and film. We read the same sort of books. Politically we are together.

Lionel's partner is clearly influential in all aspects of his life. Importantly, his account also reveals the development from romantic to companionate love, a transition that enduring marriages are said to go through too.

The other men from the middle cohort touched on what Michel Foucault called the 'lovers' fusion'.[10] Patrick is more explicit and more than hints that his life with his partner is as if 'two become one':

> Having a relationship in itself but also having a relationship with this person has given me self-confidence and made me feel that I am a real person. He is in a sense my identity. He has shaped who I am. The person I am now is half him in a way. I find now that I can hardly separate myself.

Patrick is neither resentful of his partner's power to shape him nor jealous of the qualities that his partner has. He simply rejoices in their shared identity. There is a quality of Yin and Yang in the way he describes their union. How his partner might feel about it is another question. The last of the interviewees is Richard. He is in his late 50s and has been in a relationship for 30 years. In what might be seen as typically masculine, he uses the metaphor of building to describe it: 'Together you are creating your own atmosphere as a unit'.

Two men in their 30s and two in their 20s represent the views of the interviewees from the young cohort here. Three of them are in relationships of between two and 12 years' duration.[11] All four men are employed and none has been married.

Neville (aged 37) from the upper end of the young cohort says that his partner of 12 years 'anchors' him and 'is what life is about'. For Daniel, who is 35, a relationship is hard work but rewarding:

> To be in a relationship with someone is such a damned hard thing to do. Because nothing else really requires you to look so closely at who you are in the world. Nothing else requires you to walk around quite as nakedly in the world. [Laughs] And I do not just mean physically either.

Myles (aged 24) is more wistful: 'I do not like living alone and not sharing my adventures and life experiences and challenges with someone. It means a great deal to me to live and share life with another person'. Finally, there is Mark (aged 25), who says that he wants a relationship that is like a marriage: 'I want to be with someone in a similar capacity that a heterosexual relationship can have, that is, a committed relationship for a long period of time'.

While none of the men from the three age cohorts actually used the phrase 'central focus' to describe how a relationship gave meaning to his life, their accounts suggest relationships are meaningful because of what the other man brings to their life. Among the men who saw their relationship as the central focus of being were some who said life would be nothing without their partner. Others said that the partner gave life meaning, that he was the most important person or thing to them. To use the novelist Patrick White's phrase, the other man was the interviewee's 'solid mandala'.

And similarly, while none of the interviewees used the phrase 'joint project', the language they use to describe their relationships suggests that many of them understand it in this way. Their words did convey the sense that they understood their lives to have a similar goal, or that their shared life had a mutually agreed common purpose, which has a slightly different meaning. Older men who perhaps have had more opportunity to iron out any wrinkles in their relationship often expressed the latter meaning.

Relationships are meaningful also because they are where men can expect to experience love, companionship, intimacy and sexual satisfaction. These are aspects of an emotional life that everyone might hope for from a couple relationship and are discussed in the remaining two parts of this section.

### Love, companionship and intimacy

Of some note is the fact that only one interviewee explicitly said a relationship was meaningful to him because it was where he experienced or could express love—and this was a man from the young cohort. Jason, who is aged 35, said, 'I love the feeling of love. I like being in love even with all the rubbish that comes with it. I am a bit of a love junkie, I suppose'. It is worth reflecting on why *none* of the other men referred to love in this context. First, it is possible that they take for granted the love they have with their partner. Second, men generally are too bashful to speak openly of these things. Third, perhaps they are more comfortable speaking of companionship and intimacy. And, fourth, perhaps companionship and intimacy are what love means to them.

From the accounts of the men in this sample, it would appear that only older men value companionship, for it is only men in the middle and old cohorts who speak of companionship as a meaningful feature of their relationship. The young men do not. From the old cohort there is a man in his mid-70s, who was formerly married and who rated companionship as the most important ingredient in his relationship:[12]

> The things we share are so important, such as the jokes and the other things we do together, like when my partner gets the meals so that I can stay and work in the garden. We have a holiday house and we share that, as well as the travel we do together. Life would not have much meaning without companionship.

Like companionship, intimacy appears to be a quality that only older men value or whose value only they are prepared to acknowledge, for only men in the middle cohort, that is, men in their 40s and 50s, expressly said it made relationships meaningful. Neil who is in his mid-40s and Ivan who is 40 represent their views here. Neil said that he and his partner know each other so well they are almost like brothers: 'After almost 16 years the relationship with my lover becomes one of faith, trust and dependence'. He valued the support they gave one another and also the intimacy, which he said existed on a daily basis:

> The fact that we can still learn from each other is important and also that we still laugh together. And the fact that we can argue points to the growth and understanding that can occur. He and I are very different. What is important is the support and nurturing that comes from the intimacy that is there.

Presumably when he says that his relationship is mature because he and his partner can argue, Neil means that an argument no longer threatens its existence—that is, they can argue and not worry that one of them will take offence and desert or abandon the other. Similarly, Ivan described intimacy as closeness and sharing. His partner was his lover, best friend and mate.

What is most remarkable about these attitudes is the ease with which the men admit their respect for and attachment to their partner. There is no evidence of discord or domination of one by another; in fact, there is a strong sense of equality between partners. While they are shy of using the word, 'love', it is clear that it is the basis of many of their couple relationships. These accounts are conspicuous for how like a companionate marriage are the couple relationships they describe.

### Sexual relations

Sex makes a relationship meaningful said a group of ten interviewees.[13] Half of these men are in a relationship, the other half are single. Their views are represented here by the accounts of two men from the middle cohort and one man from the young cohort. All have been in a couple relationship at some point.

Stuart (aged 49) has been single for many years. He said that he would prefer to be speaking as a person in a relationship but he is not. And this weighs heavily with him. Stuart is also HIV positive and believes that his HIV status makes it difficult for him to have a relationship: 'I would love to be in a relationship but having HIV has limited my scope for relationships. It has been hard to find a partner who has coped with that in the past'. Stuart says that sex has become an issue for him because he has had so few relationships in the last 20 years: 'It is not always getting too much of it that is the issue or getting enough of it. It is just that it is an issue. It would take up some part of my average week'. Why 'getting sex' is an issue is not clear. What he might mean is that sex would be less of an issue for him if he were in a relationship. It would be less of a struggle because it would be part of his couple relationship. But, as it is, he must go out looking for sexual encounters and these forays are time-consuming. As he says elsewhere in the interview:

> If I want to have sex, I have to throw myself into the sexual market place. To stand a chance there one is required to have a reasonably attractive body in some shape or form. And that has become a serious issue for me because HIV has disfigured me in some ways, which has affected my body image more dramatically than anything else.

Stuart's experience confirms the observations that were made in an earlier chapter on the gay scene. Most social spaces available to gay men operate as a sexual market where a premium is placed on youth and beauty. One effect of the valorisation of youth and beauty is that those who are neither young nor beautiful can be dismissed or overlooked.

Vincent is in his early 30s. He has had a number of short-term relationships, the longest of which lasted nine months. In the following excerpt, he makes clear that he is aware of a distinction between affective relations and sexual relations but also how easy it is as a young man to confuse the two, or at least how easy it is to confuse love and sex.

> When I was younger, I mistook sex for love and did so without knowing it. Many of my sexual experiences were not emotionally satisfying but were great physically. Part of me feels that gay sex is bad but a good part of me loves it and enjoys sex. Sometimes I have sex knowing that it is not love but find it good and satisfying because of the connection. My sexual appetite can be voracious. On other occasions I could not care less.

Vincent's frankness includes his admission that there are times when he knows he wants to be loved or wants love but seeks out episodic sexual relations and finds the sexual connection 'good and satisfying'. And thus he does manage both to separate and conflate the affective and the sexual.

Ross (aged 54) was married for 13 years, and has one child and grandchildren. He and his partner have been together for seven years. He is forthright in his belief that sexual relations and relationship are interrelated. A satisfying sex life is important to him, by which he means sexual relations with, as he says, 'my lover and partner', who are one and the same. Moreover, in his mid-50s he declares that: 'It is still as important now as it ever has been'. If his sex life is on hold, when for example he or his partner is inter-state, he says, 'I feel like something important is lacking in my life'.

These stories are significant because the interviewees appear to understand sex in one of two ways. It is either as an expression of lust, as a social practice they do 'for fun', that can make them 'feel good' about themselves, or it is practised in a spiritual sense, where it is an expression of the love for their partner, which can also be fun and enjoyable, of course. While the former is simply an expression of physical desire, the latter is more an expression of companionate love.

## Permanent relationships

Donald West's *Homosexuality* was something of a bible for many gay men in the 1960s.[14] An interviewee from the old cohort remembered reading the book as a young man and said that it was West who introduced him to the word 'homosexual', which replaced the schoolboy slang word, 'poof',[15] and preceded his becoming 'camp'. How reliable *Homosexuality* was as a guide to curious, inquisitive or uncertain young men is debatable. It is not clear if West's intention was to help or to warn off young men who read his book. For example, he has the following to say about the chances a gay man might have to develop a relationship:

> The deviant who has 'come out' into homosexual society, and fully accepts his inverted feelings, has then to go through the experiences of falling in love and having affairs of greater or lesser intensity or exclusiveness. Many strive to duplicate the heterosexual model of monogamous marriage, but both nature and social circumstances work against this solution.[16]

Fifty years after its first publication, *Homosexuality* reads as though its author intended to discourage gay men rather than to offer them the consolation of good science. One page later, he says slightly more optimistically and perhaps with some accuracy that 'some of the most stable male homosexual unions are those in which the partners pursue their sexual interests independently'.[17]

Commentators writing more recently approach the topic in a different spirit. Jeffrey Weeks, for one, rejects any idea that gay men are in some way unable or unwilling to have relationships. Their capacity and propensity to develop relationships are, he says, no different from those of heterosexuals.[18] Kenneth Plummer examines the many choices available to gay men who want to live a 'gay life'. Like Michel Foucault, Plummer recognises that a variety of relationships and friendships are possible.[19] He mentions three. A gay person might want to model his relationship on the heterosexual marriage, he might choose 'to experiment with more diffuse couple relationships', or he might decide to live a single life. Most gay men will decide at some point to develop a relationship, says Plummer, because they were brought up in a society that 'highlights the value and naturalness of "coupling"—through family of origin, through education, through religion, through media—it is a difficult task for any individual to estrange himself from such concerns'.[20]

While gay men might want to develop a couple relationship, it can be difficult to find a partner. Plummer suggests three reasons for this. First, the gay milieu provides for people 'who have little in common but their gayness'; second, the attitudes and behaviours of men on the scene 'establish expectations of "casualness" in sexual relations'; and, finally, gay men have to struggle with negative views of them held by wider society.[21] In regard to the effects that social hostility has on gay men and the difficulties many have in developing relationships, Plummer says:

> Social hostility to homosexual men ... may mean the relationship has to be hidden from family and work mates; it may mean difficulties in obtaining a joint mortgage, writing a mutual will or even visiting a sick partner in hospital; it may mean a general lack of support from others when the relationship is under severe stress. As hostility decreases, so these kinds of problems diminish—nevertheless they have played a paramount role in the past.[22]

Since Plummer wrote this in the early 1980s, changes have occurred in the way gay men are treated and seen by wider society. The difficulties Plummer described affect gay men less generally or intensely than they once did. But hostility has not uniformly decreased in all classes and locations. While some men in suburbs like Darlinghurst in Sydney or Soho in London, or districts like Le Marais in Paris or New Town in Chicago will have no sense of social hostility towards gay people, there are other men in country towns, provincial cities, and less affluent suburbs of big cities who do not share the same experience of relative tolerance.

### Gay marriage

Until very recently in the West, gay people have been prohibited from marrying. Permission even to conduct relationships of varying levels of intimacy is also quite recent—in legal terms. These relationships are the primary focus of this chapter. Although discussion of gay marriage in this book is limited to this and the following paragraph, it is important to note that the prohibition against such marriages is slowly weakening. Prohibition no longer exists in a number of Scandinavian countries.[23] Britain and Canada most recently passed legislation to allow gay marriage, and, as John Boswell has shown, it once existed in societies of Ancient and Medieval Europe.[24]

The interviewees were not specifically asked a question on gay marriage because the bulk of interviews were conducted in 2002 and 2003; and it was not until mid-2004 that the matter began to attract regular coverage in the gay media—in Sydney at least.[25] The men in the sample were asked, however, to tell the story of their relationship and, notably, when they did so, none mentioned gay marriage. They were also asked how their life would be different if they were not gay, in answer to which only one man, an interviewee in his mid-20s, said that if he were not gay, he would be able to marry and have children more easily.[26] There was very little evidence, then, that the interviewees were strongly interested in or aware of gay marriage, and no one indicated any intention of actively pursuing the matter at a political level.[27] There was, however, an interest in and propensity for relationships that are remarkably like the companionate marriage.

## Relationship length

Forty-nine of the interviewees, or more than 60 per cent of the sample of 80 men, were in couple relationships, the highest proportion being in the old cohort (68 per cent), followed by the middle cohort (60 per cent) and then the young cohort (57 per cent). Of the interviewees in relationships, a small handful of only five men were in relationships of less than one year's duration, while 29 men, or over a third of the sample, were in long-term relationships—defined here as seven years or longer.[28] It is notable that in the old and the middle cohorts, there were 19 men who had been in relationships of 20 years or longer and nine men whose relationships were 25 years or longer. That over one third of interviewees were in relationships of more than seven years suggests significant longevity in couple relationships.[29]

The largest concentration of men in long-term relationships was in the old cohort, where 54 per cent were in relationships of seven years or more. In the middle cohort, 46 per cent of the men were in such relationships.[30] The young cohort had the smallest number of men in long-term relationships. While 16 of the young men were in relationships, which is almost 60 per cent of the cohort, only three of them had been in relationships of seven years or more.

The comparatively low proportion of men from the young cohort in long-term relationships is to be expected because many have not yet had time to begin such a couple relationship, especially those in their early 20s. Also, it is in the young cohort that we find the men with fewest responsibilities and as well those most heavily involved in the gay scene, which, as Michael Pollak noted, might create a special set of tensions: 'How can sexual impulses stimulated by the existence of a highly accessible and almost inexhaustible market be reconciled with the sentimental ideal of a stable relationship?'[31] They are young men, and in Western countries young men are allowed if not encouraged to prolong their adolescence, which, depending on class and family, might be marked by an absence of serious ties or commitments and the pursuit of hedonism.

## Similarity to companionate marriage

The stories of three men, one from each of the age cohorts, form the basis of discussion of the permanent relationships of men in this sample. The first man is in his mid-60s and has the longest relationship of all the men interviewed for this study. Next is a man who is in his early 50s and has been in a relationship for 11 years. Then there is a 33-year-old man who is in a relationship of five years' duration.

A prominent feature of these relationships, and the others they represent, is how similar they are to the companionate marriage—described by D'Emilio and Freedman as marriage redefined in 'more egalitarian terms': 'A successful relationship rested on the emotional compatibility of the husband and wife, rather than the fulfillment (*sic*) of gender-prescribed duties and roles'.[32] The stories of interviewees' relationships were notable for the equality between the partners and also for the absence of 'gender-prescribed duties and roles'. The last point might seem unnecessary but a perception exists in mainstream society and some gay circles that gay relationships operate in the way of the traditional marriage, that there is a division of labour along gender lines, just as sexual relations are imagined to be conducted according to the model of active (masculine) and passive (feminine) partners. In their work with working-class gay men in Australia, Connell, Davis and Dowsett found 'much joking about husbands-and-wives', while the French sociologist Pierre Bourdieu wrote: 'In the couples they form, they [gay men] often reproduce, as do lesbians, a division of male and female roles'.[33] But there are also scholars who maintain that gay relationships are *not* remarkable for gender role distinctions, and this was a strong theme in the stories of the men interviewed for this study.[34] The stories were also remarkable for what they revealed about the men's actual practice of egalitarianism.

Barry is 62, lives with his partner of almost 40 years and is representative here of the men from the old cohort. Barry is not given to hyperbole but nevertheless described his relationship with his partner as a very loving one kept alive by their each having separate interests.

> I love the trash and treasure markets and my partner is mad into musicals and I think that is how it has worked so well. He comes from the arty side of life whereas I enjoy a different type of life, and we are compatible. We have our arguments, but we have never split up over the 40 years. We have always been compatible sexually. We do not do anything now. When we were in the prime of life we used to enjoy sex very much. But it is only in the last few years, since we

both had our separate stints in hospital, he with his heart and me with my back, that there is not much sexual drive at all.

Even though Barry is proud his relationship has endured, it seems he feels obliged to refer to earlier days when sexual attraction was stronger and sex was a more important part of their relationship. It might be that he misses the intimacy or enjoyment that was part of their sexual relations and is not yet reconciled to the loss of them.

Thomas represents men from the middle cohort who are in long-term relationships. Both he and his partner are 'serial monogamists', meaning that each had had one or more significant relationships before they met. Thomas works in education and has been with his partner for 11 years. He admitted that he can resent his partner's presence but at the same time welcomes his return after an absence:

> Quite often we do not do things together and I am glad of that because he gets under my feet a lot of the time. But I like that sense that he is coming back and will tell me about what is going on and will always ask if I want a cup of tea.

In the end, it is clear that, for Thomas, his partner's company is an important, meaningful adjunct because of the other's physical presence:

> There is something warming and stable and reassuring in knowing that he is there. I like being able to reach over and put my hand in his when we are driving and the bodily contact and warmth in the bed. I like that sense of someone else being there. That is important to me.

The story of this relationship is of interest for the honesty with which Thomas described the two sides of intimacy in his relationship, and, in doing so, showed how a partner's presence can be both claustrophobic and a source of deep longing and appreciation.

Mick is 33 and his partner is 38. Here he represents the men from the young cohort who are in relationships. Both Mick and his partner are employed in the travel sector and met while at work. They have been together for five years.

> In our relationship spending time together is important and so is having someone there to care for you when you are sick. I find that in a relationship sex is not everything. You could go years without

it. Having someone to wake up with is what is important. It is also about being able to come home and cry on someone's shoulder. It is being able to spend time with a person who is there for you.

Mick's account is the closest to the idea of the 'lovers' fusion' mentioned in the first section of the chapter. His relationship is very much a joint project and his partner would seem to be the central focus of his life. It is also noteworthy that he feels compelled, like Barry (above), to refer to their sexual relations. But, whereas Barry referred to sex in order to lament its passing, Mick's purpose is to discount it, to explain that its temporary absence is not important.

There are at least two possible reasons for Mick's attitude. On the one hand, he might hold the view that sex is not crucial to the success of his relationship because he does not have a strong sex drive. On the other hand, he is relatively young, and it is always easier to do without something when its supply is guaranteed, which sexual desire seems to be in young men, than when it is not, which can often be the case for older men. Mick's situation is in direct contrast to what Barry faces, which is to accept the sad truth that his sex life is ended. That both men refer to their sex lives underlines the point made in section one: that an important meaning men attach to relationships is as the site for satisfying their sexual needs.

The significance of these stories about the interviewees' experience of permanent relationships lies in what they reveal of both the seriousness and the relative ease with which gay men conduct relationships. They revealed gay relationships that were relatively permanent and approximate the companionate marriage: 'It is impossible to miss the similarity to heterosexual marriage, and ... romantic ideology about "being the only one" for your partner'.[35] The longevity of the relationships of the men interviewed for this study and their relatively high incidence contrast with the common perception of gay relationships as flimsy or inconsequential. Some scholars have remarked on the similarities between gay and straight relationships in the late twentieth century. D'Emilio and Freedman, for example, regard a homosexual relationship as one of many options from which young North Americans might choose, and Anthony Giddens's 'pure relationship' applies equally to homosexual couples.[36]

## The 'open' relationship

In the gay world there exists a style of relationship that is now less common among heterosexual people—the so-called 'open' relationship.[37] An open relationship is one where two partners agree to live together or separately and to share their lives in most senses, that is, emotionally, physically, sexually and financially, except that they are not monogamous.

Arrangements of this type are most often but not always made by mutual consent. In order for the relationship to function 'openly', the two partners will often agree on a set of rules or conditions that govern or guide the sexual relations that they may engage in outside the relationship. Like many single, promiscuous men and women, gay men in an open relationship agree to make a division, or maintain an existing division, between their affective life, and their sexual life. A popular stereotype of gay men is that they are only interested in sex, not in relationships and that if they have relationships they are not long lasting. It could be argued that the practice of some gay men to divide their affective life from their sexual life supports this stereotype.

Historians have explained the division that some gay men make between an affective life and a sexual life as an adaptation to the social context that prevailed before sexual liberation in the 1960s and 1970s, when the clandestine way of life called for '[a]n affective and social life to be carried on without the constraints imposed by stable and lasting relationships'.[38] Like Michael Pollak and Ken Plummer, John Boswell sees a direct link between the style of relations that gay people conduct and the degree of social hostility that they have to endure:

> It is obviously very much to a gay person's advantage in hostile environments not to be part of a permanent relationship ... [T]he most effective defense against oppression will lie in fleeting and clandestine relationships which do not attract attention or provoke suspicion.[39]

Their assumption is that social practices that develop in a repressive period continue long after the restrictions and stigma that it created are removed.

Four interviewees who had open relationships were willing to discuss them. None was from the old cohort, but there were two men from the middle cohort, Donald (aged 52) and Alan (aged 47), and two men from the young cohort, Harry (aged 28) and Mark (aged 25). Three of the men, Alan, Harry and Mark, referred in their stories to rules that they and their partner use to guide sexual behaviour outside the relationship.

Alan explained the nature of the open relationship he has with his partner, Sergio, in the context of the effect HIV-AIDS has had on how they deal with casual sex. To deal with the risk, they adopted what Alan called 'rules of engagement' whenever they had sex with other men.

> As a couple, we negotiated what HIV-AIDS might mean for us. We discussed rules of engagement if we wanted to go to saunas. We took safe sex very seriously and kept ourselves informed but at the same time were not paranoid about it. We realised that there is a level of risk in all of this but that we would be open in our relationship. We talk to each other and perhaps get off on the experiences with each other as part of the trade off.

The arrival of HIV-AIDS caused Alan and his partner to systematise their sexual relations with other men. His use of the military phrase, 'rules of engagement', emphasises the sense in which many gay men regard themselves 'at war' with the Human Immuno-deficiency Virus.[40] In the spirit of cultural activism, Dennis Altman has argued that men in relationships such as Alan and his partner are more likely to practise safe sex because of their wish to protect their primary affective relationship:

> [I]t is my belief that there is a far higher acceptance of multiple partners among gay men than most other groups ... Ironically, this makes it easier to develop safe sex practices, for couples can admit to themselves that there may be risk of infection from outside liaisons without imperilling the relationship.[41]

Harry's relationship with his partner, Frank, has lasted more than three years. Frank is almost 40 but Harry (aged 28) is not concerned by the age difference. In the following extract he describes what he calls the 'little rules' that govern sexual encounters outside the relationship.

> We met three years ago. It is an open relationship with little rules. For example, we are not allowed to pick up anyone. They have to pick us up, so we have the choice to say 'Yes' or 'No'. If we are together in the same town, we pick up threesomes, we do not pick up alone. That is about it. It is the longest relationship I have had.

The rules seem designed to control the likelihood of one partner feeling jealous of the other partner's sexual adventures. The purpose of the rule that requires each partner to wait for the stranger to make an advance ('They have to pick us up') is to remove them from direct responsibility for any casual sexual encounter. And thus responsibility for it would rest with the stranger.

Mark conducts a long-distance relationship with his partner. It would be easy to assume that it is the geographic distance separating them that allows for the 'openness' of their relationship, but Mark explains this arrangement pre-dates his partner's departure overseas. Elsewhere in the interview, he explained that open relationships exist because of the absence of 'support structures for relationships in the gay community'. Mark described what he understands an open relationship to be and the rules by which he and his partner conduct their version of it.

> It is okay to have sex with a guy more than once but we cannot be in a relationship with them. We are happy to talk about who we see and what we do, though we are not so interested in the intimate details. It is *useful* and an important way of doing it, given that we have been separated for over two years. But we did it before. We used to go to saunas together and go off and have our fun and then come back and talk about it. That was useful because it helped me understand that you can have different kinds of sex. You can have more sexual sex and you can have more loving sex. In that way there is not that much to compare between the two in terms of the feelings that you get out of it. In that way I think that both of us are quite secure.

Implicit in the rules in all open relationships, no matter how they are phrased, is that the emotional intimacy of the primary relationship must be protected at all costs. Either partner may have sex with a person more than once, but again, only so long as this does not represent commitment to a new relationship. Like Alan and Sergio, Mark and his partner 'talk about who we see and what we do'.

Of the four men, only Donald did not refer to rules governing conduct of his open relationship, and this might be because the decision to open their relationship was not mutual. Donald is 52 and works in public relations. In this extract, he explains that he and his partner were experimenting with an open relationship when his partner started to become emotionally involved with the other man. Donald said he would like to believe it is possible to negotiate such a relationship but it is clear in what follows that it is not easy for him.

> The loving relationship that I have with my partner is going through a challenging time because we are exploring open relationships, which are much more than just sex outside the relationship. And that is quite a dominant theme in my life. I believe that monogamy is a social construct but I cannot help getting a bit jealous from time to time. The other man does not know what he wants, which is tricky for my partner. And then there is me and I know that, if I am just patient, things will probably work out.

This open relationship, which is working in the partner's favour, has come to dominate Donald's life because it is 'more than just sex outside the relationship'. Donald shows himself hard at work to justify and accept the arrangement when he says that 'monogamy is a social construct', but it would appear that powerlessness marks his position in the triangle.

Emotionally, the open relationship brings with it a high level of risk, for, in most cases, one partner will be more eager than the other to arrange for 'third-party' sex. The need for rules suggests that the men are aware, however, that such arrangements can cause emotional distress to one or other partner and they therefore make an effort to minimise it. The rules also seem like an attempt by the men to protect what is valuable in their relationship—for example, the intimate companionship they enjoy there and the other sources of meaning discussed in section one—while, at the same time, enabling them to take part in the sexual opportunities the scene provides.

## Conclusion

In line with the findings of other published research, the stories of the men interviewed for this study show that gay men of all ages and classes value a couple relationship. Where the findings here differ is in relation to the length of the couple relationships, which, as mentioned, are notable for their longevity. One possible explanation for the divergence might lie in the fact that the majority of men in this sample are middle class, and their lives are, on the whole, less subject to the same pressures that Connell, Davis and Dowsett identify among men in working-class milieux or that were outlined in a separate piece of research by Dowsett and in the report by Chamberlain and Robinson.[42]

In contrast to popular preconceptions, the interviewees' stories suggest that, at least for a majority of the sample, their intimate life is characterised by a strong desire to pursue a couple relationship similar to the companionate marriage. Features of companionate love present in gay relationships include, for example, love, intimacy, companionship and sexual satisfaction, qualities the men said made a relationship meaningful for them. Their belief, too, that the relationship was the central focus of their life, corresponds to the focus of the companionate marriage, that is, the 'emotional compatibility' of the two parties. Nevertheless, there is also evidence from the stories of a small group of men in this sample of an interest in open relationships, that allow for sexual adventurism as well as the security of companionate love.

Overall, the sexual and affective reality of the majority of the interviewees is one of comparative fidelity, in its external form at least. This should not seem so surprising because, as Edmund White observed in the late 1970s, the desires and aspirations of most gay men are remarkably similar to those of the heterosexual majority.[43] I would argue, however, that two recent developments have also reinforced this propensity among gay men: the impact of HIV-AIDS on their sexual behaviour and attitudes, and the greater acceptance of gay relationships in the wider society.[44]

# 8
# Friends and Family

'You sometimes see the most amazing companionships or friendships or mateships that men of various ages have built.' Ivan, 40.

## Introduction

Together with the couple relationship, which was examined in the previous chapter, there are two other important features of gay men's intimate life. The first is friendship, which the men interviewed for this study rated as their principal intimate relationship—more important than the couple relationship—and the second is what I have termed the 'gay family', which comprises families that gay men create who have been formerly married, when they take part in co-parenting arrangements, when they form what I have called a 'gay nuclear family' or, finally, when they make what is known as a 'family of choice'.

Friendship between men is now a closely monitored relationship but this was not always the case. Adult friendships between men were more frequent and less commented upon until the nineteenth century when they retreated as the family gradually became the primary source of intimate relations. The simultaneous decline of male friendship and expansion of the family as the wellspring of intimacy underlines a more recent argument, which Lynn Jamieson makes in relation to the general population, which is that the couple is now the most significant intimate relationship.[1] Her argument is slightly at odds with my research findings which, as shown in section one of this chapter, reveal friendship to be the most significant intimate relationship of the men interviewed for this study. My findings show that first, friends are

134

important to more interviewees than is the couple relationship, and that second, friends and the couple relationship are considerably more important than their birth family is to them.[2] Interestingly, my findings concerning friendship's primacy are remarkably close to those of a recent large-scale Australian inquiry that investigated the health and well-being of more than 5,000 non-heterosexual people, aged 16 to 92.[3]

Philippe Ariès has argued that the growing acceptance of homosexuality in the second half of the twentieth century—when friendship began to carry 'sexual overtones'—might have assisted the decline of 'personal friendship' between men.[4] Similarly, Henning Bech argues that words like 'friends' and 'friendship' changed meaning during the twentieth century and 'turned into purely homosexual terms, just as the reality they designated disappeared from everything but homosexuals' relations'.[5] While it was more usual 20 or 30 years ago, it is still possible today to hear a gay man's partner referred to as his 'friend'. The consequence of this 'sexualisation' of male friendship has been to draw attention to any close friendship between two males because of its homosexual potential. Personal friendships between heterosexual men are rare today because there is very little space for such a relationship in their intimate life:

> *Where* might such a friend be in a 'heterosexual' man's life? Not at home, since that is reserved for the wife and kids. Nor at work, because there he is mostly together with more than one man, and in any case work itself is the primary concern in that context. Where then? In the gaps between home and work he is usually either with his family (at the movies, for example, or on a Sunday outing); or he is alone (in the car, in the supermarket); or if he is with other men, it is always in the plural or always subordinated to some other purpose (soccer, politics). If there is room at all for a friend in a man's life, it must apparently be found in the interim between the family he was born into and the one he will later enter, in other words, in the relatively unguarded niches of boyhood and youth; and even there the possibility is vanishing, since nine-year-olds are now expected to have girlfriends. Friendship between men is a social impossibility in modern societies, at least for most males.[6]

While it could be argued that Bech is too categorical—some straight men do manage to have close male friends—the tendency *not to* is still greater among men than it is among women. And, for gay men, there is no such constraint. They may, and do, as the research for this chapter shows, enjoy intimate, non-sexual friendships with men.

Homosexual parents and the families they create are not especially new or recent developments. Barry Dank first raised the question of gay parents in the early 1970s. Then John Boswell suggested that its practice had been hidden but widespread in European societies since Antiquity. He said that, with the exception of priests and other members of the clergy, most of the gay men he wrote about in *Christianity, Social Tolerance and Homosexuality* were married and had children. The reason for the 'persistence of the belief in the non-reproductivity of gay people', he continued, lies in a tendency to notice 'what is unusual about individuals rather than what is expected'. Few people, for example, would be likely to recall that Oscar Wilde and Edward II were fathers, he argued, even though they 'devoted the bulk (if not the entirety) of their erotic interest to persons of their own gender. But the fact remains that they married and had children'.[7]

From his study of the gay milieu in a North American city, Dank identified four types of homosexual parents. The first were gay people who were formerly married: 'There are many persons who played the role of husband and father—generally before they decided they were homosexual'. Second, there were homosexual couples who raised adopted children or children from a former marriage; he found that this mainly occurred among lesbian couples. Third were couples where one parent was homosexual and they remained married. Finally, there were 'front' marriages where both man and woman were gay and decided to marry and to 'pass' as a married couple: they adopted children or had children of their own. '[S]uch marriages', said Dank, 'are for purposes of social convenience'.[8]

More recently, the definition of gay family has expanded to include persons who are neither kith nor kin. Jeffrey Weeks refers to this new social form as the 'family of choice'. Elsewhere it has also been known as the 'alternative family', and sometimes the 'elective family'.[9] Socio-logist Michael Pollak detected a gay version of the alternative family in the early 1980s:

> Little groups of friends, often former lovers who in the past have all had sexual relations with each other, form a sort of 'extended homosexual family' ... 'Brother' or 'little brother' is often the special

name for those former lovers with whom the ups and downs of life together, as well as a common vocation, have been shared.[10]

When Weeks speaks of family of choice, however, he has in mind 'extended networks of support' that gay people create: 'a sense of self-worth and cultural confidence is realized in and through the friendship networks that we describe as family of choice'. He defines family of choice as a friendship network that may also comprise relatives, as well as the lovers and former lovers to whom Pollak referred. In the eyes of Weeks's respondents, the family of choice was not a substitute and was 'as real as the family of origin'.[11]

Very few men interviewed for this study understood or used family in Weeks's sense, however. The family types that do exist more closely resemble those Dank identified and are as follows. In the first place, as mentioned in the chapters dealing with the coming-out stories of the three age cohorts,[12] all the men in this sample have stories to tell of experiences with their birth families. Second, a substantial minority of men who were formerly married have families that comprise their gay partner and children of a former marriage, or, in some cases, of two marriages, that is, where both men were formerly married and each one has children from his marriage.[13] Third, one interviewee and his partner formed a family unit with a lesbian couple and the biological child of the interviewee and one of the women. Fourth, another interviewee and his male partner created a family closely resembling the nuclear family, and referred to below as the 'gay nuclear family'. Finally, this interviewee and his partner also consciously arranged a social network that they call 'family', which consists of friends, former lovers and perhaps siblings—in other words, something that approaches Weeks's family of choice. Four of these family types are discussed in the second section of this chapter, 'The gay family'. In the first section, the discussion centres on friendship and its role as the principal relationship in the affective life of gay men.

## Friendship

Friends are without doubt the central feature of the affective life of the gay men interviewed for this study: almost two-thirds of the men in the sample declared that friends were an important feature of their lives. As mentioned in the introduction to this chapter, the fact that friendship was important to more men in this sample than a couple relationship contrasts with Lynn Jamieson's claim that the couple is *the* significant intimate relationship today.[14] There are two likely reasons that the situation for gay men differs from what might be the case more generally—that is, why friendship, rather than the couple relationship, remains their principal intimate relationship.

First, even though, as previously shown, one third of the men in this sample are in long-term relationships, the majority of them are not.[15] They are either single or they are in relationships of fewer than seven years' duration.[16] The intimate couple life of these interviewees might thus consist of a series of short-term relationships interspersed with periods when they are single. If it does or if a gay man spends the bulk of his adult life single, friends may assume a more important role in his intimate life, as they also tend to do for single women. Friends are likely therefore to represent a source of constancy between relationships or indefinitely. In other words, friends may provide a web of intimacy that other gay men, who are in permanent couple relationships, find within their relationship.

This picture is reinforced by the second reason the intimate life of gay men might differ from the general one Lynn Jamieson outlined—which is that the majority of interviewees in this sample do not regard their birth family as an important source of meaning.[17] This might be a legacy of coming out: the type of relations gay men maintain with their birth family largely depends on the level of acceptance or rejection they experienced when they announced their homosexuality to them. Friends will take the place in their intimate lives that their families vacate if that response is negative. Roger (aged 44), for example, said that he would probably replace family with friends:

> I do not find my biological family, except for my mother, in any way important. I rarely see my sisters and their children. There would be half a dozen people who I would regard as my family, but I have never lived with them [Laughs] and could not bear to.

Friends might therefore assume a pre-eminent role in the intimate lives of the men in this sample, and among gay men more generally, because relatively few of them are in long-term relationships or have meaningful links with their birth family.

In the remaining parts of this section, the discussion, by age cohort, focuses on why the interviewees regard friendship as paramount. It is worth noting by way of an introduction to the discussion that each age cohort had a slightly different set of reasons for valuing friendship. Men from all three cohorts agreed, however, that social interaction was the most vital attribute of friendship. Its next most desirable quality—in the eyes of interviewees from the old and the young cohorts, but *not* the middle one—was the mutual exchange of care and support.

One possible reason for this difference might concern the value we place on friendship in times of crisis. Friends can provide a support network when our lives are out of balance or in peril because of accidents or employment or accommodation difficulties. Because young people and old people are more vulnerable to events of this nature, it makes sense that the men from the young and old cohorts emphasised the mutual exchange of care and support, as one of the desirable qualities of friendship and the men from the middle cohort did not.

## Old cohort

For the men in the old cohort, social interaction was the single most important attribute of friendship, followed by the mutual exchange of care and support.[18] In the following discussion, five men, all in their 60s, speak about the importance of social interaction with their friends; then one man in his 70s describes the place of giving and receiving in friendship.[19]

Terrence is proud that he and his partner, Jock, regularly host parties for their friends and acquaintances: 'Out in the back room we have had 28 people for sit-down dinners on a couple of occasions. One was for my 60th birthday. I also did it for Jock's birthday'. It is a tradition with their friends to have lunch with Terrence and Jock at Christmas: 'We also have twenty-six for Christmas. We have the waifs and strays in the gay world'. Lindsay similarly places a great value on his circle of friends and on maintaining contact. 'I place a lot of emphasis on keeping in touch with people. I telephone people to say "Hello" every week.' From his description, Lindsay appears to be the hub of his circle of friends:

> I maintain quite a lot of correspondence on the Internet with friends and people that I have known in places I have lived before. The 20 or 30 that I keep in contact with are very important. I would do something every day towards nurturing them or keeping in touch.

Maurice (aged 65) also values his friends and says that 'without friends life would be dreary'. His circle is smaller than Lindsay's, for he believes that 'you do not have time for more than two or three close friends'. Charles's consciousness of the value of friendship has particular poignancy. In the six months before our interview, two of his close long-term friends had died: 'Doug who I met when I was 22. That is 46 years ago. And Clarke who I knew for 47 years died in New York last week. So it has not been a good six months'.

Slightly at variance with the other men, Brendan understands friendship in the context of his Christian beliefs: 'we come to understand our spirituality through our friendships and through our love for other people'. Nevertheless, Brendan echoes the views of other men in the old cohort when he says that friends make life worthwhile. He also believes—in a somewhat doctrinaire fashion, perhaps—that a person can only experience what is good in life in the company of friends: 'I love the things that are associated with friendship, like a meal with friends. You cannot experience music and wine on your own; you only experience them with friends'.

An understood moral economy of giving and receiving is the unspoken value all men in the old cohort, and many in the other cohorts, place on, and hope to find in, friendship. Harold, who said that friends were crucial because they were 'relationships where you share and give and receive', represents these views here. He described an incident that occurred before our interview—the sort that is a commonplace in the lives of people in their 70s—when because he lives a considerable distance from his nephew, he had to call on a friend for help when he was in hospital: 'I was in for two weeks because my heart played up a bit. One friend in particular came and got everything from home for me and did everything for me'. In heterosexual families it is not uncommon for elderly relatives to be able to count on their children or grandchildren for help when they are in need. This is not the case, however, for men like Harold, and also single women, who have to make arrangements with their friends for mutual support. Harold is proud of his relationship with his friend, which is platonic, because it is one of those relationships that, he says, 'gives meaning to my life'.

### Middle cohort

Social interaction is also regarded as friendship's prime attribute by the interviewees from the middle cohort. However, unlike the views of the men from the old cohort, only one man from this cohort regarded the exchange of care and support as important, and a large group of men understood social interaction as significant because it provides continuity or substance to their lives.[20] Their sentiments are represented here by the stories of two men in their 50s and three in their 40s.[21]

Enduring friendships are meaningful for Bill (aged 52) because they provide a degree of consistency in his life: 'They have always been there in an unquestioning way and the sense that they have been has always been there'. For Nigel (aged 49), too, 'friends are probably the most important thing in life'. And old friends are especially important: 'I can talk to them and say things that they understand'. James's account is slightly different from Bill and Nigel's in that, as a young adult, he made a project of forming friendships. He is 45 and grew up in a large country town. He lived in London in his 20s and now lives with his partner in a southern capital city. During the course of the interview, he reflected on how few friends he made when he was a teenager and that, when he left the boarding school he attended, he made friends a 'career for a time in my life'.

> One of the directions I wanted to take when I left school was to find friends. Most of my friends at school were people who were on the outside. When I left school I was not thinking about work or career. I was desperately looking for friends. That was the really important part. I am pretty sure that these friends were gay or bisexual. I think in retrospect that the motivation to look for alternative people was part of my search for gay sex. It was the gay sexuality. It was the gay identity. That would have been a part of what I was doing.

James is not indiscriminate in the friends he makes and yet also admits to a confusion of sex and friendship. He is proud that he still has friends in London whom he sees whenever he travels to the United Kingdom. 'I tend to hold on to people who I want to keep as friends.'

In the remaining accounts from the middle cohort two interviewees explain how social interaction has augmented their lives. Michael (aged 52) was a gay liberation activist in his youth. He says that he cannot imagine how life would be without friends. Perhaps rather grandly, he says that they are 'existence': 'They reflect you. It is a matter of sharing. I share my life with my friends and they share their life with me'. Jerome (aged 49) says that he recently met a man who is 35 and has no gay friends:

> He lives with a lover, but I am astounded that none of his friends are gay. I do not understand how he lives because I could not do it. I need people to talk to. I need to be able to have a girlie laugh with someone or need to have a shriek! I need to have other people around me that are the same.

Jerome likes the company of people who share similar values, sense of humour and sexual identity. Part of the reason he needs to be able to socialise with friends with whom he can share 'a girlie laugh' or 'a shriek' might lie in the fact that he is a manager in a large company where all the other senior managers are heterosexual. His social life is less exclusively gay now than it was: 'When I was younger it had to be totally gay. I was not interested otherwise'. He was certain that he would never reach a stage when he does not need gay friends: 'I would always need to have gay friends, and I think when I get older or retire that this need may be even more important'.

### Young cohort

As with the other cohorts, the interviewees from the young cohort regarded social interaction with friends as the essence of friendship. For them, it provided an opportunity to share views and values and common interests. Friends were also valuable to them because of the support they gave each other, a quality that the men in the old cohort referred to as well.[22] Their views are represented here by the stories of two men in their 30s and two in their 20s.[23]

Friendship was paramount for the two men in their 30s because, in the words of one of them, it provided them with 'new ideas or new outlooks'. It was the relationship they most value because it allowed them to test out their beliefs and build their sense of self. Robert is 38 and lives in an inner suburb of a capital city. He and his partner have been in a relationship for three years and have lived together for two. For Robert, the value of friends partly lies in their capacity to challenge him and to act as a catalyst for change: 'I find that my friends and the new people I meet stimulate me'. Friends of long standing are particularly valuable because 'they share your history with you. In many ways my friends provide a shared narrative to life. For other people that would be the gay community but for me because I came out late it is my friends'. Elsewhere in the interview he indicated that his mother was not accepting of his homosexuality.

The other man in his 30s is Daniel. He says that his friends are 'like mirrors' in the sense that their views reflect his influence on them, and vice versa. He does not mean that he has a narcissistic relationship with them: 'I think that I most clearly get a sense of my place in the world from the relationships I have with my friends'. Thus the connection with them is reciprocal. Moreover, Daniel describes the influence his friends have on him in terms similar to those that Robert uses— that is, they act as catalysts for change and personal development:

> I have friends who genuinely challenge me to explore bits of me that
> I would not otherwise explore, or challenge me to do things that

I would not otherwise do. If I think back, it has been the friends who have performed that function that I most value.

Like the men in the old cohort, the young men also value friends because of a moral economy that exists of recognised giving and receiving. Mark, who is 25, and Ian, who is 28, represent those views here. Mark is a university graduate and has been with his partner for four years. He says that friends have been indispensable to him since he left secondary school—for the exchange of care and support, and the company they provide. 'I love reading and I love thinking but I love being with my friends more. I enjoy the interaction and the support and just "hanging out."' Ian gives a more detailed account of the value of mutual exchange in friendship. He believes friends and family are similar in importance: together they provide a 'support network that is always there':

> They are people to go to when you need help and someone to bounce off. I have a close family. I have a close-knit group of friends, although a lot of them have moved interstate recently. I have lost about six friends in the last six months. Trying to re-build a circle of friends can be difficult and it is something that I am trying to do because it is important to do it.

What does Ian's extract tell us? In the first place, both his family and friends are 'close-knit' groups. Second, he regards each as an indispensable source of support and succour. Third, proximity is vital for the maintenance of his friendship group, because frequent interstate travel is impractical and costly and because it is incompatible with the close and immediate social interaction that he and his friends, and perhaps also other single people in their 20s, require in order to maintain their friendships.

## The gay family

In the discussion that follows, gay family is understood to have four meanings. First, it may refer to a group of people comprising the children and partner of a gay man who was previously married or in a heterosexual relationship; it is discussed under the sub heading, 'Formerly married men'. Second, it may comprise a group consisting of two sets of parents—a gay couple and a lesbian couple—who between them conceive and give birth to a child, and is discussed under the sub heading, 'Co-parenting'. Third, a gay couple may create a gay nuclear family consisting of themselves and children; this is discussed under the sub heading 'Gay nuclear family'. Finally, a version of the gay family here takes the form of an extension of Jeffrey Weeks's family of choice, that is, a group of people comprising friends, relatives, lover and perhaps former lovers of a gay man.

### Formerly married men

Men who were formerly married comprise slightly less than one fifth of the sample.[24] In all, just over 60 per cent of the formerly married men are in the old cohort. Of those, four were married for more than 30 years and all have children. Two of them, Leslie (aged 74) and John (aged 65), are in gay relationships of 20 years or longer. In the middle cohort, there are five men who were formerly married. The man in this cohort who was married for the longest period of time (20 years) is a 50-year-old with two sons and two daughters. All such men in the middle cohort have children from their former marriages. One, Ross (aged 54), has two grandchildren as well. Among the young men, none has been married. There are in the young cohort, however, two men who belong to different forms of the gay family and their circumstances are discussed later in this section of the chapter.[25]

The stories the men tell about relations with their children and wife vary. At one extreme are stories of men retaining close contact with their children or with their children and their wife, while at the other extreme there are men who do not mention them at all. Two interviewees stand out as making considerable effort to maintain relations with their children and their former wives as well as with their birth family. They are Ross (54) and Terrence (64). Ross lives with his partner, Glenn, and his former wife lives in a neighbouring suburb. He keeps in touch with his ex-wife for a number of reasons. First, their 'similar ideas about parenting' help them to maintain contact, and then their two grand-daughters 'keep us together', he said. In addition, he keeps alive connections with his birth family: 'I have a good family life and I enjoy the memories and the feelings that I have from my family'. He specifically keeps in touch with his mother and sister. Ross says that his relationships, and especially his relationship with Glenn, give him the sense that they are a 'family unit', which is made easier by the fact that, as he said, 'my daughter and grand-daughters like Glenn as much as I do'.

Terrence is older than Ross by a decade. He never told his parents about his homosexuality or his relationship with Jock, his partner. He was married for 20 years and has two adult children. He is now in the 22$^{nd}$ year of his relationship with Jock. Terrence said that his relations with his daughter are very good but are somewhat distant with his son, who, he said, 'rings every now and again but not as much as I would like him to'. Before Terrence's mother died, she always made a point of including Terrence and Jock in family gatherings, even though she did not know, or, if she did, she did not let on that she knew, about their relationship. Terrence said that his mother and Jock 'got on a treat': 'Jock was great to her. Even when she was in a nursing home and with dementia, he would spend time with her'. He said that his sisters accept him and his relationship with Jock, even though the one who lives in the country is, as he said, 'a bit precious and born-again'.

None of the formerly married men shares a house with his children, wife, siblings, or parents. As well, not one of the men has created a household comprising himself, his partner, and his children from a former marriage, though most of the men relate stories about their children or their partner's children staying with them. None has created a formally constituted alternative family of this type *under one roof*. Their kinship relations are more loosely based.

## Co-parenting

A less well-known form of family is the one created when two homosexual couples agree to be co-parents.[26] Two couples, one of gay men and the other of lesbians, will between them conceive and give birth to a child. There are other configurations. For example, a gay man may donate sperm to lesbian or heterosexual couples that want to conceive, or to a single straight woman—providing them with the so-called 'gift of life'.[27] The man may choose to have no relations with the child or may wish to be fully involved in its life and upbringing.[28]

Parenting experiments such as these are not uncommon nowadays. What is remarkable, however, is that people are 'yearning to have children' by such unconventional means, 'often to the exclusion of all other interests', when the birth rate is falling, and also that they want to create non-traditional family arrangements at a time when the divorce rate is rising.[29]

Only one interviewee in the sample had a story to relate of being a co-parent. Because of the significance of this social experiment, the discussion here is devoted to the experience of that interviewee, who, with his partner and two lesbians, is a parent of a small child. Tony (aged 33) works in a professional occupation and lives with William, his partner, who is 38. They have been together for nine years. Tony says that he cannot imagine his life without a set of relationships that are important to him, among which are those with his partner, daughter and co-parents, mother and siblings, and friends.

Asked to tell the story of his daughter's life, he began by saying that he had always known he would be a parent: 'I did not know how it would happen but I always knew that I would. It was something that was very important to me'. He helped his parents bring up his younger siblings and 'enjoyed spending time with kids'. Tony admitted that he was more determined than his partner to begin the project of having a child: 'My partner put it out of his mind. It was not until I started talking about it that it came on to the agenda. I drove it in our relationship'. Through mutual friends, Tony and William met a lesbian couple who also wanted to have a baby.

The two couples did not undertake the project of having a child lightly. First, they agreed to spend 12 months getting to know each other, during which time they spent six months together in family therapy. 'It was an incredible journey we went through', said Tony. 'There were lots of tears. It was an amazing way to get to know people.' Second, they drew up a formal agreement of their 'understandings of issues about child rearing'. And, as Tony said, everything was covered: 'From what football club she would follow to what school she would go to, what religion she would belong to and what name she would have'.

In retrospect, Tony believes the decision to record formally their understandings about their child's upbringing was vital not simply as 'a process of documentation', as he called it, but because it allowed them to discuss areas of potential conflict. Such parenting experiments are known to be complex, if not problematic.[30] If there had been any disputes, said Tony, 'it would have been a red light' for him and his partner. In the end, the process achieved two things for the parents: first, it was a means of understanding each other, and, second, the document made clear that all the parents were to have 'a say in bringing up the child. We all agreed that the four of us have those rights'.

After a 'cooling-off' period, the two couples met and agreed to conceive. Their daughter was born in 2003. In the following extract, Tony describes how he and William share their daughter with her mothers. He also admits to feeling resentful when he has to 'give her up' for what feels like a very long time each week.

We see her one day every weekend and on Wednesday nights we have family dinner. No one is allowed to miss family dinner. As my daughter gets older we will have her more and more. When she is three she will start to do sleepovers with us without the girls. By the end of primary school it will be 50-50. It has been difficult for me because I want to be a full-time parent and the only reason I compromised is because it is in her best interests. It breaks my heart to have to drop her off every Sunday night. Last Sunday we were saying goodbye and she said that she did not like saying goodbye to daddy. It will get better.

At present Tony and William are only part-time parents. Tony clearly wants a more equal share of time with his daughter but seems reconciled to the program that the four parents agreed to while she is an infant. At present, the child seems to be a pawn in their arrangements. How the girl will wish to divide her time and live her life when she grows older is another question. Exciting as the experiment is, all four parents will have to come to terms with allowing the child to be herself. As Richard Sennett and Jonathan Cobb observed in *The Hidden Injuries of Class*, treating children as possessions or puppets is a dangerous social practice: '[Living] a vicarious life through one's children ... carries with it enormous dangers. For children are not merely extensions of oneself, embodiments of one's dreams, but independent beings themselves'.[31]

Social experiments such as this are evidence, says Jeffrey Weeks, of a generational shift in the gay milieu.[32] In the past, gay parents were mainly women or men, like those discussed in the previous part of this section, who had children from a former heterosexual relationship. Nowadays, however, gay and lesbian couples are more willing to use each other's reproductive capabilities to have children in arrangements such as Tony described. As well, a 'reproductive technology' has developed that is, according to Elizabeth Beck-Gernsheim, 'clearing the way for new forms of parenthood'.[33] In the following, she outlines some of the ethical choices it creates:

[S]hould the possibilities of artificial insemination be open only to married women, on the grounds that marriage still offers the best protection for the child's welfare? Or should they be open to anyone who so wishes—including unmarried and homosexual couples or women without a partner—on the grounds that the child's need will be for care and affection, not an official rubber stamp? Or is the idea to uphold in principle the right of the most diverse lifestyles to exist, but to require, in the name of the child's welfare (defined how?), at least a stable partnership for the application of medical technology to planned parenthood?[34]

In Australia and many other countries, despite the parenting experiments of gay and lesbian couples and single women, reproductive technology is still largely restricted to straight couples, and the public debate about other forms of parenthood has not yet progressed beyond platitudes and stereotypes.[35]

**Gay nuclear family and family of choice**

The discussion here about the remaining two categories of the gay family —the gay nuclear family and the family of choice—relies on the testimony of only one interviewee from this sample: a man from the young cohort who is in his mid-30s. While what he has to say in relation to family of choice is interesting, and corroborates Jeffrey Weeks's claim that such social experiments are taking place in the West, it is important to note that its practice is not widespread among Australian gay men, as represented by those in this sample.

Moreover, as the discussion in the first section showed, the overwhelming majority of men interviewed for this study regarded friendship as the paramount relationship, which, on the whole, they kept separate from their other intimate relationships. There is very little evidence of the interviewees 'blending' the elements of their intimate lives in the way that Michael Pollak described in his outline of the 'homosexual extended family' or that Jeffrey Weeks suggested in his definition of family of choice. And, as mentioned, the only interviewee who referred to his friendship network as 'family' is Joseph, who is the subject of the following discussion on 'gay nuclear family' and family of choice.

*Gay nuclear family*

Joseph and his partner are foster parents of two children. Joseph is 35, works in the health sector and lives in a capital city. He and his partner have been together for 11 years. Joseph says his family is important to him 'both in the biological sense and the constructed sense'. He means birth family when he uses the word, 'biological', to describe one part of his family, and, when he speaks of family in the 'constructed sense', he is referring to the nuclear family that he and his partner have created, and also to his family of choice, as we shall see below. In the following extract he explains why his constructed family can be defined as a nuclear family.

> I have quite consciously constructed a family in the last few years with my partner and our two kids. I am not a traditionalist in thinking that the nuclear family is the only way to go but I think that a household with more than one adult that cares for kids is a family.

Joseph's definition differs from accepted understandings of nuclear family in the same way that do heterosexual families with adopted or fostered children and as de facto couplings do—that is, he does not require that the children and adults be kin, viz. related by blood or marriage. Joseph and his partner, Scott, are foster parents. Neither church nor state has sanctioned their relationship. Nonetheless, Joseph believes that he has 'constructed a family ... with my partner and our two kids'. What he seems to be saying is that he has collected together the component parts of a family and assembled them in such a way that they serve their intended purpose, which Joseph believes is to provide love and care for the children. This has been one of the principal functions of the modern family since it came into being in the late Middle Ages, or, as Georg Simmel, explained: 'The major social purpose of a secure marriage was obviously the better care for the offspring which it could guarantee, and which already led to marriage-like unions in the animal world'.[36] Finally, Joseph boasts, as would any parent, that he loves that he can provide the boys with 'something that feels like a family'. And there is evidence that gay couples and lesbian couples have been and are raising children with the same purpose in mind.[37]

### Family of choice

As mentioned, this term is used to describe a form of friendship network that includes not only friends, but also relatives, lovers and former lovers. While it is true that both straight and gay people may be experimenting with this relatively new social form, it has a different meaning for gay people as Weeks explains:

> [T]here are clear overlaps between homosexual choices and the choices of many self-identified heterosexuals. But for non-heterosexuals the idea of a *chosen* family is a powerful signifier of a fresh start, of

affirming a new sense of belonging, that becomes an essential part of asserting the validity of homosexual ways of life.[38]

Some gay people may create a family of choice to *substitute* for their birth family, although this is not Joseph's situation, and it is not the situation of Weeks's respondents.[39] Joseph explains that his family of choice exists side by side with his birth family. In effect, it is an extension of his birth family. He sees more of his family of choice because his parents and siblings live interstate. 'They are scattered all over the place', says Joseph. When explaining why his birth family is important to him, it is clear that Joseph sees it as a source of his identity (and origins): 'They are a big part of my sense of self in terms of where I have come from and what it means to be me now'. It is at this point in the interview that Joseph expounds on how his family of choice exists along side his birth family.

> But I see my family as broader than the people who I am related to by blood. I include in it some of the heterosexual friends that I have had for decades. One in particular was a best friend at school and still is a best friend. He and his wife live around the corner from us now and I see them absolutely as family. My ex-partner and some of my close friends are family to me in the same way.

## Conclusion

When it was not safe for gay men to be open about their sexuality, they often married or had de facto heterosexual relationships, kept their sexuality a secret and became parents. This is the origin of the most common form of gay family and is well represented in the life stories of men in this sample.

When times were more propitious, some of these men separated from their wives or female partners. One of the options that could then have been available to them was to establish a gay family with their same-sex partner and their children. Notably, none of the men in this sample created such a gay family *under one roof*. A more common story was for the interviewees to create a looser intimate network, which they still termed 'family', where the members met regularly or occasionally—for example, for a weekly dinner—but did not live together as a household.

The interviewees' experience with three other forms of gay family, viz. co-parenting, gay nuclear family and family of choice, was largely restricted to two young men, both of whom were in their 30s. Children were involved in both cases. While these social experiments help to re-frame and extend notions of the family, the men's motives appeared more related to their own needs, particularly in the case of the interviewee and his partner who arranged with a lesbian couple to be co-parents of their own child. One interpretation of their endeavours is that, notwithstanding the care with which they prepared for parenthood and looked after the child, the interviewee and his partner seem to have created a family to provide for their own satisfaction. If this is so, it may suggest that a couple relationship alone will not fully satisfy the affective needs of all gay men—that some might want more and might hope to find it in this type of gay family.

Friendship, on the other hand, was central and crucial to the affective lives of the vast majority of men interviewed for this study. Its chief attributes were social interaction and mutual exchange of care and support. For the men in the old and young cohorts, these were the bases of their support networks.

How the interviewees understood social interaction varied by age cohort. In the old cohort it was the means by which the men maintained their social networks. By contrast, the men from the middle cohort understood it as a source of continuity and substance in their life projects. The young men, meanwhile, regarded social interaction as friendship's most significant attribute because—as with most young people, gay and straight—it is with friends that they exchange views and share values and common interests. In doing so, it seems that they engage in a process of developing and reinforcing their sense of self and self worth. In other words, the young gay men seem to be testing out their identity, as young homosexuals, through social interaction with friends, gay and possibly straight. Few, if any, men in the older cohorts made similar claims.

One explanation for this difference may lie in the life stages of the interviewees. Apart from those who came out later in life, it was among the young cohort that we found the greatest concentration of men most recently out. As discussed in Chapters 2, 3 and 4, coming out is not an overnight transition. It can take some men as long as 20 years, or more, to complete. Among other things, coming out often involves a sorting through of old friends and the making of new ones, a re-working of identity. This reconstitution of identity may take many forms. For most it will involve the selection of friends who share similar values and views. Of importance to men who have come out or who are coming out are friends who, in the words of an interviewee from the young cohort, provide a 'shared narrative'. The reason therefore that there might be fewer men or none in the middle and old cohorts who see this as an important quality of friendship is that many more of them have completed their coming out and are likely, therefore, to be more certain of their sexual identity and who they are in the world.

# 9
# Life as an Old Gay Man

'There used to be the notion that old gay men were sad and lonely but I think that has evaporated and now they are seen as no more or less sad than anyone else is.' Chester, 71.

## Introduction

At the heart of this chapter are two aspects of human identity that are rarely joined together: homosexuality and ageing. In the earlier discussion of the gay scene, and from time to time in other chapters, I have shown that a powerful public narrative exists that portrays homosexuality in terms of youthfulness and young bodies. And for this reason, being gay is rarely associated with growing old or being old. Jeffrey Weeks was one of the first scholars to discuss the story of age segregation and ageing in the gay milieu. Writing in the early 1980s, he related how old gay men were invisible because the focus of the gay milieu was on youthfulness.[1]

The purpose of this chapter is to establish what if any link exists between the interviewees' gayness and the ease or difficulty with which they live their lives as old men. Because of the changing circumstances of gay men's lives, which, over the second half of the twentieth century have included a marked reduction in social hostility towards homosexuality and a greater acceptance of gay men in most Western countries and of their so-called 'lifestyle', it makes sense that the final chapter in this book should examine how gay men have experienced and might expect to experience old age—the penultimate stage according to Simone de Beauvoir in any person's life.

The central argument of this chapter is that age segregation occurs among gay men because the gay scene valorises youthful bodies and

worships the cult of the body even more than Western society does generally. But if they avoid the scene and its youthful emphasis—and
depending on their occupation, career and relationship status—it is possible for gay men's lives in the West to be remarkably similar to those of
their heterosexual counterparts, and for gay men to experience age and
ageing similarly. The only intimate relationships generally absent from
the middle age and old age of most gay men are those with their own
children or grandchildren, but, as mentioned earlier, even these relationships may be part of some gay men's intimate lives.[2] In addition,
some scholars have suggested that, because of their coming-out experiences or the discrimination they may have faced during their life, gay
men often manage later life relatively well, if not better than their
heterosexual equivalents.[3] Not all members of the old cohort examined
here have come out but the majority had.

For many years now, scholars in the Social Sciences have argued that
ideas such as 'youth' and 'age' are cultural products and that the life
stages they describe are not necessarily determined by our biology
alone; that is, the meaning we ascribe to them depends on the value
the society we belong to accords them.[4] Marxist scholars, for example,
maintain that, while old age comes to all people, how a person experiences it is directly affected by her or his material circumstances.[5] And,
in the case of many of the world's indigenous people, for instance,
high infant mortality rates and adult mortality rates are a direct consequence of their impoverishment and have nothing to do with their
genetic dispositions.[6]

A person's attitude to and experience of age and ageing is also likely
to vary according to his or her age and sex and generation. In this
sample of interviewees, for instance, the facts of being old and having
experienced the process of ageing are the lived experiences of men in
the old cohort. For members of the middle cohort and the young
cohort, however, ageing and old age are largely imagined conditions,
for, as Norbert Elias wrote,

> normal age groups ... often have difficulty in empathizing with
> older people in their experience of ageing—understandably. For most
> younger people have no basis in their experience for imagining how it
> feels when muscle tissue gradually hardens and perhaps becomes fatty,
> when connective tissue multiplies and cell renewal slows down.[7]

The men in the middle cohort seem to have greater empathy for the
experiences of the old cohort by virtue of their own lived experience

and their place in the life course. But, because old age is so far removed from their experience of life, and empathy for the old is not encouraged in Western society today, the men from the young cohort appear to regard it only in abstract terms, if it enters their purview at all.

A large majority of men in this sample said that old gay men were viewed and treated as Other.[8] At least three quarters of men in each cohort reported that old gay men were either invisible and ignored or treated with contempt in the gay milieu; the accounts of these interviewees are considered in the third and fourth sections of this chapter. Another group of men, comprising one fifth of the sample, said that old gay men were viewed as predatory beings, a prevalent, negative stereotype that has a long history; these accounts are discussed in section five of the chapter.

Alongside the public narrative of the old gay man as predatory is another one that portrays old gay men as lonely; this persists in the gay milieu as well as among heterosexuals.[9] It is clear that while a very small number of men were aware of this narrative or knew gay men who lived lonely lives, it is not supported by the lived experience of the men in this sample and for this reason is not discussed in this book.[10]

Modifying these negative images of old gay men, but only very slightly, is the fact that one third of the men in the old cohort said they felt younger gay men respected and admired them, while a smaller number of men in the young and middle cohorts said that old gay men were treated with respect or admired; these positive views of the interviewees are the subject of the second section of this chapter. In the first section, a selection of men from the three age cohorts explains what age they regard as old and how they experience or understand it.

## What old age means

More than half the men in this sample understood ageing as a process of physical decline. When asked what picture they had of themselves as old gay men, 43 interviewees associated old age with infirmity and frailty.[11] The second most mentioned indicator of ageing was the deterioration of external appearances (for example, skin or hair), to which 17 men referred, or just over one fifth of the sample.[12] A substantial majority of those interviewed for this study therefore understood ageing to be associated with the slowing down or deterioration of the body.[13]

All interviewees were asked if they regarded themselves as old, and their answers are revealing.[14] In the old cohort, two men said they regarded themselves as old and four gave equivocal answers. Both men who regarded themselves as old are in their 60s. Interestingly, none of the men in their 70s did.[15] Failure to identify themselves as old may arise from a dissonance between the internal view they have of themselves and the external view others have of them, which, Simone de Beauvoir explained, is the 'complex truth' of old age:

> [T]he words 'a sixty-year-old' interpret the same fact for everybody. They correspond to biological phenomenon that may be determined by examination. Yet our private, inward experience does not tell us the number of our years; no fresh perception comes into being to show us the decline of age.[16]

Men from the old cohort who reported experience of Beauvoir's 'complex truth' described it almost as she did. For example, Gerald, who is in his mid-70s, found the interview question difficult to answer because 'when you look out at the outside world, you do not really see yourself as old or getting old'. It was other people, said Gerald, whose 'perceptions of you dictate that you are getting old':

> I believe that because I have white hair and have had for some years, there is a tendency for younger people on public transport to give you their seats. We [Gerald and his partner] are both still physically active. We are not bedridden; we are not crippled; we are not suffering ill health, which means that we are able to be active in lots of ways and as a consequence we do not see ourselves as old.

Six years younger than Gerald, another man, Geoffrey, also shares a similar understanding of the distance between the way others view him and his internal view of himself:

> I look in the mirror and think, "Who is that dreary old bugger looking out at me?" When I do not have a mirror, I still feel 25, but looking in the mirror I think, "Oh, God! Look at me. I am falling to pieces". And that is how you think about old people.

Geoffrey's self-analysis is both insightful and fascinating for two reasons. First, his concern about the dissonance between the two realities that shape his identity is more deeply personal than Gerald's, and, as such, is evidence of what Chris Shilling calls the effect of the 'body as a mask', which involves 'the imposition of negative stereotypes which make people acutely self-conscious about their bodies'. Second, by spelling out the link between his own experience as an ageing man and his knowledge of how ageing people in general are treated, Geoffrey reveals the genesis of social relations that give rise to ageism: 'corporeal signs of ageing are saturated with negative images and these images appear to be determined to mummify our experience of ageing.'[17]

In the next stage of the discussion in this section, the focus initially is on the lived experience of the men from the old cohort, that is, people who would generally be considered old, even if very few of them see themselves as such. Their stories concern the association they make between ageing and physical decline. When the discussion turns to deterioration of external appearances, the focus shifts to stories from the middle cohort and young cohort.

### Old cohort: ageing and physical decline

When the 14 men from the old cohort who associated physical decline with ageing spoke about it, they did so in the context of either an illness, and the incapacity it caused them, or a more general reduction in their physical capabilities. In this part of section one, two men discuss old age in the context of illness and then three men speak about how it may lead to reduced capability.[18]

The two men made aware through illness of what old age might mean are Reginald (aged 79) and Edward (aged 60). Reginald worked all his life in mundane occupations and is now retired. He lives with his partner of nine years in a working-class suburb of a major capital city. Edward writes for a living, has a boyfriend of six years and lives in an upper-middle-class suburb in a capital city. Reginald says that, for as long as he can look after himself, he will not regard himself as old. But his first experience of what old age may mean occurred when he recently fell ill: 'I couldn't get out of bed without help and I suddenly realised what was going to happen to me'. His fear of dependency is well founded, according to Elias:

> The way in which people come to terms, as they grow older, with their greater dependence on others, a decrease of their power potential, differs from one person to the next ... But it is perhaps useful to remember that some of the things old people do, in particular some of the strange things, have to do with their fear of losing power and independence and especially of losing control over themselves.[19]

Edward was also made aware of how illness may change a person's understanding of his or her future life course and what he calls his or her 'place in the queue'. He recently experienced a serious health scare:

> My hearing deficits, sight failure, the cancer, all of these happened because I am not as young as I used to be. When I was almost 60, I had to think that I might be going to die, and that means you think about where your place is in the queue. As other people die around you, you get a sense of being closer to the head of the queue. However, I do not have that immediate sense of feeling old and decrepit.

The interviewees who associated old age with a general reduction in physical capabilities did not appear to experience it until they began to approach 70. Vernon (aged 75) is the oldest man to relate an account of the general physical decline he has experienced as he ages. He does not regard himself as old but confesses he can no longer do what he could when he was younger. One way he measures the effect of age is by the reduction in his sexual performance: 'I have not been able for 12 years to be the active partner in any relationship, so certainly I have felt my age'. Chester did not begin to think about age until his 70th birthday. And now, at 71, while still not regarding himself as old, he has begun to notice 'a certain diminution of physical things and little aches and pains and illnesses'. Ronald's life path is similar to Chester's. Still in his 60s, he does not regard himself as old. He feels and sees himself as healthy, and yet, like others at his age, knows that his body can let him down: 'Various things are wrong with me, but because I am still relatively healthy I do not tend to think of myself as old'.

These men who discussed physical decline in the context of illness seemed to understand their recent experience of illness as a foretaste of the loss of mobility or independence that they anticipate will accompany old age. The other interviewees from the old cohort simply described a general slowing down as they aged or an increase in 'aches and pains'. There was nothing revelatory about their stories, except a perception that the advance of old age might take many people by surprise.

### Middle and young cohorts: ageing and the deterioration of external appearances

Considerably more men from the middle and young cohorts connected old age with the deterioration of external appearances. In fact, only two men from the old cohort referred to external appearance at all, while nine men from the young cohort and six men from the middle cohort did so. Because appearances seem thus to matter more to the younger men in this sample, their views form the basis of the discussion in this part of section one. They are represented here by the accounts of one man from the middle cohort who is in his early 50s, and two men from the young cohort who are in their 30s.[20]

Declining appearances were particularly important for Donald, who represents the views of men like him from the middle cohort. He is concerned about losing his looks as he ages, and is determined not to let his body deteriorate, as have the bodies of gay men he has seen in the sauna, 'whose elasticity has really gone'. 'Their bodies are everywhere. Frankly I do not find it pretty and I hope I do not do that. My body is still in good trim and I have a real commitment to keeping it trim into my 70s.' Donald knows that he is ageing when he looks in the mirror, but intends to grow old 'gracefully': 'I am determined not to do nips and tucks. I want to be fairly gracious. I do put a bit of blonde in my hair but there will be a point where I will be gracious and grey'.

Tony and Paul represent men from the young cohort. Both are aged 33 and are in relationships. Tony is university educated and Paul left school after he completed Year Seven. Tony is a high-income earner, whereas Paul works in a low-status, low-paid occupation. Tony is also the more articulate and says it is difficult to age as a gay man because 'the gay world focuses on young, beautiful people and the lifestyle that goes with that. As you get older as a gay man, you have to find a new space to be in'. Either in spite or because of this awareness, he intends to have plastic surgery to keep himself youthful: 'I plan to have my first bit of work next year when I am 35 and I plan to have it every five years after that'. Paul is less vain than Tony. He accepts that a 'loss of physical appeal' accompanies ageing, but believes that a man can compensate for this as he acquires emotional maturity.

It is understandable that there should be more men in the young cohort than in the other cohorts who associate declining appearances with old age. These men are in the full flush of youth and are valorised in both the gay milieu and wider society for their youthfulness. If Ariès is correct, and adolescence is the most privileged state, then Michael Mittenauer is also correct to argue that, by a remarkable inversion, the young have now become society's role models:

Youth as a period of particularly intense consumer activity is certainly relatively new. It also has to do with the sharp increase in leisure time in recent years. In the use of this leisure time, young people have taken on the role of models for society. They are, so to speak, the leisure specialists to whom everyone turns.[21]

## Positive views of old gay men

It is a sad but true fact that only 15 men, or slightly less than one fifth of the men in this sample, reported experience or knowledge of old gay men being treated with respect or admired in the gay milieu.[22] Interviewees from all three age cohorts had stories to tell of the positive regard in which old gay men are held.[23]

Only three men from the young cohort reported evidence of old gay men being treated well by other gay men. Their views are represented here by the account of one man, Myles, who is in his early 20s and single. He finished university two years ago and works full-time. Myles said that few of his contemporaries respected old gay men or accepted that they 'went through a difficult time to get to where we are today'. He has 'enormous respect for them', however, for making life easier for him and other young men.

The middle cohort is represented by Patrick and Graham, who are in their 50s. Both men are semi-retired and are in long-term relationships, which in Graham's case has lasted more than 25 years. Patrick explains that his understanding of how old gay men are treated does not include 'any experience of the broader community' and is limited to 'what [former Australian Prime Minister] John Howard would call the intellectual elite or the "chattering classes"'. Among the latter, he has found that young gay men 'generally respect old gay men'. He described this general feeling of respect thus: 'Older men are judged by what they did, how they behaved and their achievements. Whether or not they are gay is not a deciding factor'. Graham has a more intimate understanding of the respect that may exist for old gay men. Although he does not yet describe himself as old, he has been the mentor for some years of a man who is 20 years his junior: 'I would not call it a father-son relationship but it is a relationship in which he seeks my support, affection and encouragement in all aspects of his life'. Their friendship continues while each maintains separate, stable, intimate relationships.

In the old cohort, a total of seven men, or slightly less than one third of the cohort, reported experience or knowledge of being treated well as old gay men. Their views are represented here by the accounts of four men, all of whom are in their 60s. Two are retired and two work part time.[24] Three are in long-term relationships and all live in capital cities.[25] In Kelvin's experience, he has found young gay men 'friendly and affectionate but not in a sexual way'. Kelvin is single and his young homosexual friends often 'drop in to talk and so on. Perhaps they think I have some accumulated wisdom'. Terrence and John live in different cities and relate similar stories. Both know how severely the scene limits relations between the generations. And yet both know from personal experience how rewarding friendships can be with younger men. John says that he and his partner have found 'tremendous acceptance from young people'. His explanation for good relations is simple: 'There are young people who gravitate towards older people and it is a terrific relationship based on mutual respect'. Terrence and his partner socialise with a group of young gay men they met through Terrence's daughter. 'They always come here for Christmas', he says. 'They are in their 30s. We often have breakfast together on a Sunday morning with a heap of young gays.' The third man from the old cohort is Oscar and his story is slightly different from the others'. He believes that he commands the respect of younger gay men because at 65 he is still able to take part in the social practices of the scene and be less affected than are younger men by its physical demands: 'I can still go out and party all night and wake up better than most'. Oscar usually goes out with his partner and a friend: 'I have more energy than the two of them put together and they are younger than me. I think that ageing is a state of mind. Though, there are some days when this body says it is not a state of mind'.

That so few men from the young cohort and relatively few men from the middle cohort had knowledge or evidence of old gay men being treated with respect or admiration strongly suggests that age segregation still prevails in the gay milieu. More than 20 years ago, Raymond Berger identified one of its negative effects as preventing 'older and younger gay men from checking out their possibly erroneous assumptions about each other'.[26] The story from the representative of the young cohort was at best equivocal, while the stories from the middle cohort were only slightly more encouraging. Surprisingly, the four men who spoke for the old cohort did have truly positive accounts to relate of strong, beneficial relations with young men.

## The old gay man as invisible

Slightly less than half of the men interviewed for this study reported knowledge of old gay men being treated as though they did not exist.[27] In this section, the discussion begins with a summary of accounts from men representing the views of the young cohort, followed by similar accounts from the middle cohort. In these accounts, the interviewees describe treatment of old gay men that they have witnessed; some reveal how they may have treated old gay men themselves, and others explain why old gay men are not welcome to socialise with them. Finally, a small group of men from the old cohort explains why they believe they are excluded from gay social spaces.

**Young cohort**

Eleven men, or almost 40 per cent of the young cohort, had stories to tell of old gay men being treated as though they were invisible.[28] Their stories are represented here by three men in their 20s and two men in their 30s. Mark is 25 and says that in night clubs, which he calls the 'mainstay of the gay community', the focus is on 'cruising, picking up [sexual partners] and meeting people'. He rationalises these social practices, saying that because a man's ability to find new sexual partners is directly related to his 'youth and beauty', older gay men are ignored or overlooked. Ian (aged 28) concurs. Young gay men only speak to other young men, he said, and will have nothing to do with old gay men.

Troy (aged 24) is experienced in the scene. He speaks frankly about gay social practices, old gay men and age. He was educated at a private school. Troy reiterates Mark's claim that old gay men are excluded because they are neither young nor beautiful. But he is more direct and even a little hostile in his view of them. Old gay men are excluded because they do not have what he calls 'the visual'. He confesses that he and his friends 'make derogatory comments about old gay men'.

> They are not particularly accepted in the younger gay world. A lot of younger gay boys have a different lifestyle, and, as some of the older gay men are not as fast-paced and because nothing is new to them and they are not as easily excited, there is not as much in common and therefore the association between the two groups is disjointed.

According to Troy, youthfulness and physical stamina separate young and old gay men because older men cannot keep pace with young men and have different interests. Troy did not say at what age a man ceases to be young but later in his interview he does say that older men who kept their bodies trim, who did not 'let themselves go', were not necessarily regarded as old in the eyes of young men. This would explain why men in their 40s can participate on the scene, and continue to do so, within reason, for as long as they 'have the body' and can 'keep pace' with younger men. In these men's minds, then, a youthful appearance is virtually as good as being young, is almost the same as being like them.

Young gay men often hold youthful older men in high esteem because, in addition to having the required 'visual' and 'pace', they are also likely to be more established (in a career or life) and therefore able to offer the young men security, if they are seeking a relationship. They might also subsidise their mutual interests, such as social engagements, introductions, drugs and alcohol, if it is a looser arrangement the young men seek.

Two men in their 30s actually used the metaphor of invisibility to explain the nature of relations between old and young gay men. Daniel is 35 and, in the following extract, draws on Soviet history to conjure a powerful image of the effect that being overlooked has on older people in the gay milieu:

> During the Communist era of the Soviet Union people were air-brushed out of photographs. If you had a family photo taken by a gay man, the old would be air-brushed out. It is a bit like dying: you are not dead but you might as well be. They are notable by their absence.

Robert (aged 38) works with older gay men and describes them as 'good people' but knows that they are regarded as invisible in the gay community: 'the scene is a hostile environment for older men because most young men look straight through them or do not see them'.

### Middle cohort

A similar number of men from the middle cohort knew of old gay men being treated as though they did not exist.[29] They also reiterated what some of the men from the young cohort said: that the gay focus on youth and beauty was the reason young gay men overlooked or ignored old gay men. Their views are represented here by the accounts of five men in their 50s.

Noel, who is 58, said 'the image of being gay is a young man in his late teens or early 20s or an older man who is able to look young'. Ross, meanwhile, justified the youthful emphasis of the gay scene on the grounds that gay culture 'appreciates youth, muscular development and athleticism', and that these qualities were most often to be found in young or youthful men. Des likewise identified the cult of the body as the reason for the exclusion he has experienced as a 50-year-old man: 'On the scene a lot of people are into muscle, youth and good looks and when they see someone like me they see someone who is dumpy and grey and needs a face lift'.

Coupled with the misplaced belief that a person must be young and beautiful in order to be gay is an illusion young men have that they will never grow old. Richard and Henry are in long-term relationships. Richard has been with his partner for 30 years and Henry has been with his for ten years. Richard says that gay men 'glorify youth and go to endless trouble to make themselves look young and beautiful'. He is critical of the superficial values in the gay milieu: 'I find it repulsive. That is what I do not like about the so-called homosexual community. They do not think about ageing. They only think about staying young'. Henry agrees: 'they do not give a lot of thought to what they may require in order to live satisfied lives as older men'. Henry suspects that this indifference arises from a false belief young gay men harbour, which is that 'they will not grow old, either because they ignore the bleeding obvious that everyone dies or because they think that they will not survive to old age'.

### Old cohort

Men from the old cohort have direct experience of being treated as though they were invisible, and almost 60 per cent of them spoke about it.[30] The reason they gave for the marginal position old men occupy in the gay milieu was the same as the younger men identified, that is, an emphasis on youth and beauty. The accounts of five men in their 60s represent their views here. These men gained a knowledge of the gay scene in bars, clubs and saunas in Sydney, Melbourne, Canberra and Hobart.

Terrence is 64 and feels out of place in a gay venue. He liked dancing in his youth but stays away from gay dance clubs nowadays. Clive (aged 65) also knows that he is no longer 'hot property' in certain saunas: 'I am far too old and flabby and do not make the grade. It is a form of discrimination, based on very cheap values'. Brendan is in his 60s as well. He maintains that the accent on youthfulness in the gay milieu—where one has 'to live life to the full and live it now'—means that people overlook the fact that gay men grow old and are old. Lindsay concurred: 'The premium placed on attractiveness and youth in the bar and club scene means that to be old and gay is regarded negatively'.

In addition to these men who feel excluded from gay social spaces because of their age, another group of men in the old cohort, while aware of why they are unwelcome on the scene, expressed no distress because of it. It did not appear to concern them that they were not welcome to socialise with young men or in clubs and bars. One reason for this might be that they had accepted their own 'social obsolescence'. A consequence of the social practices of the scene is, as we have seen, to make commodities of its patrons: intimacy and sex are exchanged like goods and services in a market, and one of the effects of its youthful aesthetic is to signal when the commodities are out of date, when their worth has expired.[31]

For gay men, social obsolescence is that age when they are no longer welcome or feel out of place on the scene. Lindsay described it as follows: 'When you get to a certain age, you just drop out of the public gay scene and divide your time between the dogs and doing the garden'. Nonetheless, he was aware of some old men on the scene in the city where he lived who refused to allow such prejudice to keep them from attending gay events or participating in the social practices of the milieu. He recalled one man, who was 72 and who

> pops up at every conceivable homosexual event, often dressed in his net tee-shirt, his baggy shorts and cap. He is like a heroic father figure. Everyone knows who he is. People are fond of him. His is a kind of elder of the tribe.

The age at which a person 'drops out' of the scene would vary, of course, according to his involvement in it and individual response to it.

Another man who refuses to be intimidated by the social power of the young is Ronald. He is 68 and believes a considerable social distance separates him and young men. Moreover, because he objects to their social practices, he is not sure if he wants to bridge the distance: 'I cannot relate to the young gay scene of discos and drugs. I have this image of younger homosexuals as fairly pleasure-oriented in a way that I am not all that sympathetic to'. He admits to knowing few young gay men but that, when he does meet them in social spaces that are not alienating (for example, at dinner or with friends), he is always 'interested in their world outlook'. He does not expect young men to be interested in him because he was not interested in men his age when he was young. While genuinely happy to meet them, he finds himself prevented from doing so because the social spaces of the gay milieu are anathema to him as are the social practices of the young men who make the scene the principal site of their social engagement with other gay men.

## The old gay man as contemptible

Twenty-six interviewees (almost one third of the sample) had knowledge of old gay men being treated with contempt in the gay milieu—
largely on the scene.[32] Many more interviewees from the younger
cohorts reported witnessing such treatment. The most likely reasons
for this behaviour are first, that few if any men from the old cohort go
on the scene and, second, that in any sample of gay men, there is
bound to be a higher proportion of men aged 20–49 who are likely to
participate in the scene, and therefore have current knowledge of its
social practices, than men who do in their 60s and 70s. The discussion
that follows is organised such that representatives of the young and
middle cohorts speak first, followed by those of the old cohort.

### Young cohort

Almost 40 per cent of the young cohort reported evidence of contemptuous behaviour towards old homosexual men or were aware of contemptuous attitudes towards them. They are represented here by two
men in their 30s and two in their 20s. Tony and Vincent are in their
30s. One of them is Aboriginal, the other is not. The stories they relate
concern social interaction between men of different ages on the scene.
Both men have knowledge of the Melbourne scene and some experience of the scene in Sydney as well.

The behaviour towards old gay men, says Vincent, is appalling: 'I still
cannot understand why people treat older gay men with such disdain.
Whether it is at the sauna, on chat rooms or at bars, you observe dismissive behaviour'. Culturally, he struggles with the prejudice against
age, which he noticed when he first started going out: 'It is foreign to
me because as an Aboriginal person I was taught to respect elders from
day one. Even though a lot of those traditional values are twisted nowadays, we are still brought up to respect our elders'. Tony says he suspects young homosexual men are dismissive because they think old
gay men should not be on the scene. This is supported by North
American research into the same phenomenon.[33]

Angus and Jack are in their 20s and both are from capital cities.
Between them, they have knowledge of the scene in the mainland cap-
itals of the east coast and some country towns of New South Wales.
Both have seen how contemporaries and friends treat old men but say
there are two sides to the story of the contemptuous treatment of old
men. They admit that in bars and clubs young men often scorn old gay
men but they argue that old men 'deserved' the treatment they

received because either they should not be in the same place with the young men or, if they are, they should realise that young gay men are not interested in them sexually.

For Angus, the disjunction between the generations exists because of the body culture of the scene and the predatory manner of older gay men: 'I am sick of getting hit on by older guys who maintain this ridiculous image of "mutton dressed as lamb"'. He explained that people his age understood the phrase 'mutton dressed as lamb' to refer to men in their 40s or 50s who,

> have had plastic surgery or maintain a ridiculous tan because they think it makes them look young or who go to a gym four days a week. They are trying to live up to an ideal of youth that is not even true. It is something I could not do and I am 23.

Angus objects to the manufactured attempts by middle-aged men to appear young and the flawed performance of youthfulness they represent. What he identifies is one of the problems of a culture that glorifies youth and the young: there is no place to grow old. Young men seem repelled by what they see as any attempt by older men—like Aschenbach in Thomas Mann's story *Death in Venice*—to appear younger than they are.[34] Interestingly, it is not old men as such who repel them but any man who attempts to hide his true age—to masquerade as young, and hence the reference to mutton and lamb.

At 22, Jack is the youngest man in the sample. He is thoughtful and socially compassionate but nonetheless feels that his social space is invaded if he has to share it with old men. He sees them as intruders. And, in the case he describes, he is critical of old men, not just middle-aged men pretending to be 20. And, like Angus, he is annoyed by the artificial look they present in public.

> If I see 60-year-old gay people wearing tight tee shirts or leather or exposing flesh, my reaction is that I do not want to end up like that. People should act their age. Young people do these things. Why are 60-year-olds here interrupting our social space? Gay clubs are seen as young spaces or where beautiful people hang out. That is not meant to prejudice old men but they do not fit the criteria of *cool* in the top social set of the gay world.

In order to treat old people with indifference or hostility, those who are not old must see them as belonging to a 'different species', according to Simone de Beauvoir. And once it has been determined that they are different, it is possible to shut them out.[35] The process where the young men interviewed for this study shut out or distance older men from their presence is accentuated by the fact that they do not report having observed any old men on the scene whose lives they wanted to emulate or signalled what they themselves might become. Perhaps the young men are upset when they see old homosexuals on the scene because old men should be somewhere else—at home in bed with a hot water bottle perhaps, but certainly not in a bar at midnight or later. This prejudice against the old enjoying themselves is not restricted to the gay world, for, says Beauvoir, there is a general 'desire' that old people

> should conform to the image that society has formed of them. They are required to dress themselves in a certain way and to respect outward appearances. More than any other, it is in the sexual aspect of life that this repression makes itself felt.[36]

And here we have it. The young men might resent old men on the scene because it is a sexual market place and the presence there of old bodies somehow detracts from the beauty of the young. Does the presence of the old taint the nature of the exchange that takes place in the sexual market place? Or does their presence remind young people that they too will age?

### Middle cohort

Stories from the middle cohort reporting knowledge of contemptuous treatment of old gay men raised themes similar to those from the young cohort. Richard (aged 58) said the attitude toward old homosexual men was 'absolutely disgusting' and that 'the homosexual community by and large despises the old'. According to Glen (aged 49), young homosexual men treat old homosexual men 'with very little respect and probably worse than straights treat old homosexuals'. Simon (aged 46) has observed among young homosexual men on the scene what he described as a 'kind of gloating at being younger' and what he calls 'a bit of attitude' simply because they are young. Meanwhile, Matthew (aged 42) said that some young men seem to despise old gay men because of what they represent: 'I suspect they frighten them. They see in them what they are eventually going to become themselves and they do not like it'. Ivan simply says that attitudes on the scene are 'pretty atrocious' because most people on the scene are only interested in body image.

Neil (aged 46) believes that old gay men are not sufficiently appreciated for what they endured in the years before gay liberation. And, as he explains in the following extract from his interview, he sees a direct link between their suffering before gay liberation and the relative ease with which gay people may enjoy being homosexual today.

> In the gay community, old gay men are not appreciated for living their lives as gay men and the influence that has had on freedoms we now enjoy. People do not recognise that these gay men might have wisdom. They assume that if they are single and old they are only interested in young gay men for sex. Some gay men tend to judge other people on the basis of externals and that makes the ageism in the gay community worse than it is in the general community. It is even more damaging to older gay men.

A number of Neil's observations about social relations on the scene occurred in earlier stories from the young and middle cohorts. These include the belief that people generally do not associate old age with the getting of wisdom in the gay milieu; that old people are rarely respected for having lived a long life, for having survived less tolerant times or for the contribution they have made; that personal value is frequently limited to external appearances; and, that old gay men are viewed as sexually obsessed.

## Old cohort

In contrast with the stories from the younger cohorts, the interviewees from the old cohort reported relatively little evidence of old gay men, themselves or other men, being treated with contempt. Only four men had such stories, and their views are represented here by the accounts of two men in their 70s and one man in his mid-60s.

Vernon and Harold are in their 70s. Both are single and spoke of the careless, even cruel, behaviour of young gay men. Harold related his experience on the Internet: 'I find it very offensive when you happen to be on a chat line and the second question they ask is how old you are. You are either honest or you are not. If you are honest they flip off straight away'. Vernon's account of young people's attitudes similarly relates to anonymous encounters of a sort. He related the story of a friend his age who was 'doing the gardens' one night and got into a car with another man, after which they started to have sex in the back seat. Vernon continues the story:

> Two young queens sitting on the lawn rang the police from their mobile phones and put them in. In other words, how dare 'silver

hairs' have any fun on our beat. That is terrible. It is indicative of the attitudes of some unthinking young people. It is nasty, isn't it? It is saying that their sexual hatred of old people is stronger than any sense of sexual identity.

Vernon interpreted the young homosexual men's behaviour, which *was* vindictive and hypocritical, as breaking a bond that he believes should exist between all homosexual men because of their shared sexual identity. He was genuinely shocked by their behaviour, possibly because of an earlier encounter of his own on a beat:

I do not do the bogs[37] very much these days but I did about ten years ago and there was a guy who was 35 years-old who said to me, 'Why don't you old queens fuck off?' And I said, 'You will be an old queen yourself one day and when you are, my friend, you will not be nearly as interesting as I am. And your face which is already fallen will have gone further'. I was really furious.

John (aged 65) said he had noticed an 'attitude' towards anyone who is older than 25 among young men on the scene: 'If you look at the homosexual community in general, you would say that a lot of young homosexual men do not even think about age or they see us as wrinkled old things that the world would be better off without'.

## The old gay man as predatory

A powerful public narrative exists in Western countries, which both homosexuals and heterosexuals share, of the old gay man as a predatory being. Berger describes it thus: '[O]lder gay men are said to have desperate unfulfilled sexual needs which are satisfied by preying on the young'.[38] This dominant story has a complex provenance because it comprises a number of contradictory minor narratives. One of these is that people over the age of 59 continue inappropriately to have sexual desires and sex lives, while another is that sexual relations in the old are repulsive, regardless of gender or sexuality. Beauvoir gives an instance of this:

Sadism sometimes comes into this mockery [of the old]. I was taken aback in New York, when I went to the well-known show in the Bowery, where horrible old women in their eighties sing and dance, lifting up their skirts. The audience roared with laughter: what exactly was the meaning of all this mirth?[39]

Sixteen interviewees, or one fifth of the sample, had stories to tell about how the notion of the predatory old gay man is understood and circulates in the gay milieu.[40] The majority of these were drawn from the young and middle cohorts, for only one man in the old cohort referred to it. He is Edward and he spoke of a 'well-grounded expectation' among the young that old gay men will conform to this stereotype

> until they discover that they want friendship, fun and things like that. The initial needless assumption, that the old men are being friendly because they think they can get young men into bed, is probably based on a lot of experience. It is probably empirically justified.

## Young cohort

Joseph, Drew and Adam are single and represent here the five men from the young cohort who had stories of the old gay man as a predator. Joseph (aged 35) believes that, as a community, gay men are beginning to show more signs of maturity. He sees the emergence of more 'spaces and places for older men' as an example of increased social maturity.[41] He has been in bars where 'the average age is a lot older than in some of the others'. Joseph knows, however, that one of the more enduring public narratives of the gay scene portrays old gay men in negative terms: 'If you are older, you must be a pervert or a child molester. An older man who is on his own is not seen in a positive light on the scene'. When he was 18, Drew (aged 39) had a friend who was in his late 60s and gay. His friends suspected that the older man wanted sex with Drew. It was, however, a 'purely platonic relationship'. But he knows the power of the dominant public narrative concerning old gay men:

> I have seen the writing on the wall at the beat saying, 'Fuck off all you old cunts'. It is hard because being a man you are going to have a sex drive all your life. And just because we are getting older does not mean that we should stop having sex either.

Adam (aged 24) told a similar story. He said that young gay men on the scene have a picture of old gay men as 'dirty old men'. 'It is not the sexual desire that is the ugly thing in the older man'—Adam and men his age assume that desire is constant and also a constant in the make-up of gay men—'it is the decay of the body that revolts people. And people in their 20s have not got to that point'.

## Middle cohort

Ten men, or one third of those from the middle cohort, confirmed that an assumption exists in the gay milieu that old gay men are predatory. They are represented here by the accounts of Donald and Bill, both of whom are 52.

Donald lives in a capital city and belongs to a gay social club that suffers from an absence of young members, possibly because of the public stereotype that views old gay men as predatory: 'I think it is because it is seen as an "old boys' club" and the young things suspect they will not feel comfortable or the old boys will try to crack on to them. And I find that quite sad'.

At one point in his younger days, Bill worked in a male brothel when he was travelling overseas. The brothel's clientele were mainly men in their 50s, 60s and 70s. He describes in the following excerpt what he learned about sexual and emotional desire in older men while he was a sex worker.

> The old men were still sexually active and desired physical contact but often could not get it because they could not relate to many people their own age. Two 70-year-olds or 80-year-olds do not nec-essarily want each other. They want companionship and when it came to sex they wanted a younger man.

Bill then explained that, from what he could recall, a dominant public narrative in the 1970s was that old gay men were predatory and sought 15-year-olds for sexual pleasure. This narrative conflates homosexuality and paedophilia, and has been in circulation for a very long time. Bill's experience was, however, that they were separate sexualities: 'The old gay men did not want 15-year-olds. Desire for the very young was rele-gated to fantasy and never acted upon. It was an ideal but not the reality they wanted'. Although his encounters with clients were episodic and contractual, he believes that they were often seeking a connection with him that went beyond the sexual:

> They wanted men between 25 and 35 because they were looking for more than a sexual encounter. They wanted some sort of relation-ship with someone younger because it made them feel vital. The sex

was a way of giving form to their vitality. I think the clients could relate to me on an emotional and intellectual level which made the physical more worthwhile. Those men came to the brothel for companionship and the possibility of having sex but it was also a form of surrogate family for them.

Many of his clients were married. They maintained their relationship with him by asking for him every time they visited the brothel. However, few of the sex workers employed in the brothel with Bill shared his view. Younger than he was, they 'saw the clients as "dirty old men", which was unfortunate because it denied the idea that at 70 or 80 a person could still have an active libido'.

It is clear now that what repels young men such as the sex workers to whom Bill referred and the young men about whom Adam spoke is the thought of sexual desire in an old body. Given that a negative image already exists in society of sexual desire in an old male body—the 'dirty old man'—it is relatively easy for young gay men to make use of this to disparage old gay men, whose presence in the sexual market annoys them. The young might therefore construe the presence of old bodies in the sexualised spaces of the scene as predatory because they are horrified by the thought of sexual desire combined with old flesh.

## Conclusion

The majority of men in this sample associated old age with some form of bodily decline. Where interviewees from the old cohort, who were chronologically old, resisted the notion of regarding themselves as old, this is best understood in light of Beauvoir and Shilling's argument that age is often more apparent to an outsider than it is to the person who experiences it, in other words, in terms of the dissonance that exists between the inner self and the outer self.[42]

Age segregation is a dominant feature of the gay milieu and, in particular, on the scene. From the accounts of the men in this sample, very few young gay men seem to have knowledge or evidence of old gay men being treated well in the social spaces they frequent. It is also highly significant that at least three quarters of the men interviewed for this study were aware that old gay men are treated with contempt or as invisible and ignored in the gay milieu.

From the accounts of the young gay men in this sample, it seems that they find it difficult to enjoy themselves in the presence of old people. Stories from the middle cohort underlined this prejudice: old gay men were not welcome to share social spaces with young gay men because their physical presence, their actual bodies, clashed too radically with the valorised youthful bodies of the scene. An interesting corollary to this is that, while being overlooked and ignored hurt some of the old interviewees, other old gay men did not resent it. They appeared to accept age segregation as a normal development in the life course, something that was to be expected because of the youthful focus of the gay milieu and in the wider society more generally. In the main, they did not seem to experience any sense of loss because they were not welcome on the scene. Instead many had no desire to be part of it and, on the whole, seemed content with their lives and to anticipate the future in a positive spirit.

The public narrative that depicts old gay men as lonely was not examined in this chapter, or elsewhere in the book, because so few men in the sample referred to it, and, as mentioned in earlier chapters, there was little evidence of men interviewed for this study living lonely lives, at any age. An associated negative stereotype that views old gay men as predatory was examined. While the men's stories provided no evidence of any basis for the stereotype, the very existence of such stories, as public narratives, showed how virulent and pervasive it is. An analysis of the stories suggests that the fear that lies behind them is of any association, in the imagination of the young, between sexual desire and practice, and old or ageing flesh, for, in the view of one seventy-five-year-old interviewee, 'Nobody wants to screw old men. They do not mind being sucked-off by old men. That does not affect them in the way that actually touching them and entering the body of an old man does'.[43]

# Conclusion

'You hear people say that when they die they would like to be reincarnated as something else. I want to come back exactly as I am right now. I am quite happy with everything about being gay and being me.' Drew, 39.

This book has mapped the lives of 80 gay men, aged 20 to 79, in the second half of the twentieth century. It began with an examination of what coming out meant to different generations of men and then looked at their involvement in the gay scene and community. The last three chapters examined the interviewees' intimate relationships, first with their partners in couple relationships, then with their friends and families, and finally considered their experience or views of what old age is like for a gay man.

For so many of the men, coming out was seen as transformative (akin to a form of re-birth) and as the first step they must take to establish their sexual identity as homosexuals. The interviewees' stories revealed that coming out is frequently affected by birth and upbringing: their coming-out accounts varied by age cohort, according to the year of the interviewees' birth and when they reached maturity. For example, while the statement, 'I am a gay man now but once I was married', might accurately reflect the life stories of more than a third of men from the old cohort, and is a narrative with which many in the middle cohort would be familiar, it would have little relevance to the lived experience or life path of the men from the young cohort.

Coming out, as the public declaration of one's sexuality—which is how it is now generally understood—was the creation of the 'baby boomer' generation of gay men and lesbians. Many of them understood it as both a personal act and a political statement. It was an important personal act because it freed the individual from what gay liberationists regarded as the oppressive condition of having to lead a double life, to pass as straight, to deny the truth of one's existence; they also viewed coming out publicly as a necessary act for gays and lesbians to take in order to free themselves from the social order of the time. The coming-out experiences of the 'baby boomers', as revealed here in the stories of the men from the middle cohort, were not always as straightforward as the gay liberationists promised, however, and were at times characterised by trauma or rejection. By contrast, their predecessors, represented here by the men from the old cohort, came out secretly and almost exclusively in private, if they came out at all. Some married and many lived closeted, though not necessarily unhappy, lives. Today the situation for young gay men is quite different. On the whole, the stories of the interviewees from the young cohort suggest that coming out became progressively easier during the last two decades of the 20th century—notwithstanding the increased stigma associated with being gay that the HIV-AIDS epidemic brought about. Heartening though this change is, as evidence of greater acceptance of gay people, there was still a small number of men for whom coming out was a struggle, largely because of their parents' response, and also a handful of young men who had to wait until they had left home or their home town before they came out. While all the young men interviewed for this book were aware of, and had experienced the personal significance of coming out, none described it as a political act, which gay liberationists might consider as evidence of the success of their 30-year campaign to reduce gay men and lesbians' personal experience of oppression.

Most gay men encounter the gay scene at some point in their life. Comprising bars, clubs and sex venues, it is where they can go to socialise with friends, be with other gay men, have sex or find a sexual partner. Because its primary purpose is as a sexual market for young or youthful men, participation on the scene is largely determined by age. Its attractions appeal less to men as they grow older, for its social practices are geared to the demands of the young. Interestingly, despite its primacy in the gay world—mainly due to the fact that its venues are the only safe locations for gay men to congregate in large numbers—men of all ages interviewed for this study had mixed views on the scene's worth. And those with the loudest criticisms were among the men from the young cohort, including Aboriginal and Asian interviewees who complained about the racist social practices on the scene.

A large majority of the sample recorded some level of involvement in the community institutions of the gay world. Equal numbers of interviewees, spread fairly evenly across the age cohorts, were involved in either HIV-AIDS support groups and counselling services or their local social group—the latter being particularly important for gay men living in small cities or country towns. In addition, a minority of interviewees expressed strong dissenting views. These were men who either did not agree or could not comply with the dominant gay narratives of community, and questioned its existence or challenged its purpose.

In contrast to popular stereotypes that portray gay men as sex-obsessed and incapable of sustaining couple relationships, the stories of the men interviewed for this book were remarkable for the relatively conventional, even ordinary, lives they revealed. The two central relationships in their intimate lives, for example, were the couple relationship and friendship.

A majority of the sample, including men of all ages and from all classes, reported a strong desire to pursue a couple relationship similar to the companionate marriage. It was important in their view both as the central focus of their life and because it was where they looked for love, intimacy, companionship, and sexual satisfaction. As well, a small group of men gave details of how they maintained 'open' relationships with their partners, which allowed them to combine the security of the couple relationship with a degree of sexual adventurism.

More important than the couple relationship, however, to a greater number of interviewees, was friendship, which they valued for the social interaction it provided and the mutual exchange of care and support. The latter was regarded more highly by men from the old and young cohorts, possibly because, as old people and young people are more vulnerable to fluctuations in the housing market and are more highly represented in low income groups, they are more likely to make use of informal networks of support that friends can provide. The value men in this sample placed on friendship is in contrast to how friendship is regarded between men and in general. Scholars such as Philippe Ariès and Henning Bech have argued that friendship between men is now rare, if it exists at all, while Lynn Jamieson believes that the couple relationship is now generally considered to be the premier intimate relationship. In response, I have argued that, like women, gay men might pursue same-sex friendships more easily than heterosexual men because they have less to fear if these are interpreted as sexual. And that, even though they esteem the couple relationship, friendship is likely to be more important to them because friends can provide continuity if, as is the case with the majority of men in this sample, their intimate lives are punctuated by relationships that either do not fully develop or are relatively short term—defined here as less than seven years' duration.

Even though a majority of the men interviewed for the book gave accounts of poor or problematic relations with their birth families, such stories were not uniform across the age cohorts. In the case of the 'baby-boomer' generation, weak or poor familial relations were often a legacy of the rejection that accompanied their coming out. By contrast, fewer of the men from the old cohort reported negative dealings with their families—often because their parents were dead and relations with their siblings, whether supportive or estranged, were unlikely to change. Of the three age cohorts, the men from the young cohort had the best relations with their birth families, which may reflect their level of dependence on their parents or the acceptance that greeted news of their homosexuality.

As well as couple relationships and friendship, the interviewees spoke of a third type of intimate relationship that they valued—the 'gay family'. In its best known form, it comprises a gay man who has been formerly married or in a *de facto* heterosexual relationship, his same-sex partner and their children. Three other versions were discussed, viz. a co-parenting arrangement between a gay couple and a lesbian couple, a gay nuclear family, and a family of choice. While these represented the experience of only two men from the young cohort, and therefore did not reflect widespread behaviour among the men in the sample, they are significant for what they presage and reveal about people's ability to mould or re-create the family unit to suit their intimate and affective needs.

There was no evidence from the life stories of the men in this sample that gay men led lonely or isolated lives at any point in the life course, including old age. It was for this reason that the negative public narrative that pictures old gay men as solitary, lonely figures was not investigated. By contrast, the stories of the interviewees from the old cohort revealed a group of fairly resilient men who seemed reasonably content with their lives and who anticipated the future with optimism. They disclosed that, like everyone else, they resisted the notion of being old, and tended to accept the fact only when physical decline made it impossible to ignore. For reasons explored by scholars such as Simone de Beauvoir and Norbert Elias, the younger men's views on old age lacked empathy: a large majority of interviewees was aware that old gay men are treated as Other. The stories of the men from the middle and young cohorts showed that many of the negative attitudes toward ageing and old age that exist in the wider society are accentuated in the gay world. This was especially so on the gay scene where age segregation is most prevalent.

It is significant that almost half the men in the sample were aware that old gay men are treated as though they are invisible on the scene, for it is now more than 20 years since Raymond Berger's research on old gay men drew attention to the negative effects of age segregation in the gay milieu.[1] In the young cohort, the views ranged from condemnatory to compassionate. The men in their 20s knew that theirs is the most valorised age of life in the gay milieu, as it is in the wider community and wherever the cult of youth is worshipped. Some of these young men seemed to be impatient of old gay men and were quite dismissive of them. The prevailing view among them seemed to be that it is not appropriate for old gay men and young gay men to socialise together and, that, if they do, the old men should expect a poor reception from the young men. One fact the young men overlook, however, is that old gay men *have* to socialise in the same bars and clubs with young gay men because there are no other social venues for gay men. Among the men in their 30s, there were, however, more signs of compassion for an old gay man's situation. One interviewee referred to the scene as a 'hostile environment' for old gay men. Such compassion could be seen as evidence of greater maturity and a more developed understanding of the scene's social shortcomings. The representatives of men from the middle cohort largely concurred with these observations, that is, that the cult of youth causes age segregation on the gay scene. And yet, interestingly, only a handful of men from the old cohort related experiences of being treated poorly. Where they did, however, it was personally distressing to the men involved and often occurred because they had strayed into spaces where young men predominate, such as chat rooms on the Internet or beats. In these places, the power of the old men is greatly diminished, a point Elias made most powerfully in *The Loneliness of the Dying*: 'The feeling, "Perhaps I shall be old one day", can be totally lacking [in the young]. All that remains is the spontaneous enjoyment of one's own superiority, and the power of the young in relation to the old'.[2] Two prominent themes were present in the accounts of the men from the old cohort. The first concerned this sense of marginalisation some interviewees felt because of their age. The second, and more interesting, narrative came from those men who, though aware that they were excluded from most gay social spaces, did not exhibit any bitterness or regret because of it.

As a researcher I went into the field with my own personal knowledge, and some preconceptions, about the shape gay life paths may take. During the course of my engagement with the interviewees, two dominant stories emerged concerning how age and sexuality affect a gay man's understanding of himself. His actual age will influence how he relates to the gay milieu and the wider society, and it does so in two ways. First, his chronological age will tell us something about the likely context of his coming out, how receptive society was to the idea of 'the homosexual' or 'the gay man', and how parents, friends, family and work mates may have received the news of the interviewee's sexuality, if they were told. Second, the interviewee's age directly affects how he will experience age segregation, which is particularly pronounced on the gay scene. The young man glories in it; the old man is excluded. Their age and sexuality affect relations with themselves, their families, friends, the gay world and the wider society. The effect of age and sexuality is thus both ontological and social.

Both stories strongly contradicted popular stereotypes that depict gay men as lonely in old age and sex-crazed throughout their life. What they did reveal, however, was that the lives of gay men, as represented by the interviewees in the sample, have improved considerably since the 1950s. At every stage in the life course, the men interviewed for this book demonstrated relatively positive views of themselves, their intimate relationships, and, importantly, their relations with the wider society. Such freedom to express affective relations openly and without fear is a comparatively new experience for gay men, and represents real social advancement—as many of the stories from the men in the old and middle cohorts testified. The gay identity is no longer hidden or shameful, and, while some gay men may still experience rejection when they come out, the majority does not, and, since 1997, for example, no homosexual in Australia has had to fear persecution by the state. This social change has occurred for two principal reasons. The first is gay people's continued determination to defy anti-homosexual prejudice, to come out and so contribute to the variety of gay public narratives in circulation. The second concerns the wider society's willingness, in most Western countries, to receive these narratives and to accept a greater mix of sexual stories in the public domain.

# Appendix 1: The Interview Schedule

## A. Working life

1  Would you briefly tell me the story of your working life, and what it is that you enjoy/have enjoyed about work?
2  How would you describe your standard of living?
3  Have you ever had any experience of poverty?

## B. Identity

4  Would you briefly tell me the story of your coming out?
5  What has been your experience of acceptance as a homosexual/gay man?
6  What does being homosexual mean to you, and how important is it to your sense of self [who you are in the world]?
7  How would your life be different if you were not homosexual/gay?
8  What effect has HIV-AIDS had on your sense of self [who you are in the world]?
9  How important to your sense of self is your body, your body image?
10  Now I would like to spend a moment exploring what you regard as meaningful in your life.

## C. Relationship status and meaning

11  What's the story of your [most recent] relationship? [Duration?]
12  What do you regard as the most significant aspect(s) of your [most recent] *significant* relationship? E.g., commitment; companionship; good times; love; property; sex life; shared interests; shared values; growing old together?
13  What effect has HIV-AIDS had on your [most recent] relationship?
14  What preparations or plans have you [and your partner] made for your retirement and old age, and when did you begin to make them? In particular I am thinking of preparations or plans that you have made to

secure your living arrangements, financial well being, and social life. If you have not made any such preparations or plans, do you think you will and if so, when?

## D. Experience of age and ageing

15   How do you think the general community regards old homosexuals/gay men?
16   What in your opinion is the attitude of other homosexuals towards old homosexuals?
17   Do you regard yourself as old? YES/NO.
     As you do regard yourself as old, when did you first realise that you were getting old, and what does it mean to you to be old and homosexual/gay? As you do not regard yourself as old, what age do you regard as old, and what will it mean to you to be old and homosexual/gay? That is, what picture do you have of yourself as an old gay man?
18   What effect has HIV-AIDS had on your experience of age and ageing?
19   Are you apprehensive about growing old and, if so, what are your apprehensions? Are you worried about e.g.: being poor or lonely or institutionalised in a heterosexual environment; about losing your independence or mobility, or your desire or sexual performance or lack of sexual expression?
20   Do you take any measures to hold back or retard the physical effects of ageing?
21   Think back to when you were in your 20s or 30s. *Re-phrased for 20 year olds*: Think back to when you were younger or when you first 'came out'. How did you see old homosexuals/gay men then, and how do you see them now?
22   Has growing older affected your sense of yourself as a sexually attractive man?

## E. Social life

23   What proportion of your close friends is homosexual/gay?
24   What has been your experience of or involvement in the homosexual/gay community?
25   In which homosexual/gay venue do you feel most welcomed, at ease, accepted? *Re-phrased for 20 year olds*: Is there any homosexual/gay venue where you do not feel welcomed, at ease, accepted?
26   Do you use the Internet to supplement your social life?
27   Has growing older affected your social life?
28   What effect has HIV-AIDS had on your social life?
29   What picture do you have of yourself in five/ten/fifteen years' time?

# Appendix 2: The Age Cohorts and the Interviewees

## The old cohort

Twenty-two men made up the old cohort. Six of the interviewees were in their 70s; their pseudonyms and ages are as follows: Reginald (79), Gerald (75), Vernon (75), Leslie (74), Chester (71), Harold (71). Sixteen of the men were in their 60s; their pseudonyms and ages are as follows: Geoffrey (69), Ronald (68), Charles (67), Kelvin (66), John (65), Kenneth (65), Maurice (65), Oscar (65), Brendan (64), Clive (64), Terrence (64), Douglas (63), Leonard (63), Barry (62), Lindsay (62), Edward (60). Fifteen of the interviewees in the old cohort had partners. The average length of their relationships was 20 years. Six men had been in relationships of longer than 30 years' duration and one 60-year-old man had been with his partner for 39 years. More than one third of interviewees (eight men) were previously married. Four had been married for longer than 30 years including one man (in his 60s) who had been married for 40 years. The average length of their marriages was 28 years. All but two of the men who were married had children. It is in this cohort that one might expect to see also a high proportion of retired men and, in fact, slightly more than 60 per cent of the interviewees were retired. Of the eight men who are still working, four are 65 or older and work part-time. The oldest working man is 75.

The working lives of the men in this cohort were chiefly in middle-class occupations, including as teachers, academics, and public servants. Two are self-employed small businessmen. Two had working-class jobs. A little over one third received old age pensions or sickness benefits. Slightly less than three quarters of the cohort had private superannuation (now mandatory in Australia). The average income of these men in their 60s and 70s was $35,000 per annum, which is relatively meagre by OECD standards. A number of points need to be made in relation to income. Four men earned incomes less than $15,000 per annum; five had incomes in the band $15,000–$25,000; and three had incomes not in excess of $35,000 per annum. In other words, more than one half of the cohort were low-income earners, which might be explained by the number of men who were on the old age pension. Only two men out of the 22 men in this cohort did not own their residence. More than two thirds of the old cohort held bachelor's degrees or higher.

## The middle cohort

The middle cohort comprised 30 men. Fifteen interviewees were in their 50s; their pseudonyms and ages are as follows: Lionel (59), Noel (58), Richard (58), Roy (58), Samuel (56), Ross (54), Patrick (53), Bill (52), Donald (52), Graham, (52), Kevin (52), Michael (52), Thomas (52), Des (50), Henry (50). Fifteen of the interviewees were in their 40s; their pseudonyms and ages are as follows: Glen (49), Jerome (49), Nigel (49), Stuart (49), Trevor (49), Bob (48), Alan (47), Neil (46), Simon (46), James (45), Scott (45), Roger (44), Matthew (42), Ivan (40), Ken (40). Eighteen men in the middle cohort were in relationships, the average length of which was 16 years. The average age of the partners of the men in their 50s was 52, and for the 40-year-olds is 46. Twelve interviewees in the middle cohort are single. Two men, both in their 50s, said that they had been single all their lives. Compared with the experience of the men in the old cohort, a smaller proportion of men in the middle cohort were formerly married. In the middle cohort, five men—or one sixth of interviewees—were married; half what it was in the old cohort. All formerly married men in the middle cohort had children and one man who was in his mid-50s has two grandchildren. The average length of the time they spent in a heterosexual marriage was 11 years. One 50-year-old man had previously been in a heterosexual marriage of 20 years' duration.

Five of the middle cohort were retired: two men in their late 40s, one man in his early 50s and two in their late 50s. It is clear however that not many men in this sample were taking early retirement. The youngest retiree was 49. Of the remaining men who were working, all but one was in full-time employment. That is, of the 30 men in the middle cohort, 25, or more than 80 per cent, were in full-time employment. One man did not have any superannuation of any kind. Of the others, almost half did not tell me or could not remember how much was held for them in superannuation schemes. The average annual income of the men in this cohort was $47,250. Four men earned incomes less than $15,000 per annum; another man had an annual income of between $15,000 and $25,000; and five men earned more than $25,000 but less than $35,000 per annum. That is, ten men, or one third of the cohort, were living on low incomes. Eight men had annual incomes in excess of $70,000, two of whom earned more than $85,000 per annum. The majority of men in the middle cohort owned their own residence. More than three quarters of them had bachelor's degrees or higher.

## The young cohort

The young cohort consisted of 28 men, eighteen of whom were in their 30s. Their pseudonyms and ages are as follows: Drew (39), Travis (38), Robert (38), Neville (37), Andy (37), Alex (37), Jeremy (36), Joseph (35), Jason (35), Daniel (35), Julius (34), Paul (33), Mick (33), Tony (33), Luke (32), Vincent (30), Brian (30), Adrian (30). Ten of the interviewees were in their 20s; their pseudonyms and ages are as follows: Ian (28), Harry (28), David (28), Mark (25), Troy (24), Myles (24), Lachlan (24), Adam (24), Angus (23), Jack (22). The majority of men in the young cohort were in relationships. Twelve men or slightly more than

40 per cent were single. Of those men who were single only one said that he had been single all his life, a 30-year-old who lived in Sydney. This is the age group when people traditionally devote a great deal of their time, money and energy in search of partners, and in many cases of life partners, and/or casual sexual encounters. The average age of the partners of the men from this cohort in relationships was 37 for the men in their 30s, and 28.5 years for those in their 20s. The average length of relationships for the men in the young cohort was slightly less than four years. No man in this cohort was or had been married but three men, all of whom are in their 30s, were bringing up children. One man and his ex-partner were foster parents of two teenage boys; another man and his partner were bringing up two young girls who were part of his extended family; and one man and his partner were parents with two lesbian women of a infant girl. The image of young gay men as promiscuous is at odds with the lived reality of these men.

No one in this cohort was retired. Six men were students. Three were enrolled in courses at colleges of technical and further education (TAFE) and three were at university. Half were mature-age students (all in their 30s). Of the 22 men who were in work, five had working-class jobs, and these were in transport and hospitality. Two thirds had middle-class occupations, mainly in the public sector and caring professions, such as social work, disability support and health care. All but four of the men in the young cohort had some funds invested in superannuation schemes. The average income for the men in the young cohort was $44,000 per annum, which is more than the average for the old cohort but less than for the middle cohort. Ten men, or more than one third of the young cohort, were living on low incomes, that is, on yearly incomes of $35,000 or less. Three men had incomes of less than $15,000 per annum; all of whom were students. Five men (all in their 30s) earned more than $85,000 per annum. Meanwhile, six men in the young cohort were receiving some form of government income assistance, including student, unemployment, or disability benefits. The young cohort had the lowest proportion of owners of houses or flats. Nine men owned their own residence, two jointly with their partners. Excluding the tertiary students, eight men had secondary qualifications only. Twelve interviewees had university degrees.

# Notes

## Introduction

1  Title of a North American television series based on the original British television series about the lives of a group of young gay people. In Australia, it screened on SBS Television, 2001–03 and briefly resumed in 2005.

2  *Death in Venice*, directed by Luchino Visconti, Italy, 1971. See, R. Murray *Images in the Dark: an encyclopedia of gay and lesbian film and video* (New York: Penguin Books, USA, 1996), p. 131. A recent adaptation of a similar story was set in modern-day New England, USA; see G. Adair *Love and Death on Long Island* (London: Reed International Books, 1991).

3  In particular, I am thinking of Thomas Mann's novella, *Death In Venice*, Marcel Proust's *Remembrance of Things Past*, and Oscar Wilde's *The Picture of Dorian Gray*, all of which contain somewhat cliché, though nonetheless powerful, accounts of the 'faded queen' questing after youth.

4  K. Plummer *Documents of Life: an introduction to the problems and literature of a humanistic method* (London: George Allen & Unwin Ltd, 1983), p. 68.

5  For more information on the composition of the age cohorts, see Chapter 1 and Appendix 2.

6  The three periods are the 'camp' period, the 'gay' period and the 'post-liberation' period. The camp period runs from the 1940s until the end of the 1960s; the gay period is from the end of the 1960s until the mid-1980s; and the post-liberation period stretches from the mid-1980s until the early 2000s. For more detail of the contents of these periods, see Chapter 1 and then the chapters themselves, viz. Chapters 2, 3 and 4.

7  While social maturity is largely a social construct—for example, some people are socially mature at 16 while others still appear immature in their late 30s—I have chosen the conventional coming-of-age marker, 21, as the age of social maturity for men born between 1922 and 1980.

8  A. M. Boxer and B. J. Cohler 'The life course of gay and lesbian youth: an immodest proposal for the study of lives' in G. Herdt (ed.) *Gay and Lesbian Youth* (New York: The Haworth Press, 1989), p. 326.

9  See, for example, J. H. Gagnon *An Interpretation of Desire: essays in the study of sexuality* (Chicago: The University of Chicago Press, 2004), pp. 99–129; G. Herdt *Same sex, different cultures: exploring gay and lesbian lives* (Boulder, Colorado: Westview Press, 1997), p. 158; and G. Herdt and A. Boxer 'Introduction: culture, history, and life course of gay men' in Herdt *Gay Culture in America*, p. 11.

10  J. Weeks *Sexuality and its Discontents: meanings, myths & modern sexualities* (London: Routledge & Kegan Paul, 1985), p. 198.

11  According to Edmund White and Steven Marcus, gay was originally a term that applied to women and meant 'loose' or 'immoral' as in a loose or immoral woman, that is, a prostitute. 'Gay-house', says White was a term for a brothel. 'In the past one asked if a woman was "gay," much as today one

186

might ask if she "swings."' White was writing in the late 1970s. See E. White 'The political vocabulary of homosexuality' in B. R. S. Fone (ed.) *The Columbia Anthology of gay literature: readings from Western antiquity to the present day* (New York: Columbia University Press, 1998), pp. 778–9. In *The Other Victorians*, Marcus includes an extract of dialogue between the author of *The Secret Life* (the subject of *Other Victorians*) and a 15-year-old girl showing how in mid-nineteenth-century London gay was used to mean prostitute. See S. Marcus *The Other Victorians: a study of sexuality and pornography in mid-nineteenth century England* (London: Weidenfeld & Nicolson, 1970).

12  White 'The political vocabulary of homosexuality', p. 779.

13  See J. Boswell 'Revolutions, Universals, and Sexual Categories' in M. Duberman, M. Vicinus and G. Chauncey (eds) *Hidden from history: reclaiming the gay and lesbian past* (New York: Penguin Books USA Inc., 1989), p. 35.

14  At the conclusion of their interview, interviewees completed a brief questionnaire that included a question about which of the following terms they used to describe themselves: Camp, Gay, Homosexual, Poof, Queer or any other. A very large majority chose gay. Despite the importance in the early 1990s of the new identity and social movement known as 'queer', only one man in the sample used it, a man in his mid-40s. The failure of large numbers of same-sex attracted people to adopt the term queer as an identity marker has been noted elsewhere. See, for example, R. C. Savin-Williams *The new gay teenager* (Cambridge, Mass: Harvard University Press, 2005), pp. 7–8. Interestingly, 11 men in the sample said that they did not like to be known by any term that referred to their sexuality. These comprised one man in his 70s, four men in their 60s, two men in their 50s and four in their 30s.

## Chapter 1  Collecting and Understanding Gay Life Stories

1  Australian slang word for gay men, homosexuals.

2  G. Vidal 'Tennessee Williams: someone to laugh at the squares with' in *United States: Essays 1952–1992* (London: Little Brown and Company, UK, 1999), p. 440.

3  Six men are in their 70s and 16 men are in their 60s.

4  Fifteen men are in their 50s and 15 men are in their 40s.

5  Eighteen men are in their 30s and ten men are in their 20s.

6  The exceptions are three Aboriginal men, a man who was born and brought up in South-east Asia, and another man whose parents emigrated from Southern Europe before he was born. A group of men from The Netherlands and another group from the United Kingdom came to Australia as children with their parents as part of the post-war migration scheme.

7  Sixty-four per cent of interviewees hold bachelor's degrees or higher. One fifth of the interviewees have post-graduate degrees.

8  The letter was published in *LifeBlood*, a monthly supplement that appeared in Melbourne Community Views 2001–2003. It is no longer published.

9  R. Sennett and J. Cobb *The Hidden Injuries of Class* (New York: Alfred Knopf, 1973); L. P. Hinchman and S. K. Hinchman (eds) *Memory, Identity, Community: the idea of narrative in the human sciences* (New York: State University of New York, 2001); K. Plummer *Documents of Life: an introduction to the problems*

*and literature of a humanistic method* (London: George Allen & Unwin Ltd, 1983); K. Plummer *Telling Sexual Stories: power, change and social worlds* (London: Routledge, 1995); M. R. Somers and G. D. Gibson 'Reclaiming the epistemological "other": narrative and the social construction of identity' in C. Calhoun (ed.) *Social Theory and the Politics of Identity* (Oxford: Blackwell, 1994), pp. 37–99.

10  My intention is to deposit printed copies of the transcripts and the original cassette tapes with the Mitchell Library, Sydney or the La Trobe Library, Melbourne.

11  Sennett and Cobb *Hidden Injuries*, p. 37.

12  Sennett and Cobb *Hidden Injuries*, p. 37.

13  Sennett and Cobb *Hidden Injuries*, p. 115.

14  Edward Bruner 2001 'Ethnography as Narrative' in Hinchman and Hinchman *Memory, Identity, Community*, p. 271.

15  Bruner 'Ethnography as Narrative', p. 272.

16  Bruner 'Ethnography as Narrative', p. 275.

17  See, for example, D. Altman *Homosexual: oppression and liberation* (Sydney: Angus & Robertson, 1972); D. Altman *The Homosexualization of America, the Americanization of the Homosexual* (New York: St Martin's Press, 1982); H. Bech *When Men Meet: homosexuality and modernity* trans. T. Mequit and T. Davies (Cambridge: Polity Press, 1997); E. L. Kennedy and M. D. Davis *Boots of Leather, Slippers of Gold: the history of a lesbian community* (New York: Penguin Books USA Inc., 1994); K. Plummer *Sexual Stigma: an interactionist account* (London: Routledge & Kegan Paul, 1975); K. Plummer 'Going gay: identities lifecycles and lifestyles in the male gay world' in J. Hart and D. Richardson (eds) *The Theory and Practice of Homosexuality* (London: Routledge & Kegan Paul, 1981), pp. 93–110; J. Weeks *Coming out: homosexual politics in Britain from the nineteenth century to the present* (London: Quartet Books, 1990); J. Weeks *Sexuality and its Discontents: meanings, myths & modern sexualities* (London: Routledge & Kegan Paul, 1985).

18  See, for example, G. Chauncey *Gay New York: gender, urban culture, and the making of the gay male world, 1890–1940* (New York: Basic Books, 1994); C. Moore *Sunshine and Rainbows: the development of gay and lesbian culture in Queensland* (St Lucia, Qld: University of Queensland Press, 2001); J. H. Gagnon *An Interpretation of Desire: essays in the study of sexuality* (Chicago: The University of Chicago Press, 2004); G. Herdt (ed.) *Gay Culture in America: essays from the field* (Boston: Beacon Press, 1992); G. Herdt *Same sex, different cultures: exploring gay and lesbian lives* (Boulder, Colorado: Westview Press, 1997); G. Wotherspoon *City of the Plain: history of a gay sub-culture* (Sydney: Hale & Iremonger, 1991).

19  See, for example, G. W. Dowsett *Practicing Desire: homosexual sex in the era of AIDS* (Stanford, California: Stanford University Press, 1996) and E. K. Sedgwick *Epistemology of the Closet* (Berkeley: University of California Press, 1990).

20  Bruner 'Ethnography as Narrative', p. 275.

21  A. MacIntyre 'The Virtues, the Unity of a Human Life, and the Concept of a Tradition' in Hinchman and Hinchman *Memory, Identity, Community*, p. 254.

22  Plummer *Sexual Stories*, p. 20.

23  Somers and Gibson 'Reclaiming', pp. 38–9.

24  MacIntyre 'Virtues', p. 258.
25  Somers and Gibson 'Reclaiming', p. 61.
26  Carr 'Narrative and the Real World', pp. 16–17.
27  For explanation of these terms, closet and coming out, see below in section on Chapters 2–4.
28  The eight formerly married men are Gerald (75), Leslie (74), John (65), Oscar (65), Clive (64), Terrence (64), Douglas (63), and Edward (60). For discussion of state persecution of gay people in Australia, see the chapter on the coming-out stories of the old cohort.
29  Plummer *Sexual Stories*, p. 20.
30  For discussion of 'heteronormativity', see Chapter 4. For definition of 'heterosexism', see below in this section.
31  Ken Plummer defines heterosexism as '[A] *diverse set of social practices*—from the linguistic to the physical, in the public sphere and the private sphere, covert and overt—in an array of social arenas (e.g. work, home, school, media, church, courts, streets, etc.) *in which the homo/hetero binary distinction is at work whereby heterosexuality is privileged'*. Emphasis in the original. See K. Plummer 'Speaking its name. Inventing a lesbian and gay studies.' in K. Plummer (ed.) *Modern Homosexualities: fragments of lesbian and gay experience* (London: Routledge, 1992), p. 19.
32  Sedgwick also makes the point that closet is nowadays used in other senses to connote a secret that a person keeps from others. See Sedgwick *Epistemology*, pp. 67–8, 72.
33  Chauncey *Gay New York*, p. 375, footnote 7 and pp. 6–7.
34  Chauncey *Gay New York*, p. 6.
35  Chauncey *Gay New York*, p. 375, footnote 7.
36  Chauncey *Gay New York*, p. 7.
37  For thorough description and analysis of homosexual language in Australia, see G. Simes 'The language of homosexuality in Australia' in R. Aldrich and G. Wotherspoon (eds) *Gay Perspectives: essays in Australian gay culture* (Sydney: Department of Economic History, University of Sydney, 1992), pp. 31–57. For equally thorough account of homosexual language in Britain in the nineteenth century, see Weeks, *Coming out*, ch. 3. For detailed discussion of homosexual language, sexual and social practices in homosexual sub-cultures in USA, 1900–40, see Chauncey, *Gay New York*, pp. 12–23. It is fairly clear there is an overlap between the language homosexual and gay men use in English-speaking countries and that since the 1940s North American gay men have been especially influential, that they have exerted a 'global' influence on gay sub-cultures in other countries, especially but not only English-speaking ones, because of the economic and military hegemony of the USA. Following the work of Gary Wotherspoon, it would seem that one of the first points of contact was WWII when tens of thousands of US servicemen were in Australia for rest and recreation leave or combat preparation. It was then that they passed on to local gay men the jargon of North American gay sub-cultures and knowledge of their institutions and practices. It is likely gay US servicemen had similar influence in countries where they were present in large numbers during and after WWII, such as in the UK, Holland and Germany. For discussion of their influence in Australia, see G. Wotherspoon 'Comrades-at-arms: World War II and male homosexuality

in Australia' in J. Damousi and M. Lake (eds) *Gender and War: Australians at war in the twentieth century* (Melbourne: Cambridge University Press, 1995), pp. 205–22.

38  Chauncey *Gay New York*; A. McLaren *Twentieth Century Sexuality: a history* (Oxford: Blackwell Publishers Ltd, 1999); P.M. Nardi, D. Sanders and J. Marmor *Growing up before Stonewall life stories of some gay men* (London: Routledge, 1994); and Wotherspoon 'Comrades-at-arms', pp. 205–22.

39  A. Bérubé *Coming out under fire: the history of gay men and women in World War Two* (New York: Penguin Books, 1991), *passim*; McLaren *Twentieth Century Sexuality*, ch. 8.

40  McLaren, *Twentieth Century Sexuality*, p. 143. For examination of the persecution of homosexuals in USA during the Cold War, see for example, G. Chauncey *Why Marriage? The history shaping today's debate over gay equality* (Cambridge, Mass: Perseus Books Group, 2004); L. Segal *Slow motion: changing masculinities, changing men* (New Jersey: Rutgers University Press, 1990).

41  For examples of homosexual persecution in Canada, West Germany, Britain, France and Australia, see D. Eribon *Insult and the making of the gay self*, trans. M. Lucey (Durham: Duke University Press, 2004), p. 23; McLaren *Twentieth Century*, pp. 161–3; G. Willett 'The darkest decade: homophobia in 1950s Australia' in J. Murphy and J. Smart (eds) *The Forgotten Fifties: aspects of Australian society and culture in the 1950s* (Melbourne: Melbourne University Press, 1997 and *Australian Historical Studies*, 109, 1997), pp. 120–32.

42  For discussion of 'unprecedented' gay ferment in 1970s, see Plummer *Telling Sexual Stories*, pp. 90–1, and coming out then as 'mass' activity, see G. Herdt '"Coming out" as a rite of passage: a Chicago study' in Herdt *Gay Culture in America*, p. 34.

43  Chauncey *Gay New York*, footnote, p. 8.

44  Altman *Homosexual*, p. 119; Plummer *Telling Sexual Stories*, 26.

45  For effect of HIV-AIDS on communities of gay men, see, for example, D. Altman 'AIDS and the reconceptualization of homosexuality' in D. Altman *et al. Homosexuality, which Homosexuality? Essays from the international conference on gay and lesbian studies* (London: GMP Publishers, 1989), pp. 35–48; D. Altman 'Legitimation through disaster: AIDS and the gay movement', in E. Fee and D. M. Fox (eds) *AIDS: the burdens of history* (Berkeley: University of California Press, 1988), pp. 301–15; J. D'Emilio and E. B. Freedman *Intimate Matters: a history of sexuality in America*, 2nd edn (Chicago: University of Chicago Press, 1997), ch. 15; G. W. Dowsett *Practicing Desire: homosexual sex in the era of AIDS* (Stanford, California: Stanford University Press, 1996), pp. 90–117; McLaren *Twentieth Century Sexuality*, ch. 10. For an interesting discussion of how and why HIV-AIDS affected gay men's visibility in USA, see L. Bersani *Homos* (Cambridge Mass: Harvard University Press, 1996), pp. 19–29.

46  Authors whose works cover coming-out narratives in the post-liberation period include: Bech *When Men Meet*; L. Duggan 'Queering the state' in P. M. Nardi and B. E. Schneider (eds) *Social Perspectives in Lesbian and Gay Studies: a reader* (London: Routledge, 1998), pp. 565–72; Eribon *Insult*; Gagnon *An Interpretation of Desire*; Herdt '"Coming out" as a rite of passage', pp. 29–67; G. Herdt and A. Boxer *Children of Horizons: how gay and lesbian teens are leading a new way out of the closet* (Boston: Beason Press, 1993);

K. Plummer 'Lesbian and gay youth in England' in G. Herdt (ed.) *Gay and Lesbian Youth* (New York: The Haworth Press, 1989), pp. 195–223; M. Pollak 'Male homosexuality – or happiness in the ghetto' in P. Ariès and A. Béjin (eds) *Western Sexuality: practice and precept in past and present times*, trans. A. Forster (Oxford: Basil Blackwell, 1986), pp. 40–61.

47  For discussion of the gay scene before the gay liberation period and thereafter, see, for example, N. Achilles 'The development of the homosexual bar as an institution' in P. M. Nardi and B. E. Schneider (eds) *Social Perspectives in Lesbian and Gay Studies: a reader* (London: Routledge, 1998) pp. 175–82; Altman *Homosexualization*; A. P. Bell and M. S. Weinberg *Homosexualities: a study of diversity among men and women* (Melbourne: The Macmillan Company of Australia, 1978); D'Emilio and Freedman *Intimate Matters*; G. Hekma 'Same-sex relations among men in Europe, 1700–1990' in F. X. Elder, L. A. Hall and G. Hekma (eds) *Sexual Cultures in Europe: themes in sexuality* (Manchester: Manchester University Press, 1999), pp. 79–103; Herdt '"Coming out" as a rite of passage', pp. 29–67; K. Plummer 'Going gay: identities lifecycles and lifestyles in the male gay world' in Hart and Richardson *The Theory and Practice of Homosexuality*, pp. 93–110.

48  Despite geographical and historical differences, the institutions of the gay world in many medium-sized and large western cities are remarkably similar.

49  Hekma 'Same-sex relations among men in Europe, 1700–1990', p. 97.

50  Sexualisation of the scene is examined in, for example, Bell and Weinberg *Homosexualities*; D'Emilio and Freedman *Intimate Matters*; S. Jeffreys *Unpacking Queer Politics: a lesbian feminist perspective* (Cambridge: Polity Press, 2003); Pollak 'Male homosexuality', pp. 40–61; J. Weeks *Sex, Politics and Society: the regulation of sexuality since 1800*, 2nd edn (London: Longman, 1989).

51  Emphasis in the original. Carr 'Narrative and the real world', p. 22.

52  See, for example, G. Herdt *Same sex, different cultures: exploring gay and lesbian lives* (Boulder, Colorado: Westview Press, 1997), *passim*; S. O. Murray *Homosexualities* (Chicago: University of Chicago Press, 2000), ch. 9; Plummer 'Going gay', pp. 93–110; J. Weeks, B. Heaphy and C. Donovan 'Partners by choice: equality, power and commitment in non-heterosexual relationships' in G. Allan (ed.) *The sociology of the family: a reader* (Oxford: Blackwell Publishers Ltd, 1999), pp. 111–28.

53  L. Jamieson 'The couple: intimate and equal?' in J. Weeks, J. Holland and M. Waites (eds) *Sexuality and Society: a reader* (Cambridge: Polity Press, 2003), pp. 265–76.

54  For discussion of the term, 'family of choice', see J. Weeks *Making Sexual History* (Cambridge: Polity Press, 2000), p. 213ff.

55  B. M. Dank 'Coming out in the gay world' in *Psychiatry*, 34 (1971) 180–97; Pollak 'Male homosexuality', pp. 40–61.

56  S. de Beauvoir *Old Age*, trans. P. O'Brien (Harmondsworth: Penguin Books, 1977), *passim*; N. Elias 'Ageing and dying: some sociological problems' in *The Loneliness of the Dying*, trans. E. Jephcott (Oxford: Basil Blackwell, 1987), pp. 68–91.

57  See R. M. Berger 'Realities of gay and lesbian aging', *Social Work*, (1984) 57–62; J. Weeks 'The problems of older homosexuals' in Hart and Richardson *The Theory and Practice of Homosexuality*, pp. 177–84.

## Chapter 2    The Coming-out Stories of the Old Cohort

1  A. Bérubé *Coming out under fire: the history of gay men and women in World War Two* (New York: Penguin Books, 1991), chs 1 & 6.

2  George Chauncey, public lecture at University of Melbourne on 21 Sep 2005. He argues in *Gay New York* that a similar crackdown against 'deviant' sexuality occurred in the USA during the Depression when 'Lesbians and gay men ... threatened to undermine the reproduction of normative gender arrangements already threatened by the upheavals of the 30s'. G. Chauncey *Gay New York: gender, urban culture, and the making of the gay male world, 1890–1940* (New York: Basic Books, 1994), p. 354.

3  Bérubé *Coming out under fire*, p. 255. For discussion of the terms 'fairy' and 'sissy' as they applied in the USA between world wars, see Chauncey *Gay New York*, Intro and chs 2 & 3. For discussion of effeminacy, see P. M. Nardi 'Sex, friendship, and gender roles among gay men' in P. M. Nardi (ed.) *Men's Friendships* (Newbury Park, CA: Sage Publications, 1992), pp. 173–85 and also discussion in ch. 8 for connection that is assumed to exist between homosexuality and effeminacy. Garry Wotherspoon refers to the effeminate male as one of three stereotypes of homosexual men that circulated in Sydney between the wars and in World War II; see G. Wotherspoon *City of the Plain: history of a gay sub-culture* (Sydney: Hale & Iremonger, 1991), chs 1 & 2 and G. Wotherspoon 'Comrades-at-arms: World War II and male homosexuality in Australia' in J. Damousi and M. Lake (eds) *Gender and War: Australians at war in the twentieth century* (Melbourne: Cambridge University Press, 1995), pp. 205–22.

4  George Chauncey shows that an extensive scene existed in New York from the late nineteenth century: 'Fairies drank with sailors and other working-men at water-front dives and ... "noted faggots" mixed with other patrons at Haarlem's rent parties and basement cabarets'. This world was forced underground, however, in the late 1920s and 1930s because of the Depression and an anti-gay policy pursued by the State Liqor Authority. See Chauncey *Gay New York*, ch. 12. Gert Hekma argues that likewise in Europe a 'dark age' for homosexuals descended in 1935, which lasted until 1955. In contrast to Bérubé, Hekma does not argue that the increased homosociability of military service fostered a growth in and development of gay sub-cultures and identity—because, unlike in the USA, the war in Europe brought greater and more severe persecution of gay people at the hands of Fascist regimes in Germany, Italy and their occupied territories. See G. Hekma 'Same-sex relations among men in Europe, 1700–1990' in F. X. Elder, L. A. Hall and G. Hekma (eds) *Sexual Cultures in Europe: themes in sexuality* (Manchester: Manchester University Press, 1999), pp. 91–4.

5  P. M. Nardi, D. Sanders and J. Marmor *Growing up before Stonewall life stories of some gay men* (London: Routledge, 1994), pp. 8–9. Ken Plummer and Angus McLaren share similar views about the relatively weak group formation of gay sub-cultures and gay men's stigmatised identities. See K. Plummer 'Going gay: identities lifecycles and lifestyles in the male gay world' in J. Hart and D. Richardson (eds) *The Theory and Practice of Homosexuality* (London: Routledge & Kegan Paul, 1981), p. 98, K. Plummer *Documents of Life: an introduction to the problems and literature of a humanistic method* (London: George

Allen & Unwin Ltd, 1983), p. 70 and A. McLaren *Twentieth Century Sexuality: a history* (Oxford: Blackwell Publishers Ltd, 1999), p. 187.

6   C. Kaiser *The Gay Metropolis: 1940–1996* (San Diego: Harcourt & Brace & Company, 1997), p. 27.

7   Bérubé *Coming out under fire*, p. 255.

8   Bérubé *Coming out under fire*, pp. 256–7.

9   Wotherspoon 'Comrades-at-arms', p. 212.

10  See Wotherspoon 'Comrades-at-arms', p. 214, Wotherspoon *City*, ch. 2 and C. Moore *Sunshine and Rainbows: the development of gay and lesbian culture in Queensland* (St Lucia, Qld: University of Queensland Press, 2001), ch. 7.

11  Wotherspoon 'Comrades-at-arms', p. 219.

12  For accounts of the sex that Australian men had with Australian and American soldiers during World War II, see G. Wotherspoon (ed.) *Being Different: nine gay men remember* (Sydney: Hale & Iremonger, 1986), especially 'John's story', pp. 38–50, Moore *Sunshine*, pp. 108–15 and Wotherspoon *City*, ch. 2.

13  There have always been men who do not regard themselves as homosexual but who will have sex with men when and if the occasion arises. When a man who is otherwise heterosexual has sex with a man (gay or straight), their sexual encounter has often been seen as an example of 'situational' homosexuality. Such sex between men is supposed to occur because of the absence of women to satisfy their sexual needs, and to be found in male-only institutions such as prisons and the military. This is a debatable category and explanation. For discussion of the dubiousness of the notion of 'situational' homosexuality, see H. Bech *When Men Meet: homosexuality and modernity*, trans. T. Mequit and T. Davies (Cambridge: Polity Press, 1997), ch. III, esp. pp. 20–5. Garry Wotherspoon alludes to sexual encounters between men during World War II where only one was homosexual or where both were heterosexual. See Wotherspoon *City*, ch. 2, esp. pp. 86–93.

14  Moore *Sunshine*, p. 105. John Murphy makes a similar point about the effect of war on promiscuity in general. See J. Murphy *Imagining the fifties: private sentiment and political culture in Menzies' Australia* (Sydney: University of New South Wales Press Ltd, 2000), p. 56.

15  Brisbane was the headquarters of US General Douglas MacArthur and became 'an American village' [Wotherspoon *City*, p. 96.] after the USA entered the war in 1942. For a description of the effect MacArthur and his entourage had on Brisbane, see Moore, *Sunshine*, p. 106.

16  Moore *Sunshine*, p. 106.

17  Wotherspoon 'Comrades-at-arms', p. 218.

18  Wotherspoon 'Comrades-at-arms', p. 215.

19  Wotherspoon 'Comrades-at-arms', p. 218.

20  Wotherspoon *City*, pp. 93–7.

21  R. Aldrich *Colonialism and Homosexuality* (London: Routledge, 2003), p. 241. In the UK, the term 'cottage' is used for such places and in the USA, the word is 'tea room'. Among the many works that discuss or describe sex in public places, see: A. P. Bell and M. S. Weinberg *Homosexualities: a study of diversity among men and women* (Melbourne: The Macmillan Company of Australia, 1978), p. 243; Chauncey *Gay New York*, p. 201; A. Giddens *The Transformation of Intimacy: sexuality, love and eroticism in modern societies* (Cambridge: Polity Press, 1992), p. 145; K. Markwell 'Making it "our town"

too: Novocastrian gay men and their leisure' in J. Wafer, E. Southgate and L. Coan (eds) *Out in the Valley: Hunter gay and lesbian stories* (Newcastle, NSW: Newcastle Region Library, 2000), pp. 313–18; Y. Mishima 1971 *Forbidden Colours*, trans. Alfred H. Marks (London: Penguin Group, 1971),p. 61; C. Moore and B. Jamison 'Making the modern Australian homosexual male: Queensland's criminal justice system and homosexual offences, 1860–1954', *Crime, Histoire & Sociétés/Crime, History & Societies*, 11, 1, (2007) 29–30; J. Weeks *Sexuality and its Discontents: meanings, myths & modern sexualities* (London: Routledge & Kegan Paul, 1985), pp. 220–3; Wotherspoon, *City*, p. 67.

22  L. Segal *Slow motion: changing masculinities, changing men* (New Jersey: Rutgers University Press, 1990), p. 17.

23  G. Chauncey *Why Marriage? The history shaping today's debate over gay equality* (Cambridge, MA: Perseus Books Group, 2004), p. 11.

24  D. Altman *The Homosexualization of America, the Americanization of the Homosexual* (New York: St Martin's Press, 1982), p. 2.

25  Plummer *Sexual Stories*, p. 84.

26  J. Gagnon *An Interpretation of Desire: essays in the study of sexuality* (Chicago: The University of Chicago Press, 2004), p. 122.

27  Chauncey *Why Marriage?* p. 11.

28  J. D'Emilio and E. B. Freedman *Intimate Matters: a history of sexuality in America*, 2$^{nd}$ edn (Chicago: University of Chicago Press, 1997), p. 288.

29  McLaren *Twentieth Century Sexuality*, p. 161.

30  See Kaiser *Gay Metropolis*, pp. 54–5. See also, McLaren *Twentieth Century*, pp. 145–6.

31  Gagnon *An Interpretation of Desire*, p. 112.

32  D'Emilio and Freedman *Intimate Matters*, pp. 293–4, and also McLaren *Twentieth Century*, p. 161.

33  McLaren *Twentieth Century*, pp. 161–3.

34  D. Eribon *Insult and the making of the gay self*, trans. Michael Lucey (Durham: Duke University Press, 2004), p. 23.

35  D'Emilio and Freedman *Intimate Matters*, p. 294.

36  These figures are for convictions in superior courts in Australia. Willett notes that these are likely to under-estimate the extent of the effect of police repression because they exclude people who were charged but not convicted and people who were convicted in lower courts, for example in magistrate's courts. See G. Willett 'The darkest decade: homophobia in 1950s Australia' in J. Murphy and J. Smart (eds) *The Forgotten Fifties: aspects of Australian society and culture in the 1950s* (Melbourne: Melbourne University Press and *Australian Historical Studies*, n. 109, 1997), pp. 127–8.

37  Willett 'The darkest decade', p. 128. The head of the New South Wales police force said that homosexuality was the greatest danger Australia faced in the 1950s, see Aldrich *Colonialism and Homosexuality*, p. 238.

38  Willett 'The darkest decade', pp. 124–9.

39  Wotherspoon *City*, pp. 152–5.

40  Wotherspoon *City*, p. 155.

41  Wotherspoon *City*, pp. 156–7.

42  Wotherspoon *City*, p. 158.

43  M. Gilding *The making and breaking of the Australian family* (Sydney: Allen & Unwin, 1991), p. 121.

44 For discussion of the ways in which taxation policies of the conservative Menzies government benefited and supported the middle class family in the 1950s, see Murphy *Imagining the fifties* pp. 84–9.

45 Murphy *Imagining the fifties*, p. 56.

46 Garry Wotherspoon and George Chauncey describe the prominence of drag balls in the social calendar of homosexual sub-cultures in Sydney and New York respectively. See Wotherspoon *City*, pp. 76–7 and Chauncey *Gay New York*, pp. 291–9 & *passim*.

47 Chauncey *Gay New York*, footnote, p. 8.

48 Bérubé *Coming out under fire*, p. 6.

49 Dank's interviewees, whom he styled 'self-admitted homosexuals', completed a one-page questionnaire. The men were recruited from 'a large metropolitan area in the United States' in the late 1960s. The age range of respondents is 15–69. See B. M. Dank 'Coming out in the gay world' in *Psychiatry*, 34 (1971) 180–3.

50 Dank 'Coming out in the gay world', p. 181.

51 Dank 'Coming out in the gay world', footnote 7, p. 181.

52 K. Plummer *Sexual Stigma: an interactionist account* (London: Routledge & Kegan Paul, 1975), pp. 147–8.

53 Chauncey *Gay New York*, footnote, p. 8.

54 E. Goffman *Stigma: Notes on the Management of Spoiled Identity* (Harmondsworth: Penguin Books, 1968).

55 The average age of the men in this cohort is 67 and on average they came out at 37. Interviewed in 2002, a 67-year-old would have been born in 1935 and would have come out in 1972, the year the Whitlam Labor government was elected to office and one year after gay liberation and CAMP Inc. were established in Australia. This man would have been in his final year of secondary school in 1950 or 1951 and would have been 21 in 1956.

56 See discussion of heterosexual assumption in Chapter 4.

57 The term, 'poofter', is Australian slang for homosexual. A 'poofter basher' is a person who, usually in the company of others like him, seeks out gay men in isolation and attacks them physically and violently. For discussion of gay bashing as a form of sexual violence, see, for example, R. W. Connell *Gender* (Cambridge: Polity, 2002); Plummer *Sexual Stigma*; Segal *Slow Motion*.

58 E. Goffman *The Presentation of Self in Everyday Life* (London: Allen Lane, 1969), p. 49.

59 Note that Ronald uses the verb to 'bring out'.

## Chapter 3  The Coming-out Stories of the Middle Cohort

1 Laws concerning homosexuality were amended or passed in South Australia (18 Sept. 1975), ACT (Nov. 1976) and Victoria (18 Dec. 1980). Law reform occurred in the remaining states and the Northern Territory between 1984 and 1997. The last jurisdiction to introduce homosexual law reform was Tasmania in May 1997. See G. Willett *Living Out Loud: a history of gay and lesbian activism in Australia* (Sydney: Allen & Unwin, 2000), pp. 96, 98, 155, 164, 224, 231, 237.

2   J. Weeks *Coming Out: homosexual politics in Britain from the Nineteenth Century to the present*, 2nd edn (London: Quartet Books Ltd., 1990), p. 190.

3   E. Bruner 'Ethnography as narrative' in L. P. Hinchman and S. K. Hinchman (eds) *Memory, Identity, Community: the idea of narrative in the human sciences* (New York: State University of New York, 2001), p. 275.

4   G. Herdt '"Coming out" as a rite of passage: a Chicago study' in G. Herdt (ed.) *Gay Culture in America: essays from the field* (Boston: Beacon Press, 1992), p. 34.

5   A. McLaren *Twentieth Century Sexuality: a history* (Oxford: Blackwell Publishers Ltd., 1999), p. 191.

6   Herdt '"Coming out" as a rite of passage', p. 34.

7   M. Pollak 'Male homosexuality—or happiness in the ghetto' in P. Ariès and A. Béjin (eds) *Western Sexuality: practice and precept in past and present times*, trans. A. Forster (Oxford: Basil Blackwell, 1986 ), p. 53; R. W. Connell *Masculinities*, (Sydney: Allen & Unwin, 1995), p. 218. For a comprehensive investigation of how the clone has been regarded and analysed in scholarly literature, see T. Edwards 'Queering the pitch? Gay masculinities' in M. S. Kimmel, J. Hearn and R. W. Connell (eds) *Handbook of studies on men and masculinities* (Thousand Oaks, CA: Sage Publications Inc., 2005), pp. 55–60.

8   See, for example, A. M. Boxer and B. J. Cohler 'The life course of gay and lesbian youth: an immodest proposal for the study of lives' in G. Herdt (ed.) *Gay and Lesbian Youth* (New York: The Haworth Press, 1989), p. 326; G. Chauncey *Gay New York: gender, urban culture, and the making of the gay male world, 1890–1940* (New York: Basic Books, 1994), footnote 7, p. 375; J. H. Gagnon *An Interpretation of Desire: essays in the study of sexuality* (Chicago: The University of Chicago Press, 2004), pp. 121–3; Herdt *Gay Culture in America*, pp. 1–67; P. M. Nardi, D. Sanders and J. Marmor *Growing up before Stonewall life stories of some gay men* (London: Routledge, *passim*, 1994); K. Plummer *Telling Sexual Stories: power, change and social worlds* (London: Routledge, 1995), p. 81; and E. White 'The political vocabulary of homosexuality' in B. R. S. Fone (ed.) *The Columbia Anthology of gay literature: readings from Western antiquity to the present day* (New York: Columbia University Press, 1998), pp. 777–85.

9   P. Shapiro *Turn the beat around: the secret history of disco* (London: Faber & Faber Limited, 2005), p. 52.

10   Plummer *Telling Sexual Stories*, p. 90.

11   White 'The political vocabulary', p. 777.

12   White 'The political vocabulary', pp. 777–8.

13   White 'The political vocabulary', p. 777.

14   White 'The political vocabulary', p. 785.

15   Willett *Living Out Loud*, p. 47.

16   G. Wotherspoon *City of the Plain: history of a gay sub-culture* (Sydney: Hale & Iremonger, 1991), p. 162.

17   See Wotherspoon *City*, pp. 163, 166.

18   Wotherspoon *City*, p. 166.

19   Wotherspoon *City*, p. 168.

20   Willett *Out Loud*, pp. 36–7.

21   Wotherspoon *City*, p. 169.

22   Wotherspoon *City*, p. 169.

23 D. Altman *Homosexual: oppression and liberation* (Sydney: Angus & Robertson, 1972), p. 177.
24 Altman *Homosexual*, p. 223.
25 Altman *Homosexual*, p. 226.
26 Herdt '"Coming out" as a rite of passage', p. 34.
27 Plummer *Sexual Stories*, pp. 90–1.
28 J. Rickard *Australia, a cultural history*, 2nd edn (Harlow, UK: Pearson Education Limited, 2001), pp. 232–4.
29 McLaren *Twentieth Century*, p. 190.
30 D. Altman *The Homosexualization of America, the Americanization of the Homosexual* (New York: St Martin's Press, 1982), p. 3.
31 Altman *Homosexualization*, p. 22.
32 P. Blazey [Extract from] *Screw Loose: Uncalled-for Memoirs* (Sydney: Picador Australia, 1997) in G. Aitken (ed.) *The Penguin Book of Gay Australian Writing* (Melbourne: Penguin Books Australia Ltd., 2002), p. 266.
33 J. N. Katz *The invention of heterosexuality*, with a new preface, and an afterword by L. Duggan (Chicago: University of Chicago Press, 2007), p. 5. Jonathan Ned Katz is a North American historian and self-proclaimed member of the 'baby-boomer' generation who in the early 1970s attended 'raucous weekly meetings of New York City's Gay Activists Alliance'.
34 Graham Willett acknowledges this reality and also that activists were aware at the time that this was the reality of many gay people. See Willett *Out Loud*, pp. 144–7.
35 The three men are Lindsay (62), Donald (52), and Michael (52). They represent less than 4 per cent of the entire sample, or slightly less than 6 per cent of the combined total of men in the old and middle cohorts (N=52). By any account, this is a very small proportion of men who, because of when they were born and grew to maturity, were most likely to be directly caught up in and influenced by the gay liberation movement.
36 See Willett *Out Loud*, pp. 143–7 for discussion of activists' awareness of the need to work with the bar scene because of the large numbers of gay people who participated.
37 Shapiro *Turn the beat around*, p. 54.
38 Wotherspoon *City*, pp. 214–15.
39 R. Dessaix *A Mother's Disgrace* (Sydney: HarperCollins, 2002), p. 164.
40 For more discussion of the scene, see Chapter 5.
41 Wotherspoon *City*, pp. 189–94.
42 C. Moore *Sunshine and Rainbows: the development of gay and lesbian culture in Queensland* (St Lucia, Qld: University of Queensland Press, 2001), p. 146.
43 Moore *Sunshine*, p. 150.
44 G. Wotherspoon (ed.) *Being Different: nine gay men remember* (Sydney: Hale & Iremonger, 1986), p. 23.
45 Boxer and 'The life course of gay and lesbian youth', pp. 315–55.
46 M. Foucault 'Friendship as a way of life' in *Ethics: essential works of Foucault 1954–1984*, vol. 1, trans. R. Hurley and others, ed. P. Rabinow (Harmondsworth: Penguin Books, 2000), p. 139.
47 R. M. Berger 'Realities of gay and lesbian aging', *Social Work* (Jan–Feb 1984) 58.
48 B. M. Dank 'Coming out in the gay world', *Psychiatry*, 34 (1971) 190.

49 Herdt '"Coming out" as a rite of passage', pp. 31–2.
50 K. Plummer *Sexual Stigma: an interactionist account* (London: Routledge & Kegan Paul, 1975), p. 147.
51 J. Weeks, B. Heaphy and C. Donovan 'Partners by choice: equality, power and commitment in non-heterosexual relationships' in G. Allan (ed.) *The sociology of the family: a reader* (Oxford: Blackwell Publishers Ltd., 1999), p. 122.
52 Herdt *Gay Culture*, p. 32.
53 G. Herdt *Same sex, different cultures: exploring gay and lesbian lives* (Boulder, Colorado: Westview Press, 1997), p. 110.
54 Raymond Berger refers to a similar life-course event, which he calls 'the crisis of independence'. See R. M. Berger *Gay and gray: the older homosexual man*, 2nd edn (Binghamton, New York: The Haworth Press, 1996), p. 232.
55 H. Bech *When Men Meet: homosexuality and modernity*, trans. T. Mequit and T. Davies (Cambridge: Polity Press, 1997), p. 97.
56 Bech *When Men Meet*, p. 97.
57 Bech *When Men Meet*, p. 99.
58 Bech *When Men Meet*, p. 99.
59 Altman *Homosexualization*, p. 22.
60 G. Herdt and A. Boxer 'Introduction: culture, history, and life course of gay men' in Herdt *Gay Culture in America*, p. 11.
61 Herdt *Same sex, different cultures*, p. 112.
62 K. Plummer 'Going gay: identities lifecycles and lifestyles in the male gay world' in J. Hart and D. Richardson (eds) *The Theory and Practice of Homosexuality* (London: Routledge & Kegan Paul, 1981), p. 102.
63 Plummer 'Going gay', p. 102.
64 Weeks *Coming out*, p. vii.
65 Altman *Homosexual*, p. 118.
66 Altman *Homosexual*, p. 119.
67 Emphasis in the original. Plummer *Sexual Stories*, p. 26.
68 Bech *When Men Meet*, pp. 95–6.

## Chapter 4   The Coming-out Stories of the Young Cohort

1 G. W. Dowsett *Practicing Desire: homosexual sex in the era of AIDS* (Stanford, California: Stanford University Press 1996), p. 61.
2 R. Shilts *And the band played on: politics, people, and the AIDS epidemic* (New York: St Martin's Press, 1987), p. 342. According to Shilts, on 8 July 1983 a 43-year-old man died in Prince Henry's Hospital, Melbourne. The hospital was demolished in the 1990s and has been replaced by a block of luxury flats.
3 National Centre in HIV Epidemiology and Clinical Research [NCHECR]. *HIV/AIDS, viral hepatitis and sexually transmissible infections in Australia Annual Surveillance Report 2005*, (NCHECR, The University of New South Wales, Sydney; Australian Institute of Health and Welfare, Canberra, 2005), pp. 5 & 7, see also National Centre in HIV Epidemiology and Clinical Research. *HIV/AIDS, viral hepatitis and sexually transmissible infections in Australia Annual Surveillance Report 2007* (NCHECR, The University of New

South Wales, Sydney, NSW; Australian Institute of Health and Welfare, Canberra, ACT, 2007), p. 9. By 31 December 2006, there had been 26,267 HIV diagnoses in Australia, see NCHECR *Annual Surveillance Report 2007*, p. 7.

4 According to the NCHECR, by 31 December 2006, 6,723 people had died from AIDS in Australia: NCHECR *Annual Surveillance Report 2007*, p. 38. Paul Sendziuk estimates that since the start of the epidemic in Australia, homosexually-active men comprise more than 80 per cent of HIV infections and AIDS deaths: P. Sendziuk *Learning to trust: Australian responses to AIDS* (Sydney: University of New South Wales Press, 2003), p. 8.

5 A. McLaren *Twentieth Century Sexuality: a history* (Oxford: Blackwell Publishers Ltd, 1999), p. 220.

6 J. D'Emilio and E. B. Freedman *Intimate Matters: a history of sexuality in America*, 2nd edn (Chicago: University of Chicago Press, 1997), p. 355.

7 J. Foster *Take Me to Paris, Johnny*, with a foreword by P. Craven and an afterword by J. Rickard (Melbourne: Schwartz Publishing, 2003), p. 188.

8 Foster *Take Me to Paris, Johnny*, p. 194.

9 McLaren *Twentieth Century Sexuality*, p. 196. For additional discussion of AIDS and the rise of homophobia, see D. Altman 'AIDS and the discourses of sexuality' in R. W. Connell and G. W. Dowsett (eds) *Rethinking Sex: social theory and sexuality research* (Melbourne: Melbourne University Press, 1992), pp. 43–4.

10 The men were asked 'What effect has HIV-AIDS had on your sense of self?' See Appendix 1. Interview schedule, question 8. The men who referred to connection between HIV-AIDS and gay identity are Tony (33), Ian (28), Mark (25), Myles (24), Adam (24) and Angus (23).

11 J. Weeks *Sexuality and its Discontents: meanings, myths & modern sexualities* (London: Routledge & Kegan Paul, 1985), p. 49.

12 D. Altman 'AIDS and the reconceptualization of homosexuality' in D. Altman *et al. Homosexuality, Which Homosexuality? Essays from the international conference on gay and lesbian studies* (London: GMP Publishers, 1989), p. 35.

13 Safe sex and 'safer sex' were terms for sexual practices that some scientists and many gay lobbyists recommended people having casual sex adopt in the early days of the HIV-AIDS epidemic because they were thought likely to prevent transfer of the HIV. Once this was shown to be the case, government medical authorities in many western countries adopted these guidelines and funded safe-sex campaigns among the different groups of men who have sex with men—that is, gay men as well as men who do not identify as gay. The purpose of safe-sex campaigns was to encourage gay men to engage in protected anal sex only, that is, to use a condom whenever they had such sex if they did not know the HIV status of their partner. In its early days, safe sex was recommended for anyone who intended to have casual sex, anal or vaginal. For discussion of changes in sexual practices among gay men as a response to HIV-AIDS, see Dowsett *Practicing Desire*, pp. 77–87.

14 Altman 'AIDS and the reconceptualization of homosexuality', p. 37.

15 McLaren *Twentieth Century*, p. 213. See also K. Plummer 'Lesbian and gay youth in England' in G. Herdt (ed.) *Gay and Lesbian Youth* (New York: The Haworth Press, 1989), pp. 212–13.

16  Sendziuk *Learning to trust*, p. 88.
17  Sendziuk *Learning to trust*, pp. 88–9.
18  G. Wotherspoon *City of the Plain: history of a gay sub-culture* (Sydney: Hale & Iremonger, 1991), p. 226.
19  More recently, however, rates of HIV infection have been increasing in Australia, rising from 763 cases nationally in 2000 to 998 in 2006. For the vast majority of these cases, transmission was through sexual contact between men. See NCHECR *Annual Surveillance Report 2007*, pp. 9–13. Similar increases in rates of HIV infection have been recorded in the USA—for more discussion of these, see D. M. Halperin *What do gay men want? An essay on sex, risk, and subjectivity* (Ann Arbor: University of Michigan Press, 2007), pp. 11–36.
20  For discussion of the effects of HIV-AIDS on gay men's communities, see Dowsett *Practicing Desire*, pp. 64–5 and J. Weeks 'Living with uncertainty' in A. Elliott (ed.) *The Blackwell reader in contemporary social theory* (Oxford: Blackwell Publishers Ltd., 1999), p. 277.
21  For discussion of gay communities' response to HIV-AIDS and their relationship with state and federal governments' health and research strategies in Australia, see Dowsett *Practicing Desire*, ch. 3.
22  For discussion of similar social developments in North America, see J. H. Gagnon *An Interpretation of Desire: essays in the study of sexuality* (Chicago: The University of Chicago Press, 2004), p. 123.
23  McLaren *Twentieth Century*, p. 199.
24  R. Reynolds *From Camp to Queer: re-making the Australian homosexual* (Melbourne: Melbourne University Press, 2002), p. 158.
25  Reynolds *Camp to Queer*, p. 158. M. Bartos 'The queer excess of public health policy' *Meanjin*, 55, 1 (1996 ) 126.
26  J. Weeks *Making Sexual History* (Cambridge: Polity Press 2000), p. 83.
27  Reynolds *Camp to Queer*, p. 162.
28  D. Altman *The Homosexualization of America, the Americanization of the Homosexual* (New York: St Martin's Press, 1982), p. 22.
29  Plummer *Sexual Stories*, p. 96.
30  G. Herdt '"Coming out" as a rite of passage: a Chicago study' in G. Herdt (ed.) *Gay Culture in America: essays from the field* (Boston: Beacon Press, 1992), p. 35.
31  Plummer *Sexual Stories*, p. 52.
32  In heteronormative societies, gay men, lesbians and other sexual minorities are forced to declare their difference—to come out—in order to assert their identity and existence as 'non-heterosexuals'. See, for example, L. Duggan 'Queering the state' in P. M. Nardi and B. E. Schneider (eds) *Social Perspectives in Lesbian and Gay Studies: a reader* (London: Routledge, 1998), pp. 565–72. In her article, Lisa Duggan acknowledges Michael Warner as author of the term 'heteronormative' in his *Fear of a Queer Planet* (Minneapolis: University of Minnesota Press, 1993).
33  Plummer 'Lesbian and gay youth in England', pp. 210 & 212.
34  The average age of the men in the young cohort is 33. Interviewed in 2002, they were born in 1969. On average, they came out at 21. Their coming-out year was 1990 and they were in the final year of secondary school in 1986 or 1987.

35 Dank interviewed 182 gay men. See B. M. Dank 'Coming out in the gay world' *Psychiatry*, 34 (1971) 180–3.
36 K. Plummer 'Going gay: identities lifecycles and life-styles in the male gay world' in J. Hart and D. Richardson (eds) *The Theory and Practice of Homosexuality* (London: Routledge & Kegan Paul, 1981), p. 101. Michael Pollak agrees with Plummer and says that coming out most frequently occurs between 16 and 30; see M. Pollak 'Male homosexuality—or happiness in the ghetto' in P. Ariès and A. Béjin (eds) *Western Sexuality: practice and precept in past and present times*, trans. A. Forster (Oxford: Basil Blackwell, 1986), p. 44.
37 G. Herdt *Same sex, different cultures: exploring gay and lesbian lives* (Boulder, Colorado: Westview Press, 1997), p. 158.
38 Herdt *Same sex*, p. 127.
39 Gagnon *Interpretation of Desire*, p. 123.
40 McLaren *Twentieth Century*, p. 220.
41 Herdt and Boxer interviewed 202 young males and females between the ages of 14 and 20. The average age of the sample was 18. The young people were members of Horizons Community Services in Chicago, a 'drop-in' centre for young gays and lesbians. See Herdt *Same sex*, p. 127. For details of the Chicago research, see G. Herdt and A. Boxer *Children of Horizons: how gay and lesbian teens are leading a new way out of the closet* (Boston: Beacon Press, 1993).
42 Herdt *Same sex*, p. 127.
43 See, for example, K. Plummer *Sexual Stigma: an interactionist account* (London: Routledge & Kegan Paul, 1975); Hart and Richardson *Theory and Practice of Homosexuality*; Herdt and Boxer *Children of Horizons*; and Plummer *Sexual Stories*.
44 Plummer 'Going gay', pp. 98–9.
45 See G. Herdt 1989 'Introduction: gay and lesbian youth, emergent identities, and cultural scenes at home and abroad' in Herdt *Gay and Lesbian Youth*, pp. 1–42, and also Altman *Homosexualization*, ch. 1; D. Eribon *Insult and the making of the gay self*, trans. M. Lucey, (Durham: Duke University Press, 2004), ch. 13; Plummer *Sexual Stories*, ch. 6; and, Weeks *Discontents*, ch. 8.
46 Plummer 'Going gay', pp. 98–9.
47 Plummer 'Going gay', pp. 98–9.
48 G. Wotherspoon (ed.) *Being Different: nine gay men remember* (Sydney: Hale & Iremonger, 1986), p. 122.
49 Wotherspoon 'The Loner' in *Being Different*, pp. 105–24.
50 Herdt *Same sex*, pp. 127–8. A report prepared in 2003 for the Attorney General's department of New South Wales on homophobic violence found, for example, that gay men and lesbians in New South Wales 'continue to experience high levels of homophobic abuse, harassment or violence'. New South Wales Government *'You shouldn't have to hide to be safe': a report on homophobic hostilities and violence against gay men and lesbians in New South Wales* (Sydney: Attorney General's department, 2003), p. 8.
51 For example of young gay men's experience in United States, see: R. M. Berger *Gay and gray: the older homosexual man*, 2nd edn (Binghamton, New York: The Haworth Press, 1996), p. 178.

## Chapter 5    The 'Scene'

1  For discussion of gay S&M sub-cultures in North American cities, 1970s and 1980s, see E. White *States of Desire: travels in gay America* (London: Pan Books Ltd., 1986), pp. 52, 54–6, 282–4, and *passim*; for analysis of S&M imperative in some gay men, see J. Rechy *The Sexual Outlaw: a documentary* (New York: Grove Press Inc., 1977), pp. 252–62.

2  J. D'Emilio and E. B. *Freedman Intimate Matters: a history of sexuality in America*, 2nd edn (Chicago: University of Chicago Press, 1997), p. 358.

3  In December 2007, the price of a ticket to the annual 'Red Raw' dance party in Melbourne was $70, which allowed one person entry to the venue. Additional costs would include the cost of alcohol, food and water bought at the party, drugs, costume/outfit, food, transport to and from the site, as well as entry to and alcohol bought at 'recovery' parties the following day, and possibly more drugs. Crucially, a single dose of drugs such as Ecstasy, Ice, Special K and Speed, which are popular on the dance party scene, often cost more than the price of the party ticket. For discussion of the drug culture at gay dance parties, see L. A. Lewis and M. W. Ross *A Select Body: the gay dance party subculture and the HIV/AIDS pandemic* (London: Cassell, 1995).

4  K. Plummer 1981 'Going gay: identities lifecycles and lifestyles in the male gay world' in J. Hart and D. Richardson (eds) *The Theory and Practice of Homosexuality* (London: Routledge & Kegan Paul, 1981), p. 99.

5  The work of Ridge, Minichiello & Plummer reveals weak social networks and widespread alienation among young gay men on the scene. They point out also that youthfulness is highly valued in the scene and older men are often marginalised. See D. Ridge, V. Minichiello and D. Plummer, 'Queer connections: community, "the scene", and an epidemic' in *Journal of Contemporary Ethnography*, 26, 2 (1997) 146–82. For more discussion of the competitiveness of the scene, see L. Bersani 'Is the rectum a grave?' in D. Crimp (ed.) *AIDS: cultural analysis, cultural activism* (Cambridge MA: The MIT Press, 1988), pp. 197–222; M. Pollak 'Male homosexuality – or happiness in the ghetto' in P. Ariès and A. Béjin (eds) *Western Sexuality: practice and precept in past and present times*, trans. A. Forster (Oxford: Basil Blackwell, 1986), pp. 40–61. Regarding the emptiness of relationships formed on the scene, see: T. Ayres 'China doll: the experience of being a gay Chinese Australian' in P. A. Jackson and G. Sullivan (eds) *Multicultural Queer: Australian Narratives* (Binghamton, NY: The Haworth Press, 1999), pp. 87–97.

6  See, for example, N. Achilles 'The development of the homosexual bar as an institution' in P. M. Nardi and B. E. Schneider (eds) *Social Perspectives in Lesbian and Gay Studies: a reader* (London: Routledge, 1998) pp. 175–82, and also, A. P. Bell and M. S. Weinberg *Homosexualities: a study of diversity among men and women* (Melbourne: The Macmillan Company of Australia, 1978), pp. 250–9.

7  In the state of Victoria, the change to opening hours occurred in the mid-1990s under an economic rationalist state government.

8  See below for discussion of the ethics of public sex.

9  Forty-two interviewees, or 51 per cent of the sample, reported positive views of the scene, while 41 interviewees, also equal to 51 per cent of the

sample, held negative views. Nineteen interviewees held both positive and negative views. The cohort where there was the greatest overlap between those holding both positive and negative views was the young cohort.

10 Twenty-nine men, or more than one third of all interviewees, said they did not go on the scene; 16 men, or more than 50 per cent of those who spurned the scene, were from the old cohort, while eight were from the middle cohort and five were from the young cohort.

11 R. M. Berger *Gay and gray: the older homosexual man*, 2$^{nd}$ edn (Binghamton, NY: The Haworth Press, 1996), pp. 228–9. J. H. Gagnon *An Interpretation of Desire: essays in the study of sexuality* (Chicago: The University of Chicago Press, 2004), p. 122. K. Plummer *Sexual Stigma: an interactionist account* (London: Routledge & Kegan Paul, 1975), pp. 160–1, 166. Pollak 'Male homosexuality', p. 46. J. Weeks 'The problems of older homosexuals' in Hart and Richardson *The Theory and Practice of Homosexuality*, pp. 179, 181–2. M. S. Weinberg and C. J. Williams *Male Homosexuals: their problems and adaptations* (New York: Penguin Books Inc., 1975), pp. 309–13.

12 Twenty-three interviewees (or 82 per cent) from the young cohort said they participated on the scene, while 22 men (or 73 per cent) from the middle cohort said so, as did six men (or 27 per cent) from the old cohort.

13 White *States of Desire*, p. 66.

14 P. Ariès *Centuries of Childhood* (Harmondsworth: Penguin Books, 1973), pp. 28–9.

15 Among the men interviewed for this study, 13 were formerly married and 14 are parents. The families and relationship status of interviewees are discussed in a later chapter.

16 Of the 42 interviewees with positive views of the scene, 19 were from the middle cohort and 17 were from the young cohort.

17 Leather clubs or bars were popular meeting places for gay men in the 1960s and 1970s, especially for those gay men known as 'clones' (see Chapter 3), and in the Castro area of San Francisco, Greenwich Village, New York, and Berlin. Leather bars continue to prosper even as their clientele ages. For discussion of sexual practices and rituals of leather bars in 1970s, early 1980s, see Pollak 'Male homosexuality', pp. 44–5.

18 J. Boswell *London Journal 1762–63*, ed. and intro. by F. A. Pottle (London: The Folio Society, 1985), p. 211.

19 The verb 'to cruise' and the noun, 'cruising', are widely accepted gay terms in English-speaking countries. Meaning to look or hunt for sex, cruising can occur anywhere: in bars or clubs, beats or sex venues, but also anywhere in public, including beaches, swimming pools and gymnasiums, department stores, supermarkets, streets and public transport. Like the heterosexual 'chase' or a flirtatious encounter between a man and a woman, cruising, while opportunistic, is not always intentional. When it is intentional and for it to be successful cruising or the act of being cruised requires an ability to understand and correctly interpret signals that a person's clothes, behaviour, body language or eye contact convey. Cruising entered the wider lexicon when a North American film by the same name was released in 1980. For details of *Cruising* and the controversy it caused, see R. Murray *Images in the Dark: an encyclopedia of gay and lesbian film and video* (New York: Penguin Books, USA, 1996), pp. 401–2.

20  G. Chauncey *Gay New York: gender, urban culture, and the making of the gay male world, 1890–1940* (New York: Basic Books, 1994), pp. 195–6, 202.

21  M. Foucault 'Sexual choice, sexual act' in *Ethics: essential works of Foucault 1954–1984*, vol. 1, trans. R. Hurley and others, ed. P. Rabinow (Harmonds-worth: Penguin Books, 2000), p. 151.

22  D. Altman *The Homosexualization of America, the Americanization of the Homosexual* (New York: St Martin's Press, 1982), p. 82.

23  S. Jeffreys *Unpacking Queer Politics: a lesbian feminist perspective* (Cambridge: Polity Press, 2003), pp. 57–61, 63, 66–72 & 77. For a survey of some of the counter arguments and more libertarian views, see D. M. Halperin *What do gay men want? An essay on sex, risk, and subjectivity* (Ann Arbor: University of Michigan Press, 2007).

24  Lindsay (62), Thomas (52), Henry (50), Alan (47), Neil (46) and Mark (25).

25  D. Altman 'AIDS and the discourses of sexuality' in R. W. Connell and G. W. Dowsett (eds) *Rethinking Sex: social theory and sexuality research* (Melbourne: Melbourne University Press, 1992), p. 42.

26  Altman *Homosexualization*, pp. 79–80.

27  Berger *Gay and gray*, p. 39.

28  The 17 men from the young cohort with positive views of the scene were Travis (38), Neville (37), Andy (37), Jeremy (36), Joseph (35), Julius (34), Tony (33), Mick (33), Adrian (30), Ian (28), Harry (28), David (28), Mark (25), Troy (24), Myles (24), Lachlan (24), and Jack (22).

29  Neville (37), Joseph (35), Julius (34), Mick (33), Tony (33), David (28) and Jack (22).

30  The 20 men from the young cohort reporting negative views of the scene were Drew (39), Robert (38), Neville (37), Andy (37), Jeremy (36), Travis (38), Alex (37), Jason (35), Julius (34), Tony (33), Mick (33), Luke (32), Vincent (30), Brian (30), David (28), Ian (28), Mark (25), Myles (24), Angus (23), Jack (22).

31  Robert (38), Jeremy (36), Tony (33), Luke (32), Brian (30) and Angus (23).

32  E. T. May 'Myths and realities of the American family' in A. Prost and G. Vincent (eds) *A History of Private Life, vol. 5. Riddles of Identity in Modern Times*, trans. A. Goldhammer (Cambridge, MA: Harvard University Press, 1991), p. 581.

33  Jason (35), Mick (33), Luke (32) and Mark (25).

34  This is the case for working-class men in particular. See C. Chamberlain and P. Robinson *The Needs of Older Gay, Lesbian and Transgender Persons*, a report prepared for the ALSO Foundation (Melbourne: Centre for Applied Social Research, RMIT University, 2002), pp. 15–16 & 31–2.

35  Pollak 'Male homosexuality', p. 48.

36  Earlier in the chapter, market segmentation was discussed in relation to the development of the gay scene since the 1970s. The most obvious segmenta-tion in the night club scene as a whole is between gay and straight bars and clubs. So-called 'mixed' bars and clubs also exist, which, in moderately large urban centres such as Melbourne or Manchester, tend to be located in the CBD or inner city suburbs, and attract a young, inner urban crowd. They are generally safe places for middle-class gay men to socialise with their straight friends.

37  Altman *Homosexualization*, p. 21. Gilbert Herdt also argues that the gay bar was the 'pivotal social context' for gay men in the camp period. See G. Herdt

'"Coming out" as a rite of passage: a Chicago study' in G. Herdt (ed.) *Gay Culture in America: essays from the field* (Boston: Beacon Press, 1992), p. 32.

38  Neville (37), Andy (37), Myles (24) and Angus (23).
39  Ayres 'China Doll', pp. 89–90.
40  Ayres 'China Doll', p. 95.
41  In 1978 Berger interviewed 112 older homosexual men. See Berger *Gay and gray*, pp. 26–7 & 156.
42  The researchers interviewed eight men (aged 19–27) who were of Chinese ancestry and had arrived in Australian as migrants from various South-east Asian countries. See Ridge, Hee & Minichiello '"Asian" men on the scene', pp. 46–7.
43  'Gym bunny' refers to young gay men who devote much of their recreation time at gymnasiums to achieve shapely, muscular bodies.
44  Bell & Weinberg *Homosexualities*, p. 73.
45  Plummer 'Going gay', p. 106.
46  Pollak 'Male homosexuality', p. 44.
47  Reginald (79), Geoffrey (69), John (65), Michael (52), Kevin (52), Glen (49), Alan (47), Scott (45).
48  For discussion of middle-class disdain for pubs, see R. Sennett *The Fall of Public Man* (New York: W.W. Norton & Company, 1992), p. 215.
49  Vernon (75), Chester (71), Oscar (65), Kenneth (65), Barry (62), Graham (52), Trevor (49), Nigel (49), Simon (46), James (45).
50  A 'Twinky' is a pretty, possibly slightly effeminate young gay man.
51  For discussion of masculine 'collectivities' such as sporting clubs and the armed forces, see H. Bech *When Men Meet: homosexuality and modernity*, trans. T. Mequit and T. Davies (Cambridge: Polity Press, 1997), pp. 44–55.

## Chapter 6   Community Life

1  Interviewees were asked to describe their experience of or involvement in the gay community. See Appendix 1: Interview Schedule, question 24.
2  N. Achilles 'The development of the homosexual bar as an institution' in P. M. Nardi and B. E. Schneider (eds) *Social Perspectives in Lesbian and Gay Studies: a reader* (London: Routledge, 1998), p. 176.
3  D. Altman *The Homosexualization of America, the Americanization of the Homosexual* (New York: St Martin's Press, 1982), p. 8.
4  D. Carr 'Narrative and the real world: an argument for continuity' in L. P. Hinchman and S. K. Hinchman (eds) *Memory, Identity, Community: the idea of narrative in the human sciences* (New York: State University of New York, 2001), p. 22.
5  Carr 'Narrative and the real world', p. 22.
6  K. Plummer *Telling Sexual Stories: power, change and social worlds* (London: Routledge, 1995), p. 87.
7  The numbers of interviewees involved in HIV-AIDS support groups and other counselling services were fairly evenly spread across the age cohorts, with seven men from the old cohort, nine men from the middle cohort, and six from the young cohort.

8 The numbers of interviewees who expressed community involvement through their local social group were also fairly evenly spread across the age cohorts, with six men from the old cohort, seven men from the middle cohort, and nine from the young cohort.

9 There was a preponderance of men from the young cohort in this category; one was drawn from the old cohort, five were from the middle cohort, and 12 from the young cohort.

10 Three men were from the old cohort, four came from the middle cohort, and one from the young cohort.

11 ALSO is the acronym for the Alternative Life-style Organisation. Established in the early 1980s in Melbourne, ALSO is best known for the warehouse parties that it hosted and that were a prominent feature of the gay scene in the late 1980s and 1990s. Funds raised from the parties went towards the fight against HIV-AIDS. It is now known as the ALSO Foundation and is one of many gay lobby groups. The Peter Knight Centre is a community centre in Melbourne that supports PLWHA.

12 R. W. Connell *The Men and the Boys* (Sydney: Allen & Unwin, 2000), p. 190.

13 R. Sennett and J. Cobb *The Hidden Injuries of Class* (New York: Alfred Knopf. 1973), p. 113.

14 Sleaze ball is an annual dance party held in Sydney at the start of spring.

15 Drew (39), Robert (38), Travis (38), Jason (35), Tony (33), Mick (33), Brian (30), Harry (28), and Adam (24).

16 B. Anderson *Imagined Communities: reflections on the origin and spread of nationalism* (New York: New Left Books, 1991).

17 As discussed in the previous chapter, it was mainly men from the young cohort who understood the scene as community activity. Because this was examined there and because very few older men said the scene constituted their experience of or involvement in the gay community, there is no further discussion of it here.

18 The rapid growth and success of the warehouse (dance) party phenomenon in the 1980s can be explained as both a defiant and an affirming statement by gay men en masse in face of the HIV-AIDS epidemic. See L. A. Lewis and M. W. Ross *A Select Body: the gay dance party subculture and the HIV/AIDS pandemic* (London: Cassell, 1995), ch. 7.

19 See G. Willett *Living Out Loud: a history of gay and lesbian activism in Australia* (Sydney: Allen & Unwin, 2000), pp. 202–6.

20 Plummer *Sexual Stories*, p. 41.

21 Melbourne's gay and lesbian festival, Midsumma, runs from mid-January to early February each year. It includes social, cultural and sporting events such as book readings, plays, swimming and athletics competitions, a street party and film festival, as well as a family carnival and dance party. In 2008, among community and political organisations with stalls at the carnival were ANZ bank, Australian Labor Party, Honda Australia, IBM, Melbourne Sexual Health Clinic, Multicultural Centre for Women's Health, PLWHA Victoria, RSPCA, Tourism Queensland, Tupperware, Uniting [Church] Care.

22 For discussion of background to and factors affecting gay migration, see J. Chetcuti 'Relationships of interdependency: immigration for same-sex partners' in R. Aldrich and G. Wotherspoon (eds) *Gay Perspectives: essays in*

*Australian gay culture* (Sydney: Department of Economic History, University of Sydney, 1992), pp. 165–79.

23  The eight men in this group were Reginald (79), Gerald (75), Charles (67), Noel (58), Michael (52), Donald (52), Des (50) and Jason (35).

24  This group of 18 interviewees comprised five men from the old cohort, seven men from the middle cohort, and six men from the young cohort.

25  Jack (22), David (28), Neville (37), Matthew (42), Richard (58), Brendan (64), Oscar (65) and Kelvin (66).

26  E. Goffman *Stigma: Notes on the Management of Spoiled Identity* (Harmondsworth: Penguin Books, 1968).

27  Goffman *Stigma*, p. 32.

28  For discussion of the nature, pros and cons of life in a gay ghetto, see M. Pollak 'Male homosexuality – or happiness in the ghetto' in P. Ariès and A. Béjin (eds) *Western Sexuality: practice and precept in past and present times*, trans. A. Forster (Oxford: Basil Blackwell, 1986), pp. 52–6 and E. White *States of Desire: travels in gay America* (London: Pan Books Ltd., 1986), pp. 37–8, 57, 61–2, and *passim*.

29  Connell *The Men and the Boys*, p. 97.

30  Lewis & Ross *A Select Body*, pp. 184–5.

31  N. Elias 'Introduction: a theoretical essay on established and outsider relations' in N. Elias and J. L. Scotson *The Established and The Outsiders: a sociological enquiry into community problems*, 2ⁿᵈ edn (London: Sage Publications Ltd., 1994), pp. xvi & xx.

32  In *Gay and gray*, Raymond Berger cites the cases of older gay men who were disenchanted by infighting in gay community organisations. He also argues that older gay men tend to be marginalised by the younger members. See R. M. Berger *Gay and gray: the older homosexual man*, 2ⁿᵈ edn (Binghamton, New York: The Haworth Press, 1996), pp. 38 & 229.

33  Pollak 'Male homosexuality', p. 46.

34  Goffman *Stigma*, p. 35.

35  Goffman *Stigma*, pp. 50–1.

36  Lewis Coser *The Functions of Social Conflict*, 1976.

37  R. Sennett *The Corrosion of Character: the personal consequences of work in the new capitalism* (New York: W.W. Norton & Company, 1998), p. 143.

## Chapter 7  Couple Relationships

1  D. Altman *The Homosexualization of America, the Americanization of the Homosexual* (New York: St Martin's Press, 1982), pp. xi–xii; K. Plummer 'Going gay: identities lifecycles and lifestyles in the male gay world' in J. Hart and D. Richardson (eds) *The Theory and Practice of Homosexuality* (London: Routledge & Kegan Paul, 1981), p. 105; R. W. Connell, M. H. Davis and G. W. Dowsett 'A bastard of a life: homosexual desire and practice among men in working-class milieux' in *The Australian and New Zealand Journal of Sociology*, 29, 1 (1993) 122.

2  Forty-seven interviewees, or almost 60 per cent of the sample, chose relationship as one of the three most meaningful aspects of their life. See Appendix 1: Interview Schedule, question 10.

3   The nine men in relationships of 25 years' duration or longer comprise four
    men in their 60s and five men in their 50s.
4   Connell, Davis and Dowsett 'A bastard of a life', p. 122.
5   C. Chamberlain and P. Robinson *The Needs of Older Gay, Lesbian and
    Transgender Persons*, a report prepared for the ALSO Foundation (Melbourne:
    Centre for Applied Social Research, RMIT University, 2002).
6   G. W. Dowsett *Practicing Desire: homosexual sex in the era of AIDS* (Stanford,
    California: Stanford University Press, 1996), p. 135.
7   Of 47 interviewees who chose relationship as one of the three most meaningful
    aspects of their life, 15 men were from the old cohort (or 68 per cent of that
    cohort), 19 men were from the middle cohort (or 63 per cent of that cohort),
    and 13 men were from the young cohort (or 46 per cent of that cohort).
8   Lindsay, 62 (30 years) and Leslie, 74 (20 years).
9   Richard, 58 (30 years); Lionel, 59 (28 years); Graham, 52 (26 years); Patrick,
    53 (20 years).
10  M. Foucault 'Friendship as a way of life' in *Ethics: essential works of Foucault
    1954–1984*, vol. 1, trans. R. Hurley and others, ed. P. Rabinow (Harmonds-
    worth: Penguin Books, 2000), p. 137.
11  Neville, 37 (12 years); Mark, 25 (five years); Daniel, 35 (two years).
12  Leslie (74).
13  This group consists of three men from the old cohort, five men from the
    middle cohort and two men from the young cohort: Clive (64), Brendan
    (64), Edward (60), Lionel (59), Roy (58), Ross (54), Henry (50), Stuart (49),
    Vincent (30), and Jack (22).
14  First published in the United Kingdom in 1955, it was banned in Australia
    until 1961. When it did become available in Australia its annual sales were
    between 1,500 and 2,000 throughout the 1960s. See G. Wotherspoon *City
    of the Plain: history of a gay sub-culture* (Sydney: Hale & Iremonger, 1991),
    p. 126.
15  Short for 'poofter'. See p. 189 n. 36 and p. 195 n. 57.
16  D. J. West *Homosexuality* (Harmondsworth: Penguin Books Ltd., 1968), p. 56.
17  West *Homosexuality*, p. 57.
18  J. Weeks *Sexuality and its Discontents: meanings, myths & modern sexualities*
    (London: Routledge & Kegan Paul, 1985), p. 221.
19  Foucault 'Friendship', pp. 135–40.
20  Plummer 'Going Gay', pp. 103, 105.
21  Plummer 'Going Gay', p. 105.
22  Plummer 'Going Gay', p. 106.
23  G. Hekma 'Same-sex relations among men in Europe, 1700–1990' in
    F. X. Elder, L. A. Hall and G. Hekma (eds) *Sexual Cultures in Europe: themes in
    sexuality* (Manchester: Manchester University Press, 1999), pp. 99–100.
    Henning Bech writes that the Danish law on 'registered partnerships' has
    been in effect since it was passed in 1989. Bech argues that these develop-
    ments will lead to the disappearance of the homosexual as a type. See
    H. Bech *When Men Meet: homosexuality and modernity*, trans. T. Mequit and
    T. Davies (Cambridge: Polity Press, 1997), ch. VI.
24  See reports in the *Age*, Melbourne, 23 December 2005 and 30 June 2005.
    J. Boswell *The Marriage of Likeness: same sex unions in pre-modern Europe*
    (London: HarperCollins, 1995).

25  See, for example, *Sydney Star Observer*, 1, 8 & 15 July 2004.

26  See Appendix 1: Interview Schedule, questions 11 & 7. The interviewee was Mark (25).

27  These findings closely correspond to those of a large-scale Australian inquiry. *Private Lives: a report on the health and wellbeing of GLBTI Australians* was based on surveys conducted on-line in 2005 of 5,476 people aged 16 to 92. More than 60 per cent of respondents were male, of whom more than 80 per cent identified as gay. The report states that a very small percentage of respondents had formalised their relationships by marriage or a commitment ceremony (5–10% of men and women), 'while most others had no wish to do so'. See M. Pitts, A. Smith, A. Mitchell and S. Patel *Private Lives: a report on the health and wellbeing of GLBTI Australians* (Melbourne: Gay and Lesbian Health Victoria and The Australian Research Centre in Sex, Health and Society, La Trobe University, 2006), p. 9.

28  The five men in relationships of less than one year's duration are Jeremy (36), Luke (32), Adam (24), Lachlan (24), and Troy (24).

29  The following is a breakdown of men in relationships of seven years or longer: three men in their 70s, nine men in their 60s, nine men in their 50s, five men in their 40s, and three men in their 30s.

30  Interestingly, the largest group in long-term relationships crosses the old and the middle cohorts and comprises interviewees in their 60s and 50s. Nine men from each of these age groups, or a total of 18 interviewees, were in relationships of seven years or longer—that is, more than 60 per cent of the men in this sample who were in long-term relationships are in their 60s and 50s.

31  M. Pollak 'Male homosexuality – or happiness in the ghetto' in P. Ariès and A. Béjin (eds) *Western Sexuality: practice and precept in past and present times*, trans. A. Forster (Oxford: Basil Blackwell, 1986), p. 51.

32  J. D'Emilio and E. B. Freedman *Intimate Matters: a history of sexuality in America*, 2nd edn (Chicago: University of Chicago Press, 1997), pp. 265–6. For history of companionate marriage in English society, see L. Stone *The Family, Sex and Marriage in England 1500–1800* (London: Weidenfeld & Nicolson, 1977), ch. 8.

33  Connell, Davis and Dowsett 'A bastard of a life', p. 122; P. Bourdieu *Masculine Domination*, trans. R. Nice (Cambridge: Polity Press, 2001), p. 119.

34  See G. Herdt *Same sex, different cultures: exploring gay and lesbian lives* (Boulder, Colorado: Westview Press, 1997), p. 157; S. O. Murray *Homosexualities* (Chicago: University of Chicago Press, 2000), ch. 9; Plummer 'Going Gay', p. 105; J. Weeks, B. Heaphy and C. Donovan 'Partners by choice: equality, power and commitment in non-heterosexual relationships' in G. Allan (ed.) *The sociology of the family: a reader* (Oxford: Blackwell Publishers Ltd., 1999), pp. 111–28. For a useful survey of scholarly debates concerning gay men's masculinity, see T. Edwards 'Queering the pitch? Gay masculinities' in M. S. Kimmel, J. Hearn and R.W. Connell (eds) *Handbook of studies on men and masculinities* (Thousand Oaks, CA: Sage Publications Inc., 2005), pp. 51–68.

35  Connell, Davis and Dowsett 'A bastard of a life', p. 122.

36  D'Emilio and Freedman *Intimate Matters*, p. 359. A. Giddens *Modernity and Self-Identity: self and society in the late modern age* (Cambridge: Polity Press,

1991), p. 6. See also A. McLaren *Twentieth Century Sexuality: a history* (Oxford: Blackwell Publishers Ltd, 1999), p. 218 and J. Weeks *Making Sexual History* (Cambridge: Polity Press, 2000), pp. 220–1.

37 It was during the sexual revolution in the 1960s and 1970s that many heterosexual members of the 'baby boomer' generation experimented with similar radical, alternative sexual arrangements. Couples that engaged in 'open' sexual relations were known as 'swinging' couples or 'swingers'; married couples were said to have 'open marriages'. Herpes and then HIV-AIDS curtailed such experimentation for most of the 1980s and 1990s. See D. Allyn *Make love not war: the sexual revolution, an unfettered history* (New York: Routledge, 2001), chs 4 & 17 and *passim*.

38 Pollak 'Male homosexuality', p. 43.

39 J. Boswell *Christianity, Social Tolerance, and Homosexuality: gay people in Western Europe from the beginning of the Christian era to the fourteenth century* (Chicago: University of Chicago Press, 1980), pp. 26–7.

40 For useful examination and discussion of the variety of medical metaphors used in association with HIV-AIDS, see D. Lupton *Medicine as culture: illness, disease and the body in Western societies*, 2nd edn (London: Sage Publications Ltd., 2003), ch. 3.

41 D. Altman 'AIDS and the discourses of sexuality' in R. W. Connell and G. W. Dowsett (eds) *Rethinking Sex: social theory and sexuality research* (Melbourne: Melbourne University Press, 1992), pp. 40–1.

42 Connell, Davis and Dowsett 'A bastard of a life'; Dowsett, *Practicing*; Chamberlain and Robinson *Older Gay, Lesbian and Transgender Persons*.

43 E. White *States of Desire: travels in gay America* (London: Pan Books Ltd., 1986), p. 51.

44 See Chapter 4.

## Chapter 8   Friends and Family

1 L. Jamieson 'The couple: intimate and equal?' in J. Weeks, J. Holland and M. Waites (eds) *Sexuality and Society: a reader* (Cambridge: Polity Press, 2003), pp. 265–76.

2 Fifty-two interviewees, or 65 per cent of the sample, chose friendship as one of the three most meaningful aspects of their life. By contrast (as mentioned in the chapter on couple relationships), 47 interviewees, or slightly less than 60 per cent of the sample, chose relationship as one of the three most meaningful aspects of their life. See Appendix 1: Interview Schedule, question 10.

3 The study of 5,476 people, which was undertaken on-line in 2005, and entitled *Private Lives: a report on the health and wellbeing of GLBTI Australians*, shows that for men (gay and bisexual), the three 'best things in life' are, in order of preference, friends (19 per cent), work/study (15 per cent) and relationships (13 per cent). See M. Pitts, A. Smith, A. Mitchell and S. Patel *Private Lives: a report on the health and wellbeing of GLBTI Australians* (Melbourne: Gay and Lesbian Health Victoria and The Australian Research Centre in Sex, Health and Society, La Trobe University, 2006), pp. 60–1.

4   P. Ariès 'Thoughts on the history of homosexuality' in P. Ariès and A. Béjin (eds) *Western Sexuality: practice and precept in past and present times*, trans. A. Forster (Oxford: Basil Blackwell, 1986), p. 69.

5   H. Bech *When Men Meet: homosexuality and modernity*, trans. T. Mequit and T. Davies (Cambridge: Polity Press, 1997), pp. 73. Interestingly, this 'sexual-isation' of friendship is not so clear cut in women's friendships.

6   Emphasis in the original. Bech *When Men Meet*, pp. 71–2.

7   J. Boswell *Christianity, Social Tolerance, and Homosexuality: gay people in Western Europe from the beginning of the Christian era to the fourteenth century* (Chicago: University of Chicago Press, 1980), p. 10.

8   B. M. Dank 'Coming out in the gay world' in *Psychiatry*, 34 (1971) 182, foot-note 8.

9   J. Weeks *Making Sexual History* (Cambridge: Polity Press, 2000), pp. 212, 213, 219.

10  M. Pollak 'Male homosexuality – or happiness in the ghetto' in Ariès and Béjin *Western Sexuality*, p. 52.

11  Weeks *Sexual History*, pp. 218–19.

12  Chapters 2–4.

13  Such arrangements are known as 'overlapping' or 'serial' families. See U. Beck and E. Beck-Gernsheim *The Normal Chaos of Love*, trans. M. Ritter and J. Wiebel (Cambridge: Polity Press, 1995), p. 170.

14  Jamieson 'The couple', p. 265.

15  See discussion in chapter on couple relationships.

16  Thirty-one men, or slightly less than 40 per cent of the interviewees, were not in a relationship. Meanwhile, 20 men, or one quarter of interviewees, were in relationships of less than seven years' duration.

17  Forty-six interviewees, or close to 58 per cent of the sample, omitted any mention of family as a source of meaning. See Appendix 1: Interview Schedule, question 10.

18  Fourteen men, or 64 per cent of the old cohort, said friendship was mean-ingful. Ten men gave social interaction as the reason and four men said it was because of the exchange of care and support. The men who cited social interaction were Geoffrey (69), Charles (67), Kenneth (65), Oscar (65), Maurice (65), John (65), Terrence (64), Brendan (64), Lindsay (62) and Barry (62). Those who cited mutual care and support were Gerald (75), Harold (71), Charles (67) and Terrence (64). Two men fell into neither category and they were Chester (71) and Kelvin (66).

19  Charles (67), Maurice (65), Terrence (64), Brendan (64), Lindsay (62) and Harold (71).

20  Twenty men, or two-thirds of the middle cohort, said that friendship was meaningful. They were Lionel (59), Noel (58), Samuel (57), Thomas (52), Michael (52), Graham (52), Bill (52), Henry (50), Des (50), Trevor (49), Nigel (49), Jerome (49), Bob (48), Alan (47), Simon (46), Scott (45), James (45), Roger (44), Matthew (42) and Ken (40). One man cited mutual care and support as an important attribute of friendship and he was Bob (48).

21  Bill (52), Michael (52), Nigel (49), Jerome (49) and James (45).

22  Eighteen men, or 64 per cent of the young cohort, said that friendship was meaningful. They were Roger (38), Andy (37), Alex (37), Jeremy (36), Joseph (35), Jason (35), Daniel (35), Julius (34), Tony (33), Luke (32), Brian (30),

Adrian (30), Ian (28), Harry (28), Mark (25), Lachlan (24), Angus (23) and Jack (22). Three men cited mutual care and support as an important attribute of friendship and they were Daniel (35), Luke (32) and Ian (28).

23  Robert (38), Daniel (35), Ian (28) and Mark (25).

24  Formerly married men are: Gerald (79), Leslie (74), John (65), Oscar (65), Clive (64), Terrence (64), Douglas (63), Edward (60), Roy (58), Ross (54), Henry (50), Trevor (49), and Scott (45).

25  Tony (33) and Joseph (35).

26  See Weeks *Sexual History*, pp. 224–6.

27  For analysis of sperm banks in general and more discussion of semen as the 'gift of life' and other examples of sperm donors' motives, see D. M. Tober 'Semen as gift, semen as goods: reproductive workers and the market in altruism' in N. Scheper-Hughes and L. Wacquant (Eds) *Commodifying Bodies* (London: Sage Publications Ltd., 2002), pp. 137–60.

28  In *Australian Story* (ABC television, 29 May 2006), a gay man in Sydney, Paul van Reyk, described his role in co-parenting arrangements with or as anonymous sperm donor for ten or more lesbian couples and single women.

29  Beck & Beck-Gernsheim *Normal Chaos*, p. 173.

30  See Weeks *Sexual History*, pp. 225–6.

31  R. Sennett and J. Cobb *The Hidden Injuries of Class* (New York: Alfred Knopf. 1973), p. 132.

32  Weeks *Sexual History*, p. 225.

33  E. Beck-Gernsheim *Reinventing the Family: in search of new lifestyles*, trans. P. Camiller (Cambridge: Polity Press, 2002), p. 97.

34  Beck-Gernsheim *Reinventing the Family*, p. 7.

35  Regulations governing access to medically-assisted artificial insemination vary from state to state in Australia. They are less restrictive in New South Wales than they are in Victoria, and lesbians and single mothers, for example, may have access to this form of fertility treatment in NSW when prohibited from doing so in Victoria. See report in the *Age*, 26 April 2006.

36  G. Simmel 'On the sociology of the family' trans. M. Ritter and D. Frisby in M. Featherstone (ed.) *Love and Eroticism* (London: Sage Publications, 1999), p. 291.

37  See report in the *Age*, 16 August 2003, in which a journalist claims gay couples were using surrogate mothers in the USA to provide them with children.

38  Emphasis in the original. Weeks *Sexual History*, pp. 217–18.

39  Weeks *Sexual History*, p. 219.

## Chapter 9   Life as an Old Gay Man

1  While Weeks was one of the first scholars to investigate it, the work of the North American scholar, Raymond Berger, is regarded as definitive. See J. Weeks 'The problems of older Homosexuals' in J. Hart and D. Richardson (eds) *The Theory and Practice of Homosexuality* (London: Routledge and Kegan Paul, 1981), pp. 177–84; R. M. Berger *Gay and gray: the older homosexual man*, 2nd edn (Binghamton, New York: The Haworth Press, 1996); R. M. Berger 'Realities of gay and lesbian aging', *Social Work*, (1984) 57–62.

2 See Chapter 7. Changing laws concerning surrogacy and IVF are likely to see an increase in the number of gay people in the West who are parents.

3 See Berger *Gay and gray*, p. 232; A. M. Boxer and B. J. Cohler 'The life course of gay and lesbian youth: an immodest proposal for the study of lives' in G. Herdt (ed.) *Gay and Lesbian Youth* (New York: The Haworth Press, 1989), pp. 315–55; Weeks 'The problems of older homosexuals', p. 181.

4 See, for example, P. Ariès *Centuries of Childhood* (Harmondsworth: Penguin Books, 1973); S. de Beauvoir *Old Age*, trans. P. O'Brien (Harmondsworth: Penguin Books, 1977); N. Elias *The Loneliness of the Dying*, trans. E. Jephcott (Oxford: Basil Blackwell, 1987); D. H. Fischer 'Growing old in America' in J. S. Quandagno (ed.) *Aging, the Individual and Society: readings in social gerontology* (New York: St Martin's Press, Inc., 1980), pp. 34–49; P. Laslett *Family life and illicit love in earlier generations* (Cambridge: Cambridge University Press, 1977), ch. 5; M. Mitternauer *A History of Youth*, trans. Graeme Dunphy, (Oxford: Blackwells Publishers, 1992); C. Shilling *The Body and Social Theory*, 2nd edn (London: Sage Publications Ltd., 2005), pp. 196–6; B. S. Turner *The Body and Society: explorations in social theory* (Oxford: Basil Blackwell Publisher Ltd., 1984).

5 See, for example, C. Phillipson *Capitalism and the construction of old age* (London: Macmillan, 1982) and E. Willis *Illness and social relations: issues in the sociology of health care* (Sydney: Allen & Unwin Pty Ltd, 1994).

6 For example, see discussion of Australian Aborigines' mortality rates in I. Anderson *Koorie health in Koorie hands: an orientation manual in Aboriginal health for health care providers* (Melbourne: Koorie health unit, Department of Health, Victoria, 1988).

7 Elias *The Loneliness of the Dying*, p. 69.

8 The interviewees were asked, 'What in your opinion is the attitude of other gay men to old gay men?' See Appendix 1. Interview schedule, question 16.

9 For example, see: Berger *Gay and gray*, ch. 10 & *passim*; R. Dorfman *et al.* 'Old, sad and alone: the myth of the aging homosexual' in *Journal of Gerontological Social Work*, 24, 1/2 (1995) 29–44; J. Kelly 'The aging male homosexual: myth and reality' in *The Gerontolgist*, 17, 4 (1977) 328–32.

10 Three men referred to this narrative. Two were from the young cohort (Drew, 39 and Lachlan, 24) and one was from the middle cohort (Kevin, 52). No men from the old cohort referred to it.

11 The interviewees were asked whether they regarded themselves as old and then what picture they had of themselves as old gay men. See Appendix 1. Interview schedule, question 17. The 43 men who regarded physical decline as an indicator of old age comprised 14 men (or 64 per cent) from the old cohort, 18 men (or 60 per cent) from the middle cohort and 11 men (or 39 per cent) from the young cohort.

12 The 17 men who regarded deterioration of external appearances to be an indicator of old age comprised two men (or nine per cent) from the old cohort, six men (or 20 per cent) from the middle cohort and nine men (or 32 per cent) from the young cohort.

13 A total number of 60 men (or three quarters of the sample) understood old age as physical decline or deterioration of external appearances.

14 See Appendix 1. Interview schedule, question 17.

15 The two men from the old cohort who regarded themselves as old are Maurice (65) and Barry (62), and the four who gave equivocal answers are Vernon (75), Gerald (75), Kenneth (65) and Douglas (63).

16 Beauvoir *Old Age*, p. 316.

17 Shilling *The Body*, pp. 193 & 195. Shilling draws on the works of Franz Fanon and Mike Featherstone and Mike Hepworth when developing his notion of the body as a mask: F. Fanon *Black Skin, White Masks* (London: Pluto Press, 1984); M. Featherstone and M. Hepworth 'The mask of ageing and the postmodern life course' in M. Featherstone, M. Hepworth and B. S. Turner (eds) *The Body: social process and cultural theory* (London: Sage Publication, 1991), pp. 371–89.

18 The two who speak about illness are Reginald (79) and Edward (60), and the three who speak about reduced capabilities are Vernon (75), Chester (71) and Ronald (68).

19 Elias 'Ageing and Dying', p. 71.

20 Donald (52), Tony (33) and Paul (33).

21 Mitternauer *A History of Youth*, p. 41.

22 Fifteen men (or 19 per cent of the sample) reported knowledge of old gay men being treated with respect or admired. They comprised three men from the young cohort, five men from the middle cohort and seven men from the old cohort.

23 Adam (24), Myles (24), Graham (52), Patrick (53), Terrence (64), John (65), Oscar (65) and Kelvin (66).

24 Terrence and Oscar have part-time jobs.

25 Kelvin is the single man.

26 Berger, *Gay and gray*; p. 42. Berger conducted his research in 1978. He asked 112 respondents to answer a questionnaire, then selected 10 men to interview more thoroughly. All respondents were 40 or older and drawn from a North American 'locale' which he described as 'a four-county area, encompassing urban, suburban, and semi-rural environments'. His youngest respondent was 41 and the oldest was 77. See pp. 26, 156–7.

27 Thirty-six men (or 45 per cent of the sample) reported witnessing old gay men treated as invisible or, in the case of the older men, had experienced being so treated. They comprised 11 men from the young cohort, 12 men from the middle cohort and 13 men from the old cohort.

28 Robert (38), Neville (37), Alex (37), Jason (35), Daniel (35), Mick (33), Tony (33), Adrian (30), Ian (28), Mark (25) and Troy (24).

29 There were 12 men from the middle cohort: Lionel (59), Richard (58), Noel (58), Ross (54), Michael (52), Henry (50), Des (50), Trevor (49), Jerome (49), Alan (47), Simon (46), James (45).

30 Thirteen men, or 59 per cent, of the old cohort reported this experience: Gerald (75), Leslie (74), Harold (71), Ronald (68), Charles (67), Kenneth (65), Maurice (65), John (65), Terrence (64), Clive (64), Brendan (64), Douglas (63) and Lindsay (62).

31 See M. Pollak 'Male homosexuality – or happiness in the ghetto' in P. Ariès and A. Béjin (eds) *Western Sexuality: practice and precept in past and present times*, trans. A. Forster, (Oxford: Basil Blackwell, 1986), pp. 40–61.

32 This group of 26 interviewees comprised four men from the old cohort, 11 men from the middle cohort and 11 men from the young cohort.

33  See Berger *Gay and gray;* p. 228.
34  See T. Mann *Death in Venice, Tristan, Tonio Kröger,* trans. H.T. Lowe-Porter (Harmondsworth: Penguin Books, 1975), p. 77.
35  Beauvoir *Old Age,* p. 244.
36  Beauvoir *Old Age,* p. 246.
37  Australian slang for public toilets.
38  Berger *Gay and gray,* p. 191.
39  Beauvoir *Old Age,* p. 247.
40  The 16 men comprise one man from the old cohort, who is Edward (60); ten men from the middle cohort, who are Samuel (57), Ross (54), Bill (52), Thomas (52), Donald (52), Glen (49), Trevor (49), Stuart (49), Neil (46), Simon (46); and five men from the young cohort, who are Drew (39), Joseph (35), Harry (28), Adam (24) and Angus (23).
41  Joseph is referring to social groups such as Mature Age Gays in Sydney and Vintage Men in Melbourne.
42  Beauvoir *Old Age,* p. 315; Shilling *The Body,* pp. 195–6.
43  Vernon, 75.

## Conclusion

1  R. M. Berger *Gay and gray: the older homosexual man,* 2nd edn (Binghamton, New York: The Haworth Press, 1996), pp. 24–5, 42 and *passim.*
2  N. Elias *The Loneliness of the Dying,* trans. E. Jephcott (Oxford: Basil Blackwell, 1987), p. 71.

# Index

LaVergne, TN USA
19 January 2010
170439LV00002B/23/P